INFORMIX

A Guide for

Application Developers

Art Taylor

Tony Lacy-Thompson

For book and bookstore information

http://www.prenhall.com

PRENTICE HALL PTR, UPPER SADDLE RIVER. NJ 07458

Library of Congress Cataloging-in-Publication Data

Taylor, Art
       INFORMIX-NewEra : a guide for application developers / Art Taylor, Tony Lacy-Thompson.
         p.   cm.
      Includes index.
      ISBN 0-13-209248-4
      1. NewEra (Computer program language)   2. Application software.
I. Lacy-Thompson, Tony.   II. Title.
QA76.73.N48T39   1996   95-19206
005.75—dc20   CIP

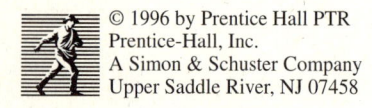

© 1996 by Prentice Hall PTR
Prentice-Hall, Inc.
A Simon & Schuster Company
Upper Saddle River, NJ 07458

Informix Press
Informix Software, Inc.
4100 Bohannon Drive
Menlo Park, CA 94025

Cover design director: *Jerry Votta*
Cover design: *Jeannette Jacobs*
Acquisitions editor: *Mark L. Taub*
Manufacturing manager: *Alexis R. Heydt*

Manager, Informix Press: *Todd Katz*

The publisher offers discounts on this book when ordered in bulk quantities. For more information contact: Corporate Sales Department, Prentice Hall PTR, One Lake Street, Upper Saddle River, NJ 07458. Phone: 800-382-3419, Fax: 201-236-7141, email: corpsales@prenhall.com

The following are worldwide trademarks of Informix Software, Inc., or its subsidiaries, registered in the United States of America as indicated by ®, and in numerous other countries worldwide: INFORMIX®; INFORMIX-NewEra™; INFORMIX-NewEra ViewPoint™ Pro; INFORMIX-SuperView™ (SuperView technology Patent Pending).

Lotus Notes is a trademark of Lotus Development Corporation. Motif is a registered trademark of the Open Software Foundation. Oracle is a registered trademark of Oracle Corporation. Windows is a trademark and Microsoft is a registered trademark of Microsoft Corporation. Other product names mentioned herein are the registered trademarks or trademarks of their respective owners.

All rights reserved. No part of this book may be reproduced, in any form or by any means, without permission in writing from the publisher.

Printed in the United States of America

10 9 8 7 6 5 4 3 2 1

ISBN 0-13-209248-4

Prentice-Hall International (UK) Limited, *London*
Prentice-Hall of Australia Pty. Limited, *Sydney*
Prentice-Hall Canada Inc., *Toronto*
Prentice-Hall Hispanoamericana, S.A., *Mexico*
Prentice-Hall of India Private Limited, *New Delhi*
Prentice-Hall of Japan, Inc., *Tokyo*
Simon & Schuster Asia Pte. Ltd., *Singapore*
Editora Prentice-Hall do Brasil, Ltda., *Rio de Janeiro*

Contents

Introduction ix
Chapter 1 The NewEra Language 1
  Object-oriented Languages 1
  What Is An Object? 2
  Encapsulation 2
  What Is a Class? 3
  Inheritance 3
        Polymorphism 4
  Informix-4GL and the NewEra Language 5
  Informix-NewEra as a Structured Language 5
  Informix-NewEra Language Improvements 5
        The include Statement 6
        External Variable Declarations 6
        Constants 6
        Variable Initialization in Declaration Statements 6
        Function Prototypes 6
        Function Parameter Improvements 7
        Dynamic Memory Allocation 8
        Custom Data Types 8
        Call By Reference 8
  Informix-NewEra Object Implementation 8
        Class Definition 9
        Inheritance 9
        Scope for Class Members 9
  Informix-NewEra Event Implementation 9
        Handler Declaration 10
        Synchronous Calls 11
        Asynchronous Calls 11
  NewEra Class Libraries 11
        The Visual Class Library (VCL) 12
        The Connectivity Class Library (CCL) 12
        Embedded SQL 13

Chapter 2 Using the Window Painter and Application Builder 15
    Object-Oriented Programming with NewEra Applications........................... 15
    The NewEra *wif* File 17
    Using the NewEra Window Painter... 17
    NewEra Event Handlers 19
    Setting Control Properties... 20
        Setting *General* Properties 20
        Setting Location Properties 23
        Setting Format Properties 24
        Setting Database Properties 25
        Setting Entry Properties 26
    Creating Event Handlers 27
    The Window Painter Code Window 28
        Other NewEra Code Blocks 28
        The pre_header Code Block 29
        The pre_body Code Block 29
        The class_extension Code Block 29
        The constructor_extension Code Block... 30
    The NewEra Window Hierarchy 30
    The Window startup Property 31
    The Menu Editor.. 31
    The NewEra Application Builder 33
    Steps in Creating a NewEra Application 34
        Create Database Schema 34
        Create Application Windows with SuperTables 35
        Create Menus and Other Controls 35
        Add Code to Glue Application Objects and Controls 36
        Create Application Reports 36
        Make Cosmetic Changes 37
    SuperTable Window 37
        Field Labels 38
        Using SuperViews 39
        Establishing Master-Detail Relationships 39
Chapter 3 A Sample Application: The Accounts Receivable Module 43
    Accounts Receivable Overview... 43
    Accounts Receivable Data Flow 44
    Accounts Receivable Application Development Issues 45

Contents   v

Locking Issues And Transaction Management 46
       Data Entry Locking Issues 47
Application Windows 48
       Customer Data Entry Window 48
       The Window Template 49
       Customer List 50
       Zip Codes Window 51
       Batch Entry Window 51
       Accounts Receivable Aging Report Window 52
Database Design 53
       The batch Table 55
       The customer Table 55
       The customer_codes Table 56
       The districts Table 56
       The terms Table 56
       The shipping_codes Table 57
       The bill Table 57
       The line_items Table 57
       The stock_items Table 58
       The journal_entries Table 58
       The security Table 58
       The security_codes Table 58
       The stock Table 59
       The zip_code Table 59
       The control Table 59

Chapter 4 The NewEra Window 61
       The ixVisualObject 62
       The NewEra SuperTable 65
       The Visual Frame Object 69
       The Text Box Control 69
       The Label Control 70
       The Button Control 71
       The Picture Button 72
       The Radio Button 73
       The Check Box 74
       The List Box 75
       The SuperField Control 78
       The SuperTable Control 80

Chapter 5 The Structure of NewEra Applications 85
    Structure of a NewEra Program 85
        The Window Object 85
        The Pre-Header Section 86
        Global Variables 87
        The main Program Block 87
        Event Handlers 88
        The Query Button Code 88
        The Retrieve Button Code 89
        The Previous Button Code 89
        The Next Button 90
        The Insert Button 91
        The Delete Button 92
        The Window Constructor 92
        The SuperTable Constructor 93
        The SuperField Constructor 95
        The ixLabel Constructor 97
        The Window Header File include File 98

Chapter 6 Creating NewEra Applications 101
    The Process of Creating a NewEra Application 101
    Create Database Schema 102
    Identify Functionality and Interaction Of Windows 103
    Create Class Libraries 103
    Create Windows 103
        The Process of Creating NewEra Windows 103
        Create Template Window 104
        Open Template Window and Set Window Properties 104
        Paste SuperTable Fields and Buttons for Table(s) and Set
            SuperTable Properties 105
        Add Additional Controls and Code 105
        Format Screen 106
        Add Code Where Needed 106
    Create Menus 106
    Add Code to Glue Applications 106
    Create Reports 106
    Make Cosmetic Changes 107
    Creating the Template Window 107
        Customizing SuperTable Functionality in the Template
            Window 110
        Adding Additional Functionality 113
        Using the Template Windows 121

Contents

Chapter 7 Creating Application Windows with NewEra 123
    Creating Simple Windows with Templates 123
        Open Template Window and Set Window Properties............. 124
        Pasting SuperTable Fields and Buttons; Setting SuperTable
            Properties 124
        Adding Additional Controls and Code 125
        Format Window 126
        Text Formatting 126
        Control Formatting 128
        Adding Code to *Glue* NewEra Controls 128
    Using the DBELIST Box Class 128
        Registering the dbelist Box 129
        The focus Event for the zip_code Field..................................... 129
    Adding Additional Functionality to the Customer Input Window 130
        Use of a Hidden SuperTable... 131
        Binding Radio Buttons to SuperTable Cells 134
        Popup Searchable List Box Window... 137
        Searching the List Box 139
        The Search Function 140
        The List Box select Event... 142
        The preheader Section 143
        The Find Next Button Handler 144
        The finish Event 144
        Using a Grid-Form SuperTable Template: The Zip Code
            Window 145

Chapter 8 Developing Interacting Windows in NewEra 153
    Batch Input Window... 153
        The Retrieve Operation 158
        The Pre-Body Code Section 160
    Adding Additional Functionality 162
        Using Transactions with SuperTables 162
        Programming Field Validations and Lookups........................... 166
        Using Help with NewEra... 168
        Using Error Logging with NewEra 169

Chapter 9 Creating Class Libraries... 175
    Building a Class Library 176
        The Database Aware List Box Class 176
        The dbelist Class Member Functions 180
    The General Use Library Functions 185
        The General Functions Header File... 185
        The General Function Source Code Module 188

Chapter 10 NewEra Reports 193
Functionality Of A/R Aging Report 194
The Accounts Receivable Aging Report 196
Running ViewPoint Pro Reports from NewEra Applications 208

Chapter 11 Extending NewEra Classes 211
Packaging the SuperTable Buttons: Extending the ixFrame Class 212
The browseFrame Class Definition 213
The browseFrame Constructor Function 214
Query Button Activate Event Handler 216
Displaying Browse Information: The Status Frame 217
The statusFrame Constructor Function 218
Extending the SuperTable Class: The browseSuperTable Class 220
The browseSuperTable Constructor 221
The browseSuperTable rowRetrieved Handler 222
Extending the Window Class 224
The browseWindow Constructor 225
Using the Extended NewEra Classes 227
Combining the Extended Classes into the Template Application 229
Changing Functionality of Extended Classes 230

Chapter 12 Migrating Informix-4GL Applications to NewEra 231
Converting Informix-4GL Applications 231
Character-Based versus GUI Screen Development 231
Informix-4GL *Events* 232
The Structure of Informix-4GL Applications 232
Informix-4GL Reports 233
Conversion of Informix-4GL Legacy Applications 233
Language Conversion 234
Isolate Screen I/O Modules 234
Converting Informix-4GL message, error and display Statements 237
Converting the Screen Forms and Browse Functionality 239

Index 241

Introduction

Informix-NewEra was designed primarily for developers of large applications. Apart from a comprehensive object-and database-oriented language, it has a set of five graphical tools. The manual set consists of eight individual books which fully describe the product and its use. This book does not intend to replace the extensive NewEra manual set. It is intended to provide a companion to the product and the manuals. The intention is to give the novice or prospective user a clear description of the process of creating an application in Informix-NewEra. Within this description will be some tips and fresh ideas for the more experienced user.

To get the most out of this book, the user should already understand the basics of the object-oriented approach and the basics of the NewEra product. Some understanding of Informix-4GL would also be helpful.

Informix-NewEra provides a complete set of object-oriented features, so the object-oriented paradigm will be described, but only at an introductory level. This will help those with limited understanding of object-oriented programming to understand the underlying architecture of the product and its applications.

WHAT IS INFORMIX-NEWERA?

Informix promotes the NewEra product with the following statement.

> "Informix-NewEra is an open, graphical, object-oriented development environment for client/server enterprise database applications."

Each word in the statement describes a facet of NewEra, and together the words describe the product. These facets are described in more detail below.

Open – through its published language and window intermediate format (WIF) specification, NewEra is open to third parties wishing to integrate their tools – language generators, window painters, CASE tools, repositories, etc. And through its ODBC compliance, NewEra is open to database servers other than Informix.

Graphical – through highly productive visual programming tools, producing fully graphical applications for both Windows and Motif. (Character-based deployment is also possible.)

Object-oriented – although this claim is heavily over-used in today's client/server tools market, few products are actually more than *object-based*. This means that they can apply object-oriented (OO) rules such as inheritance and polymorphism to visual objects, but you must then connect non-OO code segments to them. NewEra is **fully** object-oriented in that both visual and non-visual objects support inheritance, polymorphism and encapsulation.

Client/server, enterprise, database applications – NewEra is not designed for the 5-user vacation-tracking system. NewEra is architected to cope with large, complex applications that may be deployed throughout the enterprise – 100, 500, 1000 users. And for the millions of lines of high-level code needed to cope with today's increasingly complex application requirements. NewEra is designed to do all this without the need to resort to a third generation language (3GL) such as C or C++ (though you can integrate C++ code with NewEra).

Many large applications just will not fit onto a Windows PC, so NewEra is also architected to support application partitioning – the ability to split an application across both a desktop Windows machine and a UNIX server. And if additional processing power is needed, NewEra applications will run on a Unix workstation.

The Generation Game

The first generation of client/server development tools, as a reaction to the character-terminal, host-based products they were attempting to supplant, majored in three areas:

1. Visual programming: point and click, dragging and dropping objects actually on the screen without having to write code.

2. Great looking screens: exploiting the visual nature of the graphical user interfaces (GUI) to give end-users a more friendly work environment.

3. Quick prototyping: throwing together the core parts of an application in record time, almost in front of the user's eyes.

Unfortunately, their PC heritage and their ability to develop small applications quickly got them into deep water. People liked these graphical, easy-to-use applications and wanted them deployed across the enterprise. They also wanted to build large, complex applications. But the first generation products were not designed to handle "big client/server," and so they failed. They couldn't handle the complexity, and they couldn't handle the performance. In many cases the core code, usually written in a BASIC-like scripting language, was ripped out from behind the screens and replaced with thousands of lines of C code.

In contrast, NewEra inherited the core of its language from Informix-4GL, the most widely used 4GL on open systems. Informix-4GL already had plenty of experience in enterprisewide applications, and Informix took great care in rearchitecting that core to support an object-oriented paradigm, to support graphical constructs and an event-driven user interface and yet to maintain at least 75% compatible with the existing Informix-4GL language. Informix-NewEra then excels in three areas:

Scalability – by supporting rich code functionality, a fully compiled language, and (summer 1995) application partitioning, NewEra is well able to take its place in the second generation, "big client/server" arena.

Productivity – a combination of visual programming, a fully object-oriented language, and the combination of both interpreted and compiled code makes NewEra an extremely productive environment. And since complex applications are usually developed by teams, NewEra is fully integrated with Intersolv's PVCS, the leading version control product for Windows.

Extensibility – through support for Informix and third party-developed class libraries, applications and even NewEra itself can be easily extended without the need to rearchitect from the core.

The NewEra Language

The core of NewEra is the NewEra language. In developing it, Informix combined the power of their existing 4GL with object-oriented (OO) constructs and support for the graphical user interface (GUI). The language has the following features:

- It is a fourth-generation language with English-like syntax containing both procedural statements (such as `let`, and `if/then/else`) and non-procedural statements (such as SQL queries)
- It is a database-oriented language with full support for SQL
- It supports an event-driven programming style which is key to the GUI approach, as well as providing a library of graphical controls
- It is a fully object-oriented language with support for encapsulation, inheritance and polymorphism
- Applications can be written which do not require any visual interface (essential for batch reporting and application partitioning)

- It is an extensible language. Class libraries written by development organizations can add to the functionality of the language without the need for new statements or compiler versions

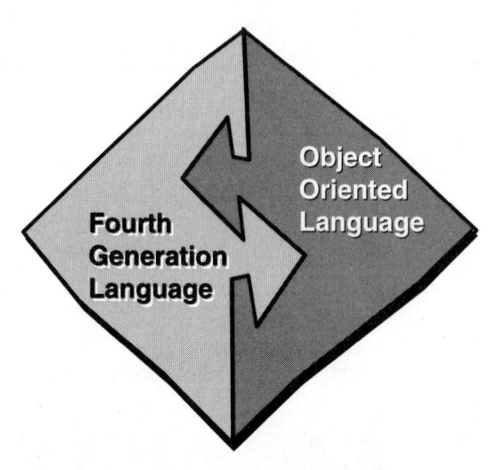

Figure I-1 - Informix-NewEra Architecture

The NewEra language also supports some 75% of the statements of Informix-4GL - all except the screen I/O statements. This makes migration of existing 4GL programs possible. It also makes migration of skills and knowledge much easier.

There is in fact a "migration spectrum," ranging from mere porting to full migration. Applications can be "ported" by just recreating all the visual objects (easy with the Window Painter) and attaching segments of Informix-4GL code to them. This produces an "object-based" program, since there are visual objects but the majority of the code is not object-oriented.

At the other end of the migration spectrum is full migration, converting existing Informix-4GL code into object-oriented code as well as recreating the visual objects. Although this may give the best paybacks in the long term, the effort required depends very much on the state of the code - in particular on how well structured the code is. In practice, the best approach is probably somewhere in between. The conversion of Informix-4GL code to NewEra is covered in more detail in chapter 12.

Flexible Transition to Objects

Revolution is a spectacular though often unproductive path to change, and many OO projects have foundered on the rocks of resistance. Because OO involves a new way of looking at application development, it is often difficult to move programmers with traditional skills over to OO, resulting in a productivity gap while they re-train.

NewEra helps you to bridge that gap by allowing you to move to OO at your own pace. Some team members can start using OO methods straight away, creating objects and methods from scratch. Other programmers who have spent many years programming in 3GLs such as C and COBOL (and 4GLs), can take a hybrid or object-based approach by creating visual objects in the Window Painter, and then attaching to them either traditional code segments or objects written by other team members.

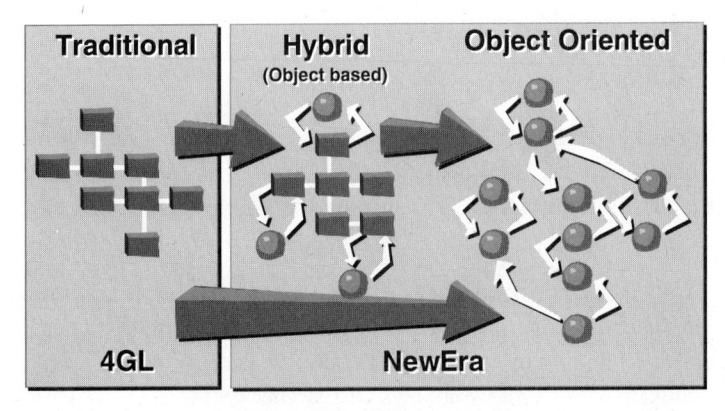

Figure I-2 - NewEra Provides a Flexible Transition to Object-Oriented Programming

Extensibility Through Class Libraries

One of the problems of traditional (non-OO) programming is that it is difficult to extend the functionality of both language and programs without major work on the part of the vendor. Incorporating new core functionality into existing programs can also be difficult for the developer.

A class is a template for an object (the cookie cutter), and a class library is a collection of classes dedicated to a particular set of tasks. Examples would be visual classes or connectivity classes. The fact that class libraries can be written in NewEra, or C or C++ allows you to take advantage of class libraries written by third parties as well as your own.

It is very easy to incorporate a class library into your application, which means that adding functionality for, say, EDI or document imaging, can be just like software clip art!

The NewEra Toolset

NewEra contains a set of tools to help you build applications. These tools are described briefly below.

- Application Builder
- Window Painter
- Interactive Debugger
- ViewPoint Pro
- Repository Browser (available in later version)

Application Builder

The Application Builder is really the programmer's console. It is where the programmer administers the development environment, making choices on code editors and compile options, and graphically managing the building blocks of the application, such as source code files, class libraries, and makefiles.

Unlike any other OOP client/server development tools, NewEra gives you a choice of compilation methods: either interpreted for faster development (compiles are quicker), or fully compiled (compiled to native object code) for faster performance and the ability to break an application down into Windows DLLs. The Application Builder allows you to specify which method to use.

In addition, the Application Builder also controls the integration with Intersolv's PVCS, the market-leading tool for version control and configuration management on Windows.

Window Painter

The Window Painter is more than just a painter, it is an integral part of the application development cycle. It contains all the elements you need to build complete applications. From point-and-click visual objects and pull down menus to database-aware controls that need no coding (such as Query, Retrieve, Insert, Delete). But what sets the Window Painter apart from other similar tools is that it actually generates code – NewEra code. Programmers can change the generated code for database-aware controls, add additional code, and see the whole program through a single view, the code view.

Interactive Debugger

The NewEra Debugger is a graphical interactive tool that allows you to inspect NewEra programs as they are running. With the Debugger you can:

- Examine the source code of NewEra programs (useful for learning about the product)
- Set breakpoints in the code
- Step over and into functions (but only NewEra functions, not C or C++ functions)
- Examine the state of a variable

The Debugger can only be used with interpreted NewEra p-code.

ViewPoint Pro

ViewPoint Pro is a graphical "no coding" power user product that is bundled with NewEra, as well as being sold separately. It allows developers to graphically manage database schemas and SuperViews, as well as manage field validation, editing criteria, and visual attributes. In its standalone version it may be used to create simple applications containing forms, menus and reports. These graphical reports may be run from within a NewEra application. More industrial strength reports need to be written directly in NewEra code.

Third Party Tools and Class Libraries

Because NewEra is such an open environment, a number of third party tools have been integrated with it already. As of March 1995, these include:

- CASE tools. Westmount's ICASE OMT is an object-oriented upper CASE tool which generates NewEra code. Other CASE tools integrations are under development.
- Testing tools. Products such as those from Mercury Interactive, Performix, Segue and SQA improve your ability to test complex client/server applications.
- Version control. Currently the PVCS product for Windows, and Atria's ClearCase is being integrated for UNIX.

The ability to integrate third party class libraries (written in NewEra, C or C++) into NewEra applications is a unique feature. A number of very useful third party libraries will become available in 1995.

HOW THE BOOK IS ORGANIZED

The book introduces you to the tools and language of NewEra by developing portions of an Accounts Receivable application. This section summarizes the chapters of the book.

Introduction – what you're reading now. Summarizes the Informix-NewEra product and the goals of the book.

Chapter 1, The NewEra Language

This chapter covers the basics of the NewEra language. This chapter covers some of the basics of object-oriented programming such as objects, classes, inheritance and polymorphism. The NewEra implementation of events is covered and there is a discussion of how the NewEra language relates to its predecessor language, Informix-4GL.

Chapter 2, Using the Window Painter and Application Builder

This chapter covers the process of developing an application from start to finish using the visual programming capabilities of the Window Painter. The steps involved in setting the general properties for a visual object are covered. The process of entering code for various event handlers and pre-header code blocks is covered.

Chapter 3, A Sample Application: The Accounts Receivable Module

This chapter describes the database schema for the accounts receivable module. The important windows to be used for the application are shown and discussed. Transaction management issues and locking schemes are discussed briefly but are shown in more detail in a later chapter.

Chapter 4, The NewEra Window

This chapter discusses the visual objects and many of the controls contained in a NewEra window. The SuperTable and Superfield controls are also discussed.

Chapter 5, The Structure of NewEra Applications

This chapter discusses the basic structure of a NewEra application. How the various components of the NewEra window interact is discussed and the code behind a complete NewEra application window is discussed in detail.

Chapter 6, Creating NewEra Applications

The process of creating a NewEra application is discussed. Steps for NewEra application development are recommended and demonstrated. The use of NewEra window templates is shown along with the process of extending SuperTable functionality.

Chapter 7, Creating Application Windows with NewEra

The process of creating NewEra windows is demonstrated, progressing from simple, single table application windows to more complex, multiple, interacting windows (chapter 8). Adding controls, using hidden SuperTables, and formatting windows is discussed and a searchable list box and a database aware list box are shown.

Chapter 8, Developing Interacting Windows in NewEra

The use of a batch data entry window is shown with multiple, interacting windows. Actions in one window will trigger activity in other, connected windows. The efforts required to use transactions with SuperTables is demonstrated. The process of using radio buttons with database interaction, and using NewEra help facilities and error logging are also shown.

Chapter 9, Creating Class Libraries

Creating and using class libraries is demonstrated through examples. A database aware list box class is shown and some general use NewEra wrapper functions are detailed.

Chapter 10, NewEra Reports

Using NewEra report writing facilities is discussed and demonstrated through examples. The development of an accounts receivable aging report is shown. The report is written to a file that is then read and displayed to a list box that allows the font size to be changed dynamically. The process of running a ViewPoint-Pro report through NewEra is demonstrated.

Chapter 11, Extending NewEra Classes

The template window example presented in earlier chapters is expanded in this chapter to take advantage of the object-oriented programming facilities of the NewEra language. The creation of a "browse" window is demonstrated, with the definition of classes derived from the NewEra SuperTable (`ixSuperTable`) class and the NewEra frame class (`ixFrame`).

Chapter 12, Migrating Informix-4GL Applications to NewEra

This chapter provides advice and information on migrating Informix-4GL legacy applcations to NewEra. It provides a discussion of the Informix-4GL character-based environment versus the NewEra GUI environment. Informix-4GL statements are associated with equivalent NewEra statements where applicable. Tips are provided for converting Informix-4GL screen logic to NewEra window facilities.

APPRECIATION

Thanks to several people for their assistance in the creation of this text. Bill Hedge provided useful technical insight and perceptive review of some key technical points. Maribeth Bray who provided consistent and timely technical review of the text. And Isie Masri who provided some last minute insights into the subtle specificity of object-oriented terminology.

Chapter 1
The NewEra Language

The NewEra language is Informix's successor to the enormously successful Informix-4GL language. NewEra is a more robust language than Informix-4GL with many language features such as constants and `include` statements that were absent from Informix-4GL. But the most significant improvement in the language is that NewEra is *object-oriented*. The structure and benefits of object-oriented languages are discussed below.

OBJECT-ORIENTED LANGUAGES

Object-oriented programming represents a paradigm shift, like moving from an Earth-centric to a Sun-centric view of the Solar System. Until the 16th century, everyone believed that the Sun and all the planets and stars went around the Earth. This model neatly explained the majority of phenomena that occurred above people's heads. There were one or two planets that seemed to stop and actually go backwards (retrograde) from time to time, but that didn't seem to have too much effect on people's lives. It was only when Kepler started questioning this Earth-centric principle and suggesting instead a solar system with the Sun at the center, that real advances in astronomy could be made (see Figure 1-1).

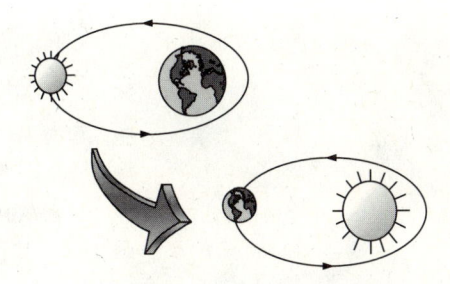

Figure 1-1 - A Paradigm Shift: Moving from an Earth-centric to a Sun-centric Approach

To cope with the increasing demands put on software development by end-users, complex systems and the need to make use of ever more powerful hardware, we need a *paradigm shift*, a new model, a new way of looking at the problem. Programmers must move away from the old way of programming and take a leaf out of the hardware vendors' book. They achieve increasingly greater levels of complexity by plugging together building blocks of pre-tested, pre-specified chips. Developers need to build software in the same way as hardware vendors build hardware – from pre-tested building blocks, or components.

WHAT IS AN OBJECT?

Objects are like cells, the basic building blocks of nature. Cells, like objects, package related information (data) and behavior (methods) together. Cells have a nucleus surrounded by various proteins and a membrane. Cells communicate with each other by sending messages, not directly to the nucleus, but to the proteins around it. This helps to protect the nucleus and ensures that it only does the tasks it was designed to do.

Complex organisms are built up of millions of cells. These cells are effectively objects and the communication with messages among cells is analogous to object-oriented *events*. These events are discussed in more detail below.

ENCAPSULATION

Packaging related data and procedures (functions) together is called *encapsulation*. It is an improved version of information hiding and it ensures that program variables are protected inside an object. No part of the system depends on knowing the internal details of any other part. No other part of the program may interfere directly with the data of an object.

Objects send each other *messages*; these messages call the object's respective methods into action, and it is these methods alone that access the required variables (see Figure 1-2 - Object Communication via Messages).

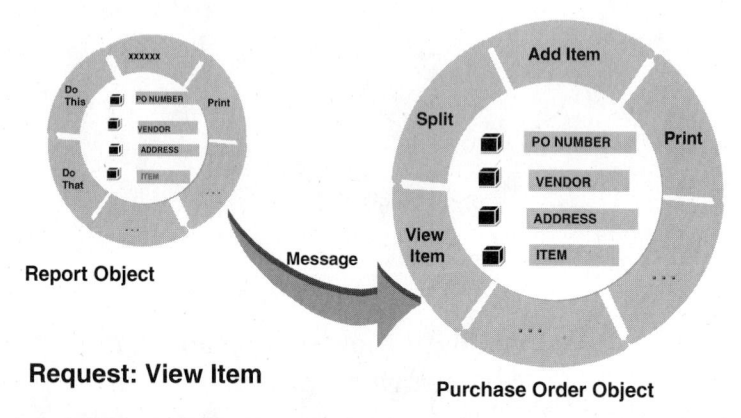

Figure 1-2 - Object Communication via Messages

Consider a VCR remote control. To play a tape you don't unscrew the lid and touch a couple of wires together, you point the remote control at the VCR and press "play". You send a message to the VCR to undertake a particular task, and you're not really interested in how it does it. The advantage here is that if you get a different model of VCR, you don't have to learn a new way of playing a tape, you just point the remote control and press play, even though the inner workings may have changed significantly. You need not know how the VCR works. The complexity is *encapsulated* in the VCR.

Encapsulation also has a significant side benefit. Because an object has both data and methods, it is very much closer to being a *real-world* object. We can talk about the Purchase Order object and its methods – add an item, view an item, print the purchase order. This approach means that programmers can talk to end-users about things they *both* understand. In fact, Grady Booch, one of the founding fathers of OOP (object-oriented programming), says:

"If you want to program in the traditional, structured way, take the specification for the project and underline all the **verbs**. If you want to program in an object-oriented way, underline all the **nouns**."

WHAT IS A CLASS?

A class is a blueprint for an object that defines the methods and variables for a particular type of object.

A radio button class defines the look, feel and behavior of a radio button object. A new instance of a radio button object may have a different label and different code may be executed in the activate handler for the button, but the button will always behave the same.

A class library is a set of reusable classes placed in a library, and dedicated to a particular set of tasks or functionality. NewEra is shipped with a Visual Class Library for Windows which contains classes for list a variety of intelligent controls: text boxes, radio buttons, check boxes, and others. The class library is where the benefits of reuse really appear.

INHERITANCE

One way that we cope with complexity is breaking complex structures down into their constituent parts. Often we find that certain objects are just specialized versions of more general objects. The class of objects known as "vehicles" have a number of things in common. They all have wheels, a motive force, and some kind of steering mechanism. We can further classify certain types of vehicles as being more specialized. The delivery truck, tank truck and fire truck are all trucks with common characteristics – they *inherit* these characteristics from the base class of trucks. But they each have individual methods which are unique.

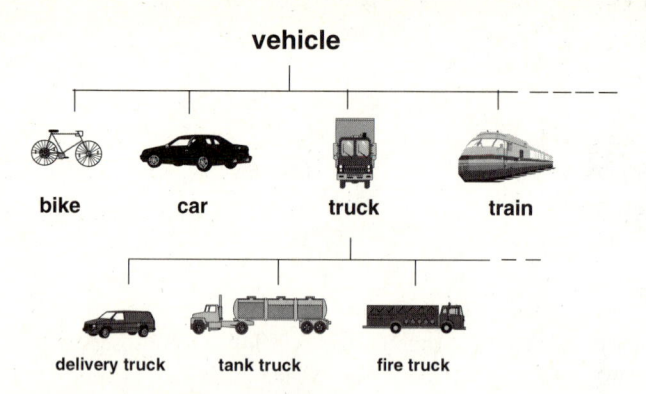

Figure 1-3 - Inheritance

Another real-world example would be a customer class. All customers have a number of things in common, but in a particular business there could be two kinds of customers: a retail customer and a wholesale customer. These are special cases of the more general customer class that inherit all of the characteristics of the base customer class, but add some extra variables and methods.

Should another class of customer be needed in the future (maybe a corporate customer), it would be easy to create this class out of the base customer class, and then add any new special characteristics. This leads to greater reuse, quality and maintainability, and rather than programming everything from scratch, we start to program *by difference*, only programming the things that have changed from previously known classes.

So inheritance defines one class of objects (the derived class) as a special case of a more general class (the *base* class). It automatically includes all the methods and variable definitions of the general class, and it may define its own methods and variables, some of which may actually *override* the inherited characteristics.

Polymorphism

Objects act in response to messages they receive. But the same message can result in different actions when received by different objects. The message "print" for example, when sent to a picture object will invoke will invoke different methods than when it is sent to a text object. This is known as polymorphism and it allows new objects or printing methods to be added without having to change the object sending the "print" message. Informix-NewEra supports this powerful mechanism.

INFORMIX-4GL AND THE NEWERA LANGUAGE

Informix-4GL was the foundation for the NewEra language. The core of the Informix-4GL language is in NewEra: the flow of control statements, the SQL data types, report writing language and a complete function call implementation. What is missing are the elegant screen interaction statements of Informix-4GL. These have effectively been replaced by the NewEra Visual Class Library (VCL).

The Informix-4GL reporting language has been left intact. This structured, block-oriented report language has a proven track record in the field.

INFORMIX-NEWERA AS A STRUCTURED LANGUAGE

The Informix-NewEra language is a structured programming language in the tradition of C or Algol. Language statements are organized in blocks with a clear and sometimes explicit beginning and end. Unconditional branches are available, but their use is discouraged. Conditional control branches lead to structured code blocks that make tracing program execution easier.

Functions can receive and return multiple parameters. These functions can be developed as black-box components, being designed for a specific function. Programmers can merely call the function, passing in the correct parameters and receiving the correct results. Programmers need not be concerned with the implementation of the function - it is a black-box.

There are clear benefits to structured programming. Maintenance is easier because programmers can clearly see the entire scope of a statement by examining the statement block.

INFORMIX-NEWERA LANGUAGE IMPROVEMENTS

The Informix-NewEra language has been improved over its Informix-4GL antecedent. These improvements are detailed below.

Improvement	Description
`include` statement	allows files to be inserted into NewEra source code modules during compilation
external variable declarations	allows global variables to be optionally recognized in other modules
variable initialization in declaration statements	allows variables to be initialized when they are declared
function parameter default values	function parameters can be declared to receive default values in the event a parameter is not passed
named function parameters	function parameters can be assigned names
function prototypes	function signatures are described to the compiler to allow compiler checking
dynamic memory allocation	memory is dynamically allocated via object instantiation

Improvement	Description
call by reference	objects are passed and assigned with a reference to the object
custom data types	class definitions are effective data types
constants	integer constants can be declared. Their value cannot be changed in the application.

The include Statement

NewEra `include` statements allow files to be inserted into a source code module where the `include` statement appears. If a full pathname is not included, the current directory will be searched for the file. Additional search directories can be added by passing the -H option to the NewEra compiler.

External Variable Declarations

NewEra allows variables to be declared global in one module, and then optionally have those variables recognized in another module using the 'external variable' declaration. This allows the scope of global variables to be restricted to those modules where the variable needs to be recognized.

Constants

NewEra allows integer constants to be declared. These constants are set at compile time and cannot be modified during program execution. This provides a level of safety and can improve the readability of the code.

Variable Initialization in Declaration Statements

Variables can be declared and initialized in a single statement in NewEra. The initialization can involve expressions including function calls. Thus an object can be declared and instantiated (created) with the statement

```
variable   vectorObj = new ixVector()
```

or a value could be assigned to a variable in a declaration as with

```
variable   x  = 1, y = 2 * 100
```

Function Prototypes

Function prototypes or signatures can be defined in NewEra. These prototypes are not required and the Informix-4GL style functions with no prototypes are still supported.

Chapter 1: The NewEra Language   7

Prototyping allows the compiler to check the values being passed to a function and can thus eliminate errors before the application is run.

Function Parameter Improvements

Function parameters can be named in NewEra and default values can be specified. When function parameters are named, they can then be referenced with the name when the function is called. If a function parameter has a default, then the parameter can be eliminated when the function is called and the default value will be used by the function, thus NewEra supports variable function parameters.

Named parameters can make function calls more readable. And the ability to assign defaults to function parameters can greatly simplify function usage as shown below.

```
function retrCustDetailRecs( customer_number integer,
                             sort_criteria char(*) : NULL,
                             filter_criteria char(*) : NULL )
     returning ixRow
```

This function prototype is for a function that retrieves detail records for a customer. Named parameters are supplied for the customer number, sort criteria and filter criteria. The design for this function stated that the most common call to the function would be to retrieve all detail records for a customer. In some cases there would be a need to filter the detail records and possibly sort the records, so the function should have the capability to retrieve records with filter and sort criteria.

It would therefore be acceptable for the function to simply retrieve all customer detail records by default. To implement the function in this manner, the sort criteria and the filter criteria are allowed to default to NULL values. The code in the function will determine that if these values are NULL, then there is no need to add sort criteria or filter criteria to the data access statement. The customer number is a required parameter and no default is supplied for this parameter. This function prototype allows the function to be called as follows.

```
variable custRec ixRow

call retrCustDetailRecs( customer_number: 13334 )
        returning custRec
```

Using named parameters with defaults simplifies this function call but yet allows the flexibility to add sort criteria and filter criteria to the function call if needed.

Dynamic Memory Allocation

Through objects, dynamic memory allocation is supported in NewEra. As objects are instantiated from a class reference, the memory for the object is assigned. When a class definition contains data variables, memory is allocated for the variable when the object is created, and the memory for the variable is created.

When an object has a NULL reference, then its allocated memory is available to be *scavenged* by NewEra. NewEra will free this memory when it sees fit to do so. The NewEra language does not explicitly provide a means of freeing memory allocated to objects. An intrinsic destructor function cannot be explicitly invoked, but a programmer can write their own "!destroy()" method. NewEra will then call this method automatically when memory for an object is deallocated.

Custom Data Types

Custom data types can be created using objects. A class could be declared to contain a reference to a complex record. Data variables could then be created to be identical to the complex record by using the class name as a data type, as shown below.

```
variable xrec,yrec,zrec myComplexRec
```

In this example, the data type `myComplexRec` is a class reference to the class containing the complex record definition. The variables `xrec`, `yrec` and `zrec` are all declared to be of data type `myComplexRec`.

Call By Reference

NewEra does not supply a generic pointer as the C language does. Though this is a much praised feature in the C language, there is danger in allowing this capability in a language. NewEra controls this feature by providing data references through objects.

Object identifiers are references to the objects. When an object is passed to a function, it is passed by reference. Likewise, when an object is assigned, it is assigned by reference. This provides a very efficient means of manipulating data variables and constants in the NewEra language and is an improvement over the Informix-4GL language which only provided function *call-by-value*.

INFORMIX-NEWERA OBJECT IMPLEMENTATION

NewEra provides *true* object-oriented facilities. NewEra *classes* can be defined that encapsulate both data and functions (methods). These classes can be used at runtime to instantiate objects of the class. Classes can be *derived* from other classes through *inheritance*.

Class Definition

NewEra classes are defined using the `class` statement. The class definition is used to package the functionality of class. The class definition can contain variables and functions (or methods). The class definition **must** contain a definition for the class *constructor* function. This function is given the same name as the class name, and is implicitly called when an object of the class is created.

Variables and functions can be declared as `public` variables that can be referenced by class members and non-class members. These class components can also be declared as `private` variables that can be referenced only by class members. And optionally, they can also be declared as `protected` can be referenced by class members and members of derived classes but not by non-class or derived class members.

Inheritance

NewEra classes support inheritance. A class can be declared 'derived from' another class. When a class is derived from another class, it inherits all of the data variables and functions of the other class.

Scope for Class Members

By using scope rules wisely, a great deal of safety can be employed in the process of encapsulation. When functions and data are packaged in class libraries, the programmer may want to restrict users from using certain portions of the library. If functions have been written to be used internally within the class library, then access to these functions can be restricted by declaring the functions and data to be `private`, or `protected` limiting access only to the class members.

If a class has been designed to be an abstract class existing essentially for other classes to be derived from its class definition, then the `protected` declaration could be used. This declaration would extend access to not only the class members of the class, but also to class members of a derived class.

INFORMIX-NEWERA EVENT IMPLEMENTATION

An *event* is used to trigger the activity of an object oriented application. NewEra events can be declared for a class using the `event` statement. The `event` statement appears in the class definition. Events can be declared to receive parameters and return values, in a manner similar to functions.

Events are placed on an event queue where they are later dispatched to the appropriate object handler. NewEra does not examine this queue until it is in a mode where it is waiting for user input, essentially in a wait loop. It then removes events from the top of the queue, determines the appropriate event handler and dispatches the event (see Figure 1-4).

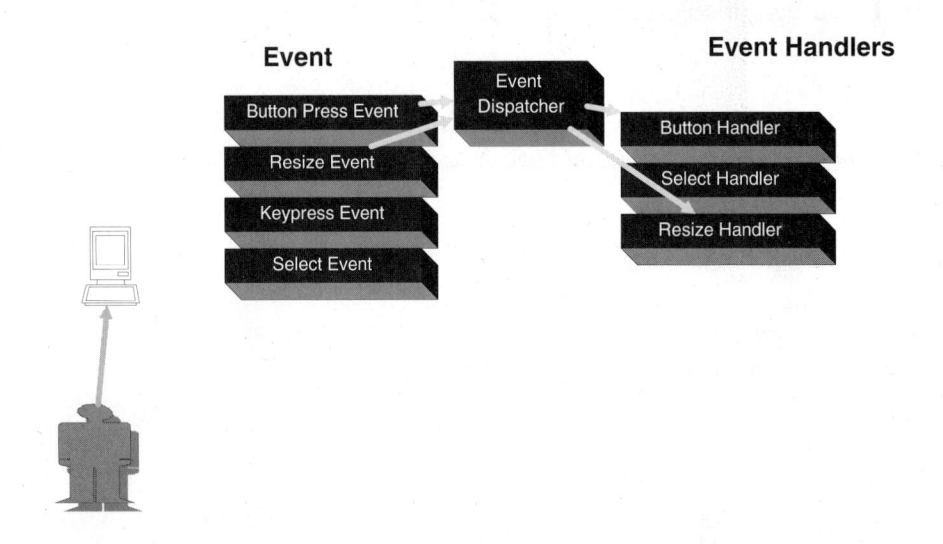

Figure 1-4 - NewEra Event Queue

Most events have default handlers assigned. These default handlers generally do not take any action. The power of NewEra and object-oriented programming is that the programmers can easily assign their own handlers for these events. And using the Window Painter, this can be accomplished through a visual point-and-click mechanism. This text provides several examples of this technique.

Handler Declaration

Handlers are declared for an event of a class. Events are then attached to the handlers using the `handle` statement. The handler **must** be a handler for the class which owns the event as shown below.

```
class myClass
function myClass::myClass()
event pickEvent()

end class

...
handler myclass::handlePickEvent() returning void
...
end handler

-- class constructor
```

```
function myClass::myClass()

handle pickEvent with myClass::handlePickEvent

end function
```

This example shows a class being created and an event, named `pickEvent`, being declared within the class definition statement. A handler is then declared outside of the class definition. Note that the handler uses the class designation in its declaration (`myClass::HandlePickEvent`). The `handle` statement is then used in the class constructor to assign the `handlePickEvent` handler to the `pickEvent` event for the class `myClass`. Had an event that was not declared to be part of the `myClass` class been used in the `handle` statement, a compile time error would have been generated.

Synchronous Calls

Handlers can be called synchronously using the `call` statement just as a function is called. This is a useful feature. As examples in this text will show, this allows handler code to be easily reused throughout the application with a simple function call.

Asynchronous Calls

Handlers can be called with an asynchronous call using the `post` statement. This places the event in a queue where it will be executed when the program begins to wait for user input.

NEWERA CLASS LIBRARIES

NewEra supplies a number of class libraries to make the task of programming applications easier. These class libraries supply much of the functionality of the NewEra language. Learning and understanding these library functions is key to mastering the NewEra language.

Many of the tasks performed by the screen interaction statements of Informix-4GL have been replaced by the Visual Class Library. In fact, the process of retrieving data from the database and manipulating the data on the screen have been combined together into a set of class libraries. Data retrieval, manipulation, validation and database updates have been reduced to a small set of class library functions.

Many data manipulation features that programmers have wanted to see in the Informix-4GL language have now been neatly packaged in Informix-supplied class libraries. String manipulation facilities, mathematical functions and dynamic arrays are all contained in well documented, easy to use class libraries. These libraries are discussed in greater detail below and throughout the text.

The Visual Class Library (VCL)

The Informix supplied VCL contains two very important classes: the SuperTable and the SuperField class libraries. These classes supply the facilities for displaying data to the window and moving data to and from the database. Data can be written to and retrieved from window fields, mirroring the functionality of the `display` and `input` statements in Informix-4GL. But the SuperTable goes beyond simple input and display of data; it is a database aware control, and has the ability to manipulate the database under control of the user.

With the SuperTable, data can be retrieved from the database table and displayed to the screen using the single SuperTable member `retrieve` function call. The database table can be updated with a single call to the SuperTable member function `apply`. Other functions exist to validate data, change query criteria and change the display mode for the SuperTable control.

The SuperField class library is part data processing in NewEra. The SuperField relates to the data entry field in the SuperTable frame. A number of events are associated with the SuperField that allow the data entry process to be controlled. A `beforeCell` event allows the programmer to enter code to be executed after the user attempts to leave the cell. Other similar events exist for the SuperField that allow a significant control over the data entry process. These events are similar to the `beforeField` and `afterField` blocks in the Informix-4GL `input` statement.

Other VCL classes relate to window objects and controls. Any of the objects that appear on a NewEra window are true NewEra objects within the language. For instance, a button control on the window is an instance of an `ixButton` class. This control can therefore be treated as an object; a reference to the control can be passed to a function and the button object could be copied to another object. Within the button object are all of the functions within the class `ixButton`. And since the `ixButton` class has inherited functions from `ixVisualObject`, these functions are available and can be used to hide and show the button as needed.

Other intelligent NewEra controls are the list box, the radio button and the check box. All of these controls are objects in the NewEra program with member data and member functions that allow the control to be manipulated.

The Connectivity Class Library (CCL)

The CCL contains a set of ODBC compliant class definitions that contain facilities for manipulating the database. Using the CCL, the database is manipulated using objects and thus has all the advantages of using objects. The CCL classes can be inherited and custom CCL classes can be created by the programmer. The object reference can be created in one function and then passed (by reference) to another function to perform the actual data retrieval.

The CCL member retrieval functions retrieve data into `ixRow` objects that are derived from the dynamic array object, `ixVector`. These objects take on any record layout necessary the structure of which can be determined at runtime. Thus, Informix-NewEra provides an easy-to-use capability to perform dynamic SQL using NewEra objects. These `ixRow` objects can in turn be passed by reference to other functions for manipulation.

An `ixRowArray` object is also available. This object is a dynamic array of `ixRow` objects. It can grow and shrink as needed and automatically performs memory allocation. A data retrieval set can be completely loaded into an `ixRowArray` and then manipulated, passing the array object by reference if needed. (In fact, this is how the SuperTable class retrieves data.)

All of the database operations of the CCL are database independent. An application written to use the Informix database could be run against an Oracle database with no changes required.

Embedded SQL

The SQL language is part of Informix-NewEra. In NewEra applications, SQL statements can be inserted just as any other language statement. Database cursors can be created and used as they are in Informix-4GL and ESQL/C.

The SQL language is a convenient and clear method of interacting with the database in Informix-NewEra. With a few lines of code and some built-in Informix-NewEra functions, the object record benefits outlined above could be used with embedded SQL.

Both the CCL and embedded SQL methods of database access are demonstrated in this text.

Chapter 2
Using the Window Painter
and Application Builder

With the Informix-NewEra Window Painter, the window is the focal point of the application (see Figure 2-1). The GUI window is composed of visual objects which *raise* events. These events control the application. An application does not take a serial, procedural path, but instead takes the execution path chosen implicitly by the user's actions. This is consistent with the GUI paradigm where the user controls the flow of the application by triggering events.

Visual objects can be simple text boxes or intelligent controls such as a radio button, list box, or a check box. All window objects are true programming objects which represent instantiations of a class. These classes have all of the properties and behavior of NewEra classes, including inheritance.

Where Informix-4GL used easy-to-remember syntax to provide for screen interaction, Informix-NewEra provides a visual point-and-click environment where screen fields and buttons are pasted into the window to perform most programming functions. Instead of writing a set of Informix-4GL statements to open and display a window and a screen form, the programmer instead paints the window and screen fields as well as any additional controls that may be needed.

Any code needed to connect the controls and window objects together is usually entered using the Window Painter. In this respect, the Window Painter is an organizing tool. The programmer simply selects the control or window object to be coded, "clicks" the item with the mouse, and a code window with a list of appropriate events is displayed. The programmer selects the event to program and can then enter the code for the event.

OBJECT-ORIENTED PROGRAMMING WITH NEWERA APPLICATIONS

The NewEra language adds an object-oriented layer to an already rich, structured language. This creates a subtle but minor conflict in the programming process: whether to use a structured, function driven style versus programming in a purely object-oriented approach. The language does not insist on either approach and provides sufficient capabilities to do both. The structured programming style is certainly amenable to legacy Informix-4GL applications being converted, but is not consistent with the object-oriented approach being used by the Window Painter.

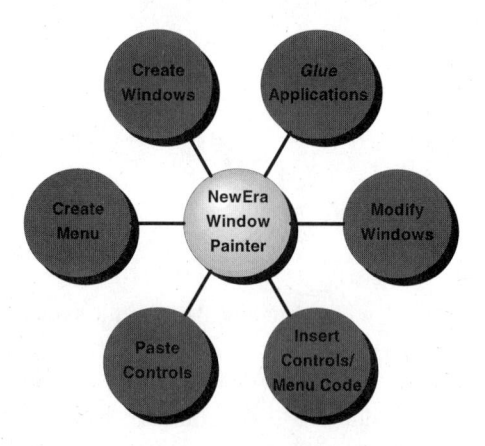

Figure 2-1 - The NewEra Window Painter as the Focal Point of Application Development

A utilitarian approach may be the best approach - to use the language facilities that best suit the task at hand. If an application has a complex set of procedures to perform, then a structured approach may best suit the application. If an application involves manipulation of a complex set of data items with complex sets of behavior, then an object-oriented approach may be best. The NewEra language has the language components to support both approaches to programming.

The capability to combine the two programming approaches in the same application yields an effective program structure. This is an approach that is effective with the NewEra language. In NewEra, the Window Painter treats the data entry window and its components as a set of objects. This is an appropriate metaphor for the GUI screen where the components interact with each other and the user controls the flow of the program by triggering events. A structured, serial, procedure driven approach would not work well in this environment (this is part of the difficulty of mapping a character-based, procedural application into a GUI application).

In the NewEra data entry window where data is retrieved through window components, an object-oriented approach is appropriate. But other parts of the same data entry application may be better suited to the procedural approach. For example, a journal entry update window may use a master-detail window with a *free-form* SuperTable as the master component and a *grid-form* SuperTable as the detail portion. The Window Painter would automatically provide most of the GUI components for this application. But as data is entered in the grid SuperTable, a total must be kept and tracked, account codes must be validated, the set of journal entries must be kept in balance and the total of the journal entries must match the batch total. This should require some structured code, preferably functions to perform each of these procedural operations. Additionally, once the journal entry operation is complete, an account update must be performed.

It would be perfectly appropriate to program this complex procedural operation using structured code. This data entry application would combine both structured application development and object-oriented code; this would effectively be a *hybrid* approach to NewEra application programming (see Figure 2-2) combining object-oriented and structured code in the same application. Conversion of legacy Informix-4GL applications to NewEra could make use of this approach.

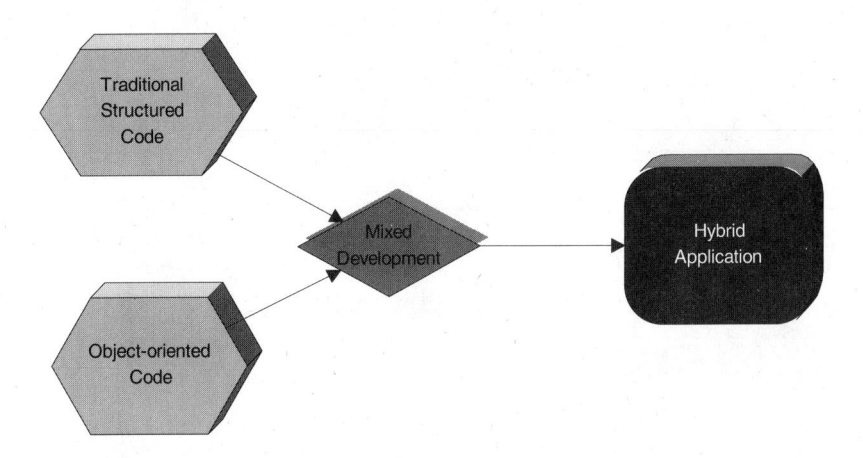

Figure 2-2 - A Hybrid Approach to Application Programming with NewEra

THE NEWERA *WIF* FILE

The NewEra Window Painter generates a *wif* (window interchange format) file. This file contains references to the properties of the window and its objects. It will also contain entries which reference the events triggered within the application and the code to be executed within those events. When the window is saved, the *wif* file is used to generate the NewEra code for the application. This NewEra code is then compiled to become the NewEra application.

The *wif* file is part of the open architecture of NewEra. Just as vendors are encouraged to create and sell object libraries for NewEra, the *wif* file is also available to be generated by other applications. A third-party Window Painter could optionally generate a NewEra *wif* file in addition to other window formats to describe the window being painted.

USING THE NEWERA WINDOW PAINTER

When started, the NewEra Window Painter presents the programmer with the window shown in Figure 2-3 - The NewEra Window Painter. There are two button bars available: the top button bar and the side button bar. The top button bar contains buttons for "new window", "file save", the "menu builder", "properties", and the "SuperTable editor". To the right of these buttons is a drop-down list box which lists the fonts available. To the right of this is a drop down list box for the font size. Next there are buttons for formatting text to bold, italics, and underline. To the right of these buttons are buttons for "align left", "align right", "center" and "free-form" alignment for the fields on the window

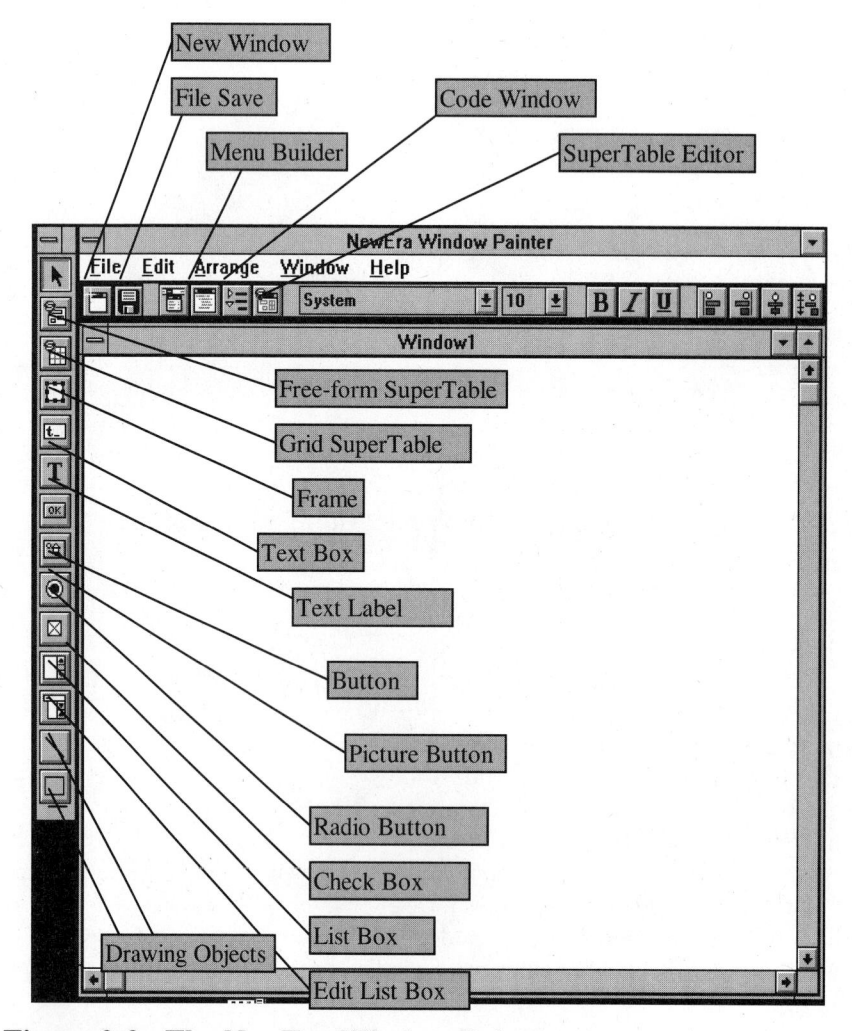

Figure 2-3 - The NewEra Window Painter

The side button bar contains buttons to paint the intelligent controls and objects available in NewEra. These objects are the free-form SuperTable, the grid-form

SuperTable, a frame object, a scrollable text box, a text label, a button control, a picture button, a radio button, a check box control, a list box, and a drop down list box.

NEWERA EVENT HANDLERS

The event handling facilities in NewEra are some of the richest in any language available. For example, the SuperField control provides events for `afterCell`, `afterDataChanged`, `CellkeyPressed`, `beforeCell`, `beforeDataChanged`, and a number of others.

Since NewEra is an object-oriented language, events are inherited from derived classes, so the `ixSuperField` class inherits the `focusIn` and `focusOut` events from the `ixControl` class and handlers can be written to handle these events for an `ixSuperField` object as though the event were part of the `ixSuperField` class.

Event handlers indirectly allow the user to control the flow of the application. A button could be used in much the way that menu items were used in character based user interfaces written in Informix-4GL. When the user selects a button, an event is triggered in the same way that a user would trigger or execute the code associated with the menu item in a character-based interface.

In order to execute code associated with a button control, an event handler must be used to handle the event associated with the `select` event for the button. The NewEra Window Painter provides an easy to access interface for coding event handlers. When the programmer uses the mouse to double-click on the control in the NewEra Window Painter, a code window will open with a drop-down list box for the events associated with the control (See Figure 2-4).

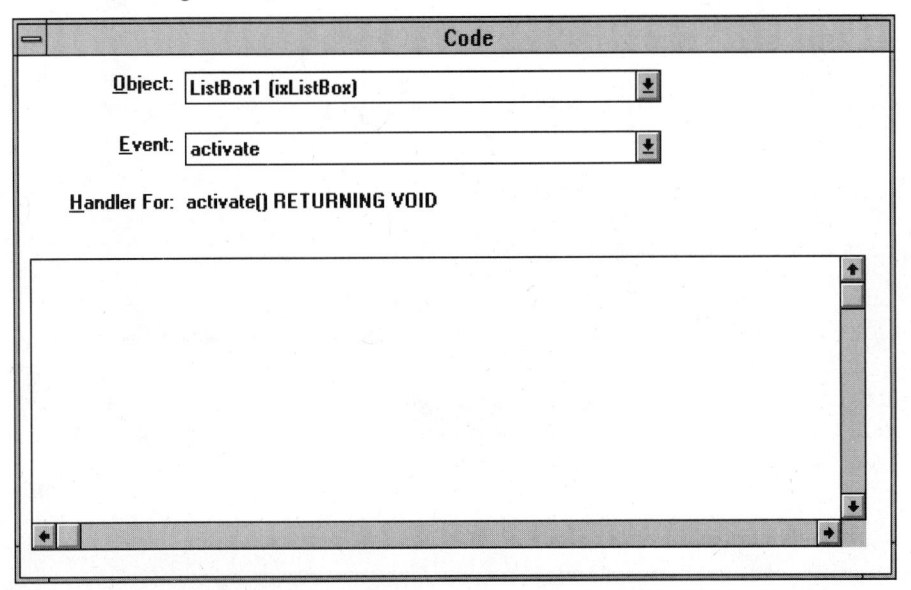

Figure 2-4 - Event Code Window

SETTING CONTROL PROPERTIES

The NewEra Window Painter allows a number of different attributes to be defined for window objects. Properties are divided into the categories of *general*, *location*, *format*, *database* and *entry*. These properties affect where and how the object will be displayed on the window and the appearance of the object. Clicking on the properties button or the top button displays the popup window shown in Figure 2-5 - The Properties Dialogue Box. The list of properties for each category may be displayed (or collapsed) by using the mouse to click on that category. Properties may then be set as described below.

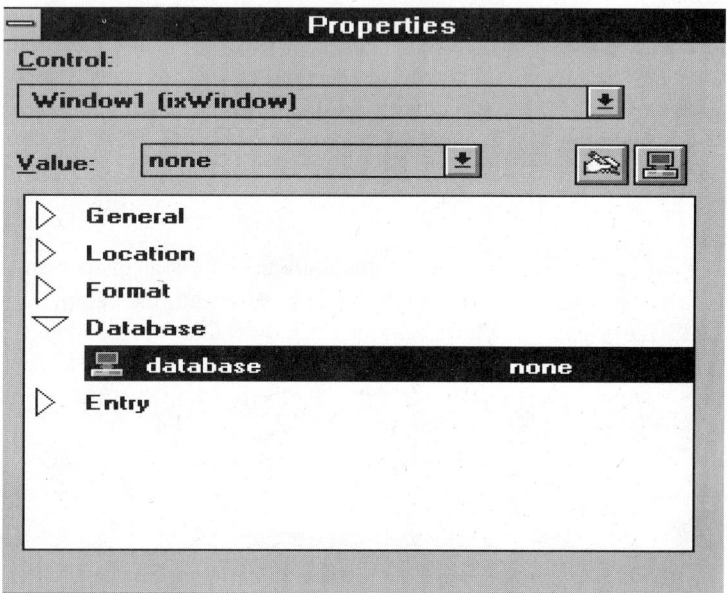

Figure 2-5 - The Properties Dialogue Box

Setting *General* Properties

The *general* properties for window objects include such attributes as the *name* of the object (the name that will be used throughout the generated code for the object), the *title* that will appear on the window for the object, and the *style* of the object. The name of the object is the label that will be used throughout the NewEra generated code for that control. It is a good policy (and makes code maintenance easier) to change this name to something meaningful for the application being coded.

For instance, the default name for a window as generated by the Window Painter could be `window1`. In the case of a customer information input application, the main window could instead be named `CustWN` (see Figure 2-6).

As a general rule of thumb, it is useful to distinguish control names with naming conventions, naming windows with an 'WN' ending and SuperTables with an 'ST' ending, and a list box with an 'LB' ending. Additionally, radio buttons could have an 'RB' ending, buttons could have a 'BN' ending and check boxes could have a 'CB' ending.

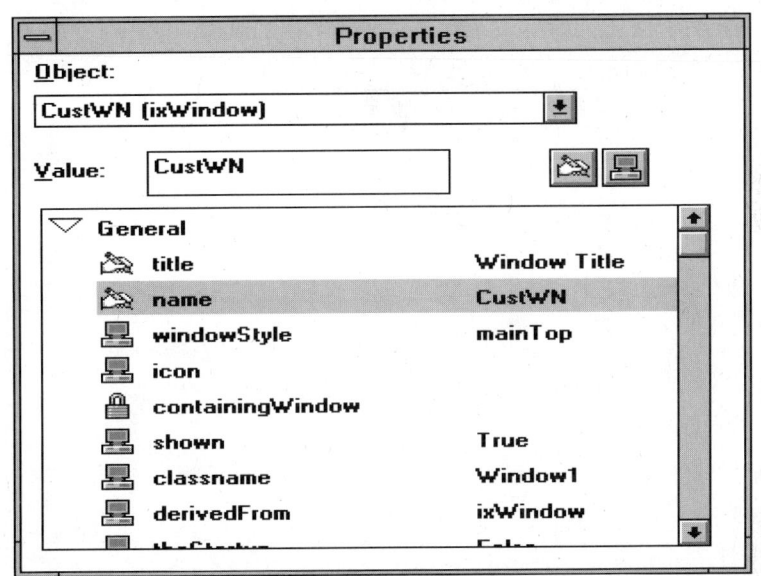

Figure 2-6 - Window Painter Properties Window

Many objects also have a property for the *title* of the control; this is the label that will appear on the window for the control (see Figure 2-7- Status Overdue Radio Button Properties). For a button control, it is the label that will appear on the button (see Figure 2-15). For a check box, it is the label that will appear next to the check box.

In Figure 2-7, the radio button has been given the name `StatusOverdueRB` by changing the name parameter in the properties dialogue box for the window object to `StatusOverdueRB`. This is a name which better reflects the function of the radio box.

Calling the `ixRadioButton isPushed` member function will return TRUE if the button is pushed, or FALSE if the button has not been pressed. This would allow the following code to be written.

```
if window1.StatusOverdueRB.isPushed() then

    -- flag the account as overdue
    update customer
    set   status_flag = "O"
    where customer_number = 13444

end if
```

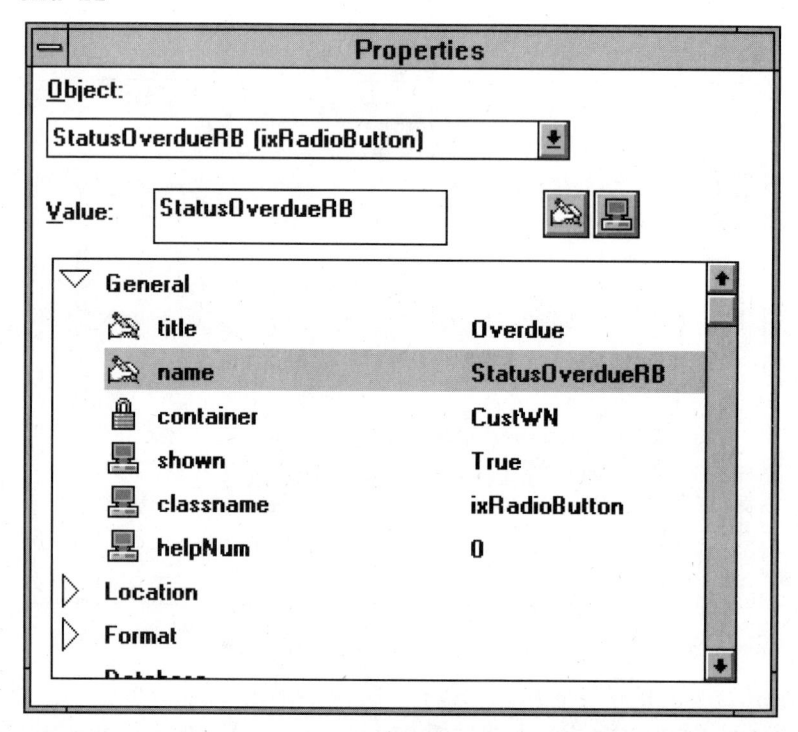

[Properties dialog showing:
Object: StatusOverdueRB (ixRadioButton)
Value: StatusOverdueRB
General:
- title: Overdue
- name: StatusOverdueRB
- container: CustWN
- shown: True
- classname: ixRadioButton
- helpNum: 0
- Location
- Format]

Figure 2-7- Status Overdue Radio Button Properties

Without this change, the Window Painter may have named the object `radio_button46`, a much more ambiguous name than the name `StatusOverdueRB`.

In Figure 2-8, the SuperTable which references the `items` table has been named `itemsST`. This allows the SuperTable member functions to be called with more meaningful statements. For example, to retrieve data from the `items` table using a SuperTable, the following code could be executed.

```
variable ok    BOOLEAN

LET ok = window1.itemsST.retrieve( QBE: FALSE )
```

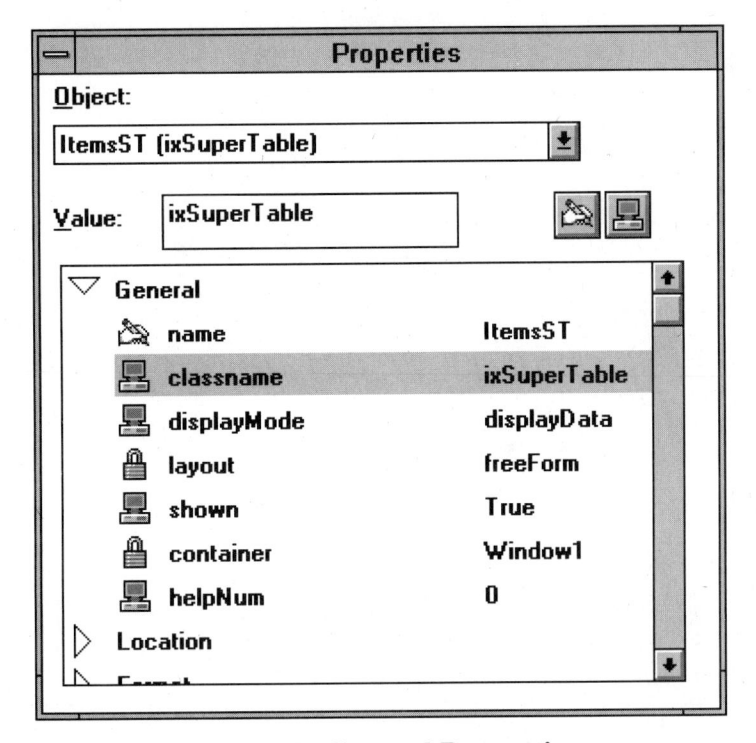

Chapter 2: Using the Window Painter and Application Builder   23

```
┌─ ───────────────── Properties ─────────────────┐
│ Object:                                         │
│ ┌─────────────────────────────────────┐ ┌───┐  │
│ │ ItemsST (ixSuperTable)              │ │ ↓ │  │
│ └─────────────────────────────────────┘ └───┘  │
│                                                 │
│ Value:   ┌─────────────┐           ┌───┬───┐   │
│          │ ixSuperTable│           │ 🖊 │🖥│   │
│          └─────────────┘           └───┴───┘   │
│  ┌─────────────────────────────────────────┐ ▲ │
│  │ ▽  General                              │ │ │
│  │      🖊  name              ItemsST      │ │ │
│  │      🖥  classname         ixSuperTable │ │ │
│  │      🖥  displayMode       displayData  │ │ │
│  │      🔒  layout            freeForm     │ │ │
│  │      🖥  shown             True         │ │ │
│  │      🔒  container         Window1      │ │ │
│  │      🖥  helpNum           0            │ │ │
│  │ ▷  Location                             │ │ │
│  │ ▽  Format                               │ ▼ │
│  └─────────────────────────────────────────┘   │
└─────────────────────────────────────────────────┘
```

Figure 2-8 - Items SuperTable General Properties

And if `Window1` had been named to `itemsWN`, then an even clearer segment of code could be used as shown below.

```
LET ok = itemsWN.itemsST.retrieve( QBE: TRUE )
```

Setting Location Properties

The "location" properties specify where the visual object will be placed on the window. They allow four parameters to be input as shown in Figure 2-9; the *height*, the *left* corner, the *top* corner and the *width*. Entries are in twips, centimeters or inches (depending on the *Preferences* choices under the *Window* menu of the Window Painter).

The top and left parameters for a given visual object are relative to the containing visual object. If it is necessary to center the window on the terminal screen, then the top and left location parameters should be set accordingly.

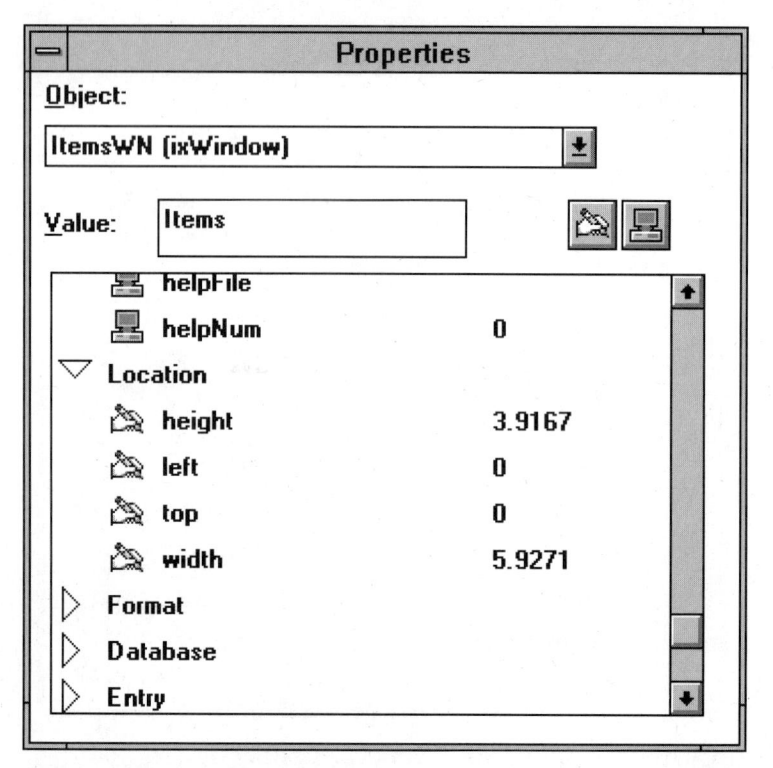

Figure 2-9 - Setting Location Properties

Setting Format Properties

The "format" properties window allows the programmer to set the color parameters, font and point size of the object (see Figure 2-10). A variety of color options and fonts may be available depending on the GUI environment.

When a visual object is painted into a window, the Window Painter uses the format properties for the containing object in the window. It is then up to the programmer, either through the Window Painter properties window or programatically using `ixVisualObject` function calls, to change these properties.

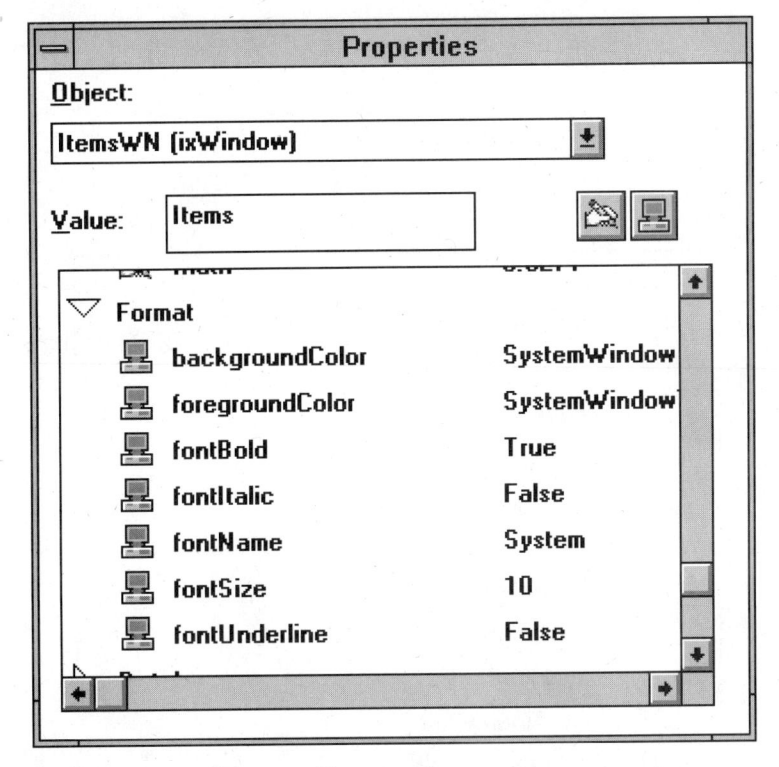

Figure 2-10 - Setting Format Properties

Setting Database Properties

The NewEra product has several *database aware* controls that interact with the database. In order for these controls to perform update functions, database properties must be set correctly. The most notable database aware control is the SuperTable.

The SuperTable controls all database interaction between the NewEra window and the database. The parameters for the SuperTable are explained later in this text.

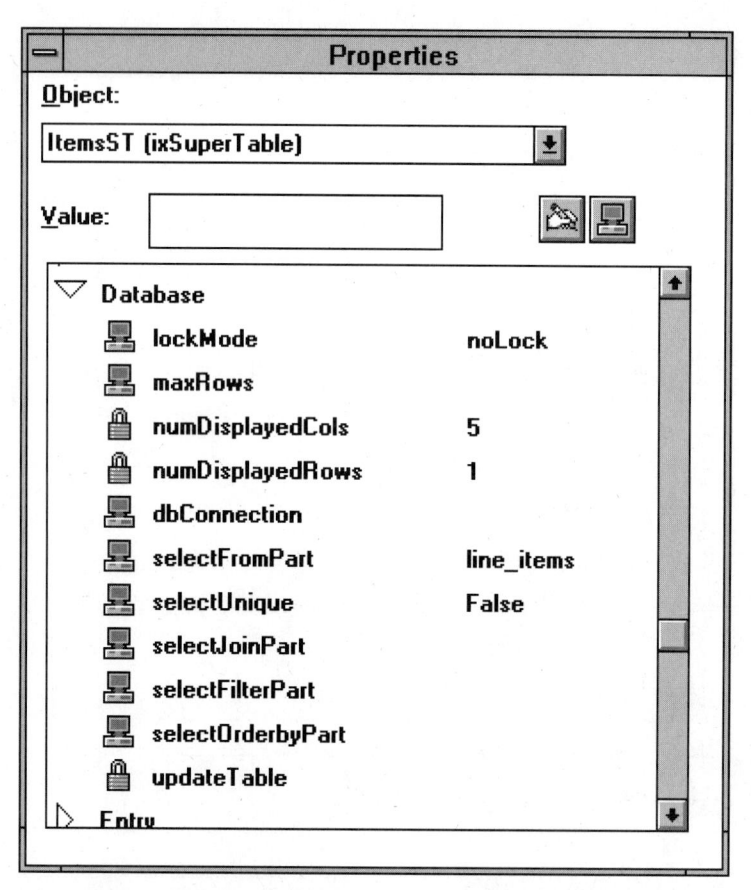

Figure 2-11 - Database Properties

Setting Entry Properties

The `Entry` property is a single property that indicates whether or not the entry capability is *enabled* or *disabled* for this control (Figure 2-12). If the entry is disabled, the control is disabled and the control can only be manipulated programmatically. If the entry is enabled, then it operates normally allowing both keyboard or programmatic manipulation.

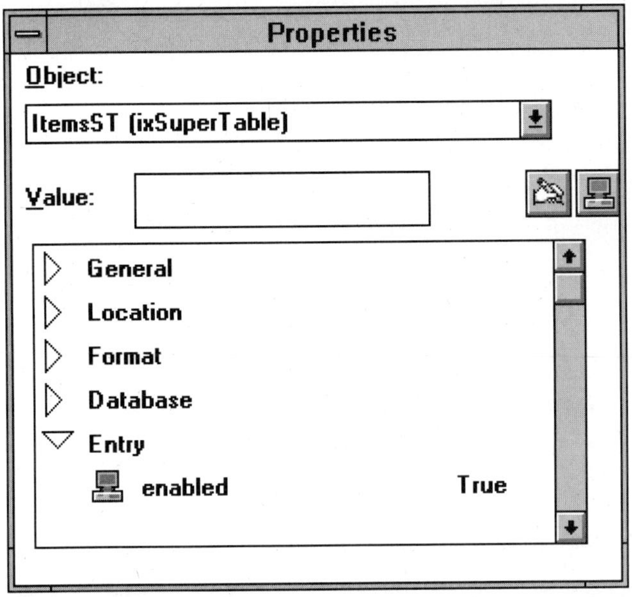

Figure 2-12 - Setting Entry Properties

CREATING EVENT HANDLERS

In order for applications to respond to events generated by controls that have been placed into NewEra windows, *event handlers* must be created. Default event handlers exist for most of the controls listed above. The NewEra Window Painter organizes the process of creating custom handlers for controls by applying a point-and-click approach to the task of programming event handlers.

When the mouse is used to click on a control in the Window Painter, a code window is displayed for that control. The available events for the control will be listed in a drop down list box in this window (see Figure 2-13). By using the mouse to gain focus into the code area, the programmer can enter NewEra code for the event.

Note that some events require a return value (often a Boolean value); the Window Painter does not check for this return value. If a return value is omitted, it will not become apparent until compile time when the signature of the event handler is checked by the compiler.

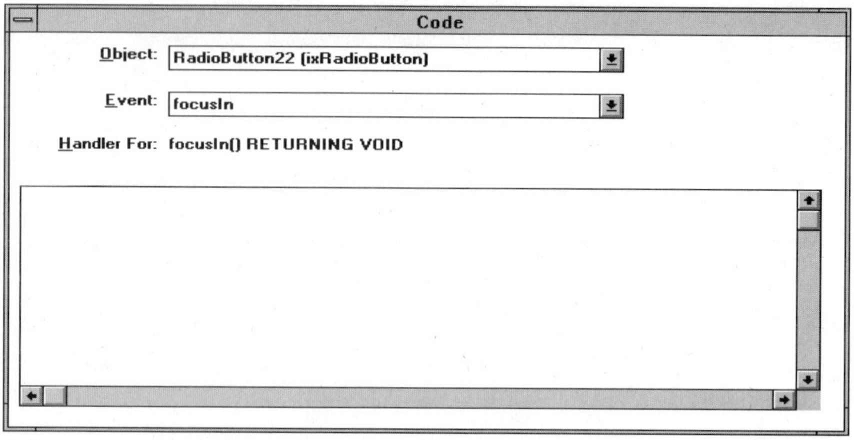

Figure 2-13 - Event Handler Code Window

THE WINDOW PAINTER CODE WINDOW

The NewEra code window provides only rudimentary editing facilities for the programmer; it is tedious to enter a large amount of code using this facility. It is better to use the code window to enter calls to functions that in turn perform most of the work for the event handler. The module containing these functions could then be linked into the application. (This approach also has the benefit of keeping the code modular and making it more maintainable.)

The GUI clipboard is available in the NewEra code window, thus allowing cut and paste operations via menu options or control keys. Code could be written in a Windows editor and then copied to the clipboard. The Window Painter code window would then be selected and made active by using the mouse click to put the cursor in the code window. The Edit option would be chosen from the Window Painter menu and the Paste Text operation chosen. This will place the contents of the clipboard into the code window at the current cursor position.

Other NewEra Code Blocks

The Informix-NewEra Window Painter allows for the insertion of several additional code blocks within the generated code. These *code blocks* can be used to insert code at certain points in the code generated by the Window Painter. They are discussed in more detail below.

Code Block	Purpose
pre_header	enter code to be inserted into start of the header file for the application. Generally used to enter include files for the application.
pre_body	inserted before the `main` program block
constructor_extension	inserted within and at the end of the constructor for the class
class_extension	inserted within and at the end of the class definition for the class

The `pre_header` Code Block

The `pre_header` code block is used to insert NewEra include files needed for the application. The code entered here would be inserted at the top of the include file.

When multi-window applications are being written, the header files for the additional windows would be inserted here. For example, if a window named `window1` displayed a window named `window2`, then `window1` would need to reference the window object for `window2` in order to call the `open` member function to open and display the window. The `window1` code would need to be able to reference the `window2` window class as an object class. This would therefore require that the `pre_header` block for `window1` code include the following entry.

```
include "window2.4gh"
```

The `pre_body` Code Block

Continuing with the above example, when `window1` starts, it would need to create an object of class `window2` and preferably have this object be referenceable throughout the application. This would require an entry in the `pre_body` code block for `window1` to declare a global variable for the `window2` object, as follows.

```
global variable window2 window2
```

The `start` event for the `window1` window would then contain the following entry to instantiate the `window2` window object. From this point in the code, the `window2` window is available to be referenced.

```
let window2 = new window2()
```

The `class_extension` Code Block

The `class_extension` can be used to add additional variables, member functions or classes to the window class. This is a convenient method for adding variables and functions to an application and limiting their scope. These components will be part of the window object and thus not conflict with other variables in the application. This is one of the primary benefits of object-oriented encapsulation.

These object components can then be initialized in the `constructor_exension` block discussed below.

The `constructor_extension` Code Block

The `constructor_extension` can be used to add initialization routines to a window. Since the constructor will be called *when* the window is created, this is effectively a 'before-window-open' event. If variables are added to the window class they can be initialized at this point. If additional windows are to be used with the window, their objects could be created at this point and then opened in the `start` event for the window.

THE NEWERA WINDOW HIERARCHY

The NewEra window object can be considered a *container* for all of the objects and controls used within the window. It inherits all of the properties of the `ixWindow` class. Within the window, there can be numerous NewEra objects which are *contained* by the window. These objects can include controls such as radio buttons, check boxes, labels, list boxes and SuperTable. NewEra frames can also be part of a window and the frames can also be containers for other objects and controls. The diagram below shows the potential visual container hierarchy for a NewEra window.

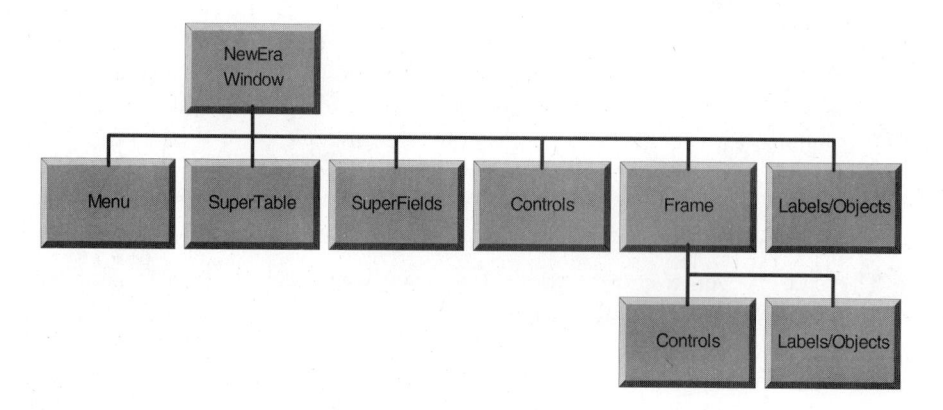

Figure 2-14 - The NewEra Window Hierarchy

The Window startup Property

If the window *startup* property is set to TRUE, the NewEra Window Painter automatically generates a global window object for the window being created and generates a `main` program block and the code necessary to open and display the window. This creates a relatively easy-to-reference container for the window. This container can then be referenced in other parts of the application such as event handlers. For example, in a window where there are two SuperTables, a SuperTable named `items_st` contained in the window named `items_wind` could be referenced as

```
call items_wind.items_st.retrieve( QBE: FALSE)
    returning retval
```

The Menu Editor

The NewEra Menu Editor creates menus in a hierarchical fashion with menus and submenus and corresponding hot-key access for the menu options. Using a point and click approach to menu development, the indentation of the menu items in the menu dialog box indicates the hierarchy of the menu items, with the menu items to the left having a higher hierarchy than those to the right. Thus menus to the right of and below a menu item represent choices for that menu item. If these menu items in turn have menu items listed below and indented to the right of them, then these menu items represent *submenus*. The list below provides an example.

```
Edit
        Copy to Clipboard
        Cut to Clipboard
        Paste to Clipboard
Payables
        Post Payables
                Print Pre-Post Report
                Print Pre-Post Audit
                Post Payables to General Ledger
```

This list represents a series of menu choices. For the Edit menu option, there are three items listed below and indented to the right of this option; these items are therefore choices for the Edit menu item.

Below this item there is an menu option for Payables. Then below this menu option there is a choice for Post Payables that is indented, thus it is an option for the Payables menu option. But below this option there are three items listed that are indented; these options are therefore menu options for the Post Payables option. The Post Payables option is a *submenu* under the Payables menu.

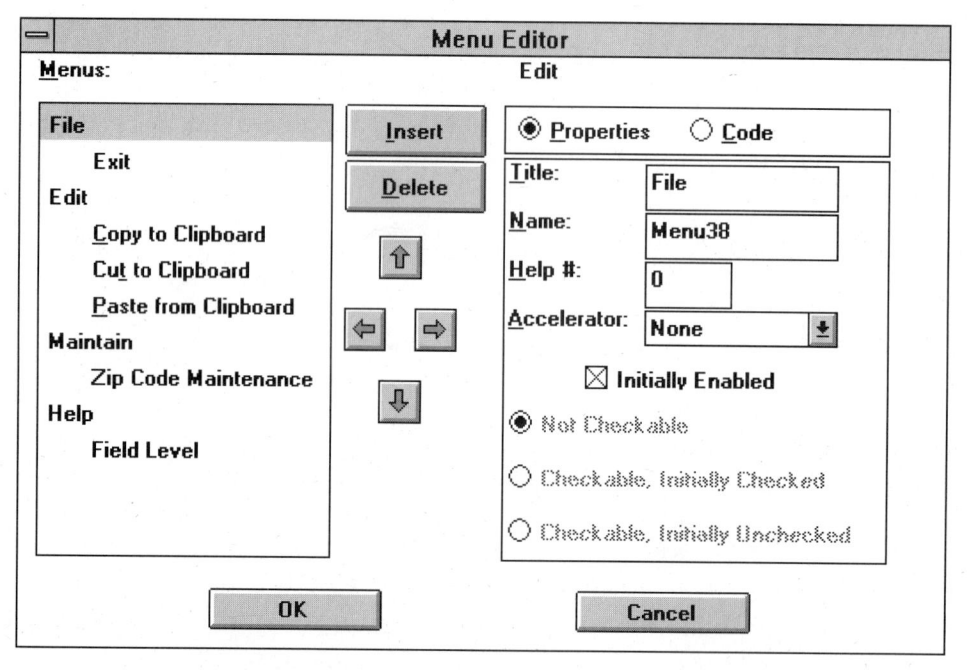

Figure 2-15 - The NewEra Menu Editor

When the radio button for *properties* is checked, the menu properties for title and name of the menu option can be entered. The title is the menu title that will appear on the window for the menu item and the name is the name of the menu object that will appear in the NewEra code. The help number to be associated with the menu option can also be entered in the properties window. This is the help number that can be used to retrieve the help for the menu application using Informix-supplied class libraries.

For any menu option, pressing the radio button for *code* opens a code window where code to be executed for the menu option can be entered. This code window is similar to the code window in the window painter but is exceptionally smaller. As with the other code windows in NewEra, there is a significant advantage to entering a function call in this window and then coding the function in another module.

THE NEWERA APPLICATION BUILDER

The application builder provides an easy-to-use, centralized repository for the code development of NewEra applications. With this tool, the various components of NewEra are pulled together to build and application. The information used to build the application is stored in a database that, if stored on a shared server, can be made accessible to all programmers working on an application.

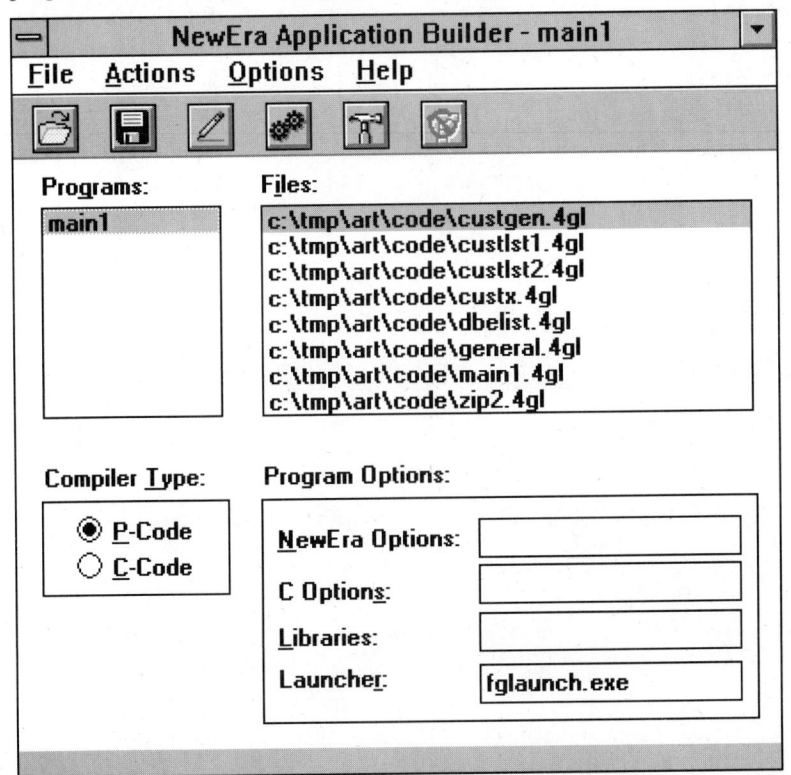

Figure 2-16 - The NewEra Application Builder

In the Application Builder, applications are developed using *projects*. A project can have multiple source code modules associated with it. When the code for an application is compiled, the user can optionally regenerate the hierarchy of the application. This is necessary if class relationships and hierarchies are changed during the development of an application.

Using a shared disk and a source code control system, a group of programmers could work together on the same client/server application. Project definitions for the applications and programs will be shared in the Application Builder among the development staff.

STEPS IN CREATING A NEWERA APPLICATION

As in any application development process, an orderly approach to development will simplify the process. This section proposes a set of steps for the development of NewEra applications.

These steps (shown in Figure 2-17) take into account the nature of NewEra application development. Since much of the development of NewEra applications centers around the Window Painter, this tool will figure prominently in the process.

- ✓ Create Database Schema
- ✓ Create Windows with SuperTables
- ✓ Create Menus and Other Controls
- ✓ Add Code to Glue Application Objects and Controls
- ✓ Create Reports
- ✓ Make Cosmetic Changes

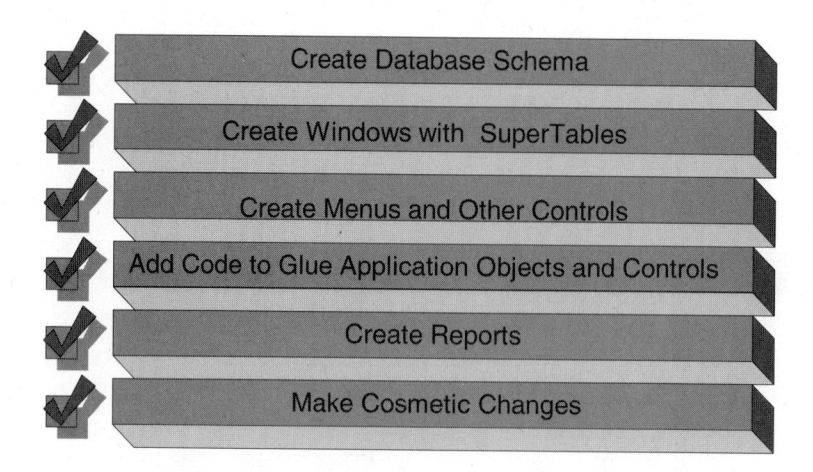

Figure 2-17 - NewEra Application Development Steps

Create Database Schema

The initial step in creating a NewEra application is, as with most database applications, create the database schema. Obviously, without a stable database structure, coding and development of the application cannot begin. The database design is the foundation on which the application will be built.

The NewEra database development tool, ViewPoint Pro, is an excellent tool for graphically developing the structure of the database. This tool allows the schema of the database tables to be entered and modified. The permissions for a table can be entered down to the column level. Attributes and integrity checks and relationships can be

Chapter 2: Using the Window Painter and Application Builder   35

entered for the table and its columns; this is known as the *SuperView*. The current version of NewEra will interpret all of the information entered for the SuperView with the exception of relationships to other tables.

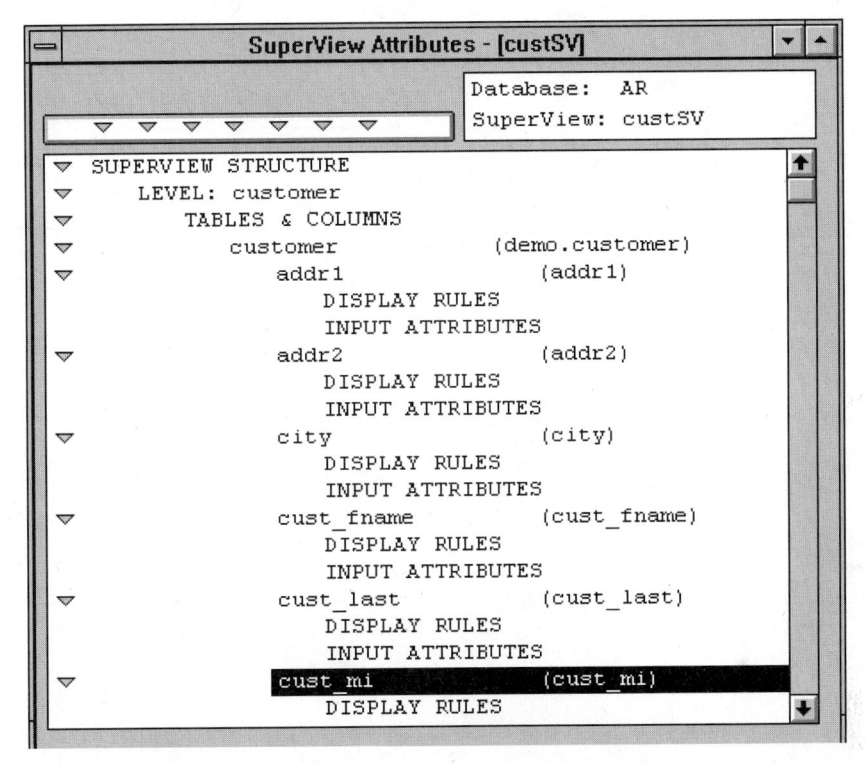

```
┌─ SuperView Attributes - [custSV] ──────────────────▼─▲─┐
│                                  Database:  AR        │
│    ▽ ▽ ▽ ▽ ▽ ▽                  SuperView: custSV    │
│                                                        │
│ ▽  SUPERVIEW STRUCTURE                              ▲ │
│ ▽      LEVEL: customer                                │
│ ▽         TABLES & COLUMNS                            │
│ ▽            customer              (demo.customer)    │
│ ▽               addr1              (addr1)            │
│                    DISPLAY RULES                      │
│                    INPUT ATTRIBUTES                   │
│ ▽               addr2              (addr2)            │
│                    DISPLAY RULES                      │
│                    INPUT ATTRIBUTES                   │
│ ▽               city               (city)             │
│                    DISPLAY RULES                      │
│                    INPUT ATTRIBUTES                   │
│ ▽               cust_fname         (cust_fname)       │
│                    DISPLAY RULES                      │
│                    INPUT ATTRIBUTES                   │
│ ▽               cust_last          (cust_last)        │
│                    DISPLAY RULES                      │
│                    INPUT ATTRIBUTES                   │
│ ▽               cust_mi            (cust_mi)          │
│                    DISPLAY RULES                    ▼ │
└────────────────────────────────────────────────────────┘
```

Figure 2-18 - ViewPoint-Pro SuperTable Editor

Create Application Windows with SuperTables

Next, the Window Painter is used to create the application windows. Since some windows may involve data relationships between two tables, these relationships would be coded within the Window Painter and added to the properties window for the SuperTable using the `joinTables` property.

Create Menus and Other Controls

If any menus are needed to support the individual windows, they are created in this step. If any menu items or buttons are to be used to *glue* the various windows together, they would also be added at this point. In this step, it is not necessary to be concerned with cosmetic issues such as whether or not a button should be a picture button; these will be resolved in a later step. It is just necessary to add the components that will be needed to create the application.

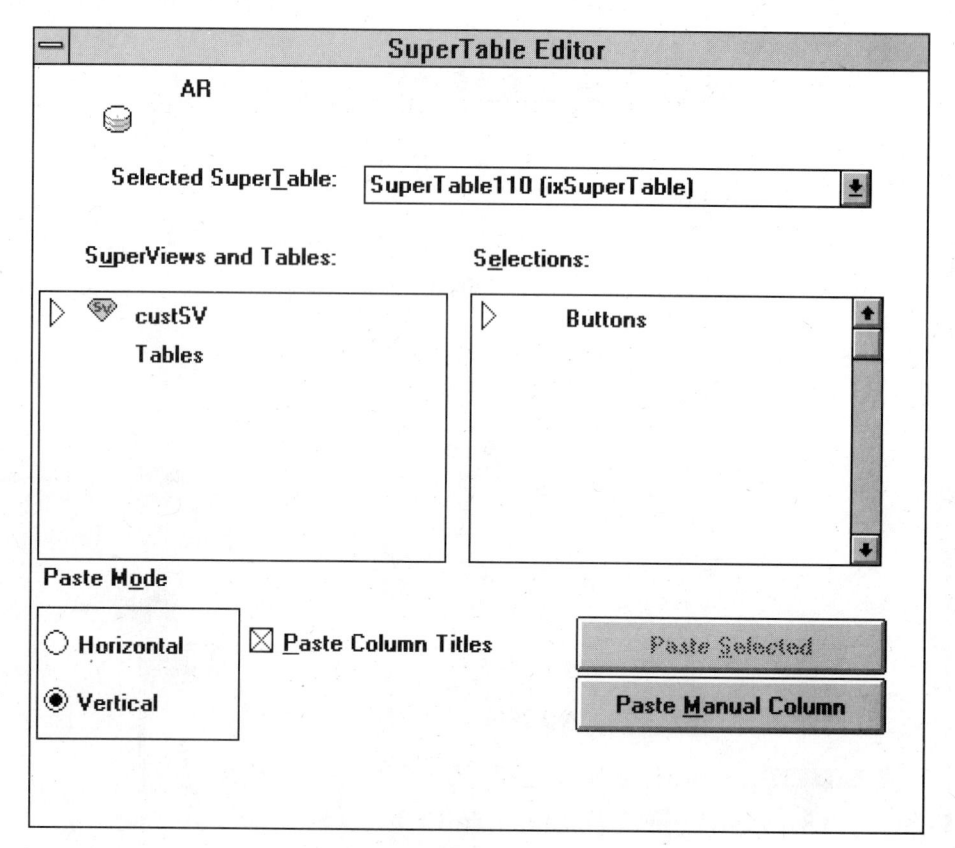

Figure 2-19 - The SuperTable Editor

Add Code to Glue Application Objects and Controls

NewEra code needed to implement the menus or buttons painted into the application in the previous step would be written in this step. If additional code is needed to further customize the application, class libraries could be written or reused at this stage and inserted into the application.

Create Application Reports

Next, reports needed for the application would be created. These could be created and tested separately and then added to the final application via menu items or buttons.

Make Cosmetic Changes

Finally, cosmetic changes would be made; this could involve making some buttons picture buttons, adding graphic logos to the window, changing icons and reformatting the application windows. Throughout the process, the application builder would be used to pull all the pieces of the application together into a single, cohesive application.

SUPERTABLE WINDOW

The SuperTable window is used to paste data entry fields into a NewEra window. These data entry fields are the intelligent, *database-aware* NewEra controls. Using a combination of fields and buttons from the SuperTable Editor, a programmer can create a complete data-entry application in a matter of minutes.

The first step in creating a form is to choose the SuperTable button on the tool panel of the Window Painter. Once this control is chosen, the programmer can then use the cursor to create a frame within the current window. This frame is created by using the cursor to click to create an anchor point, and then, while holding the left mouse button down, dragging the cursor across the window. It is important to make the frame large enough to hold the expected number of input fields, otherwise the fields pasted into the window may overlap.

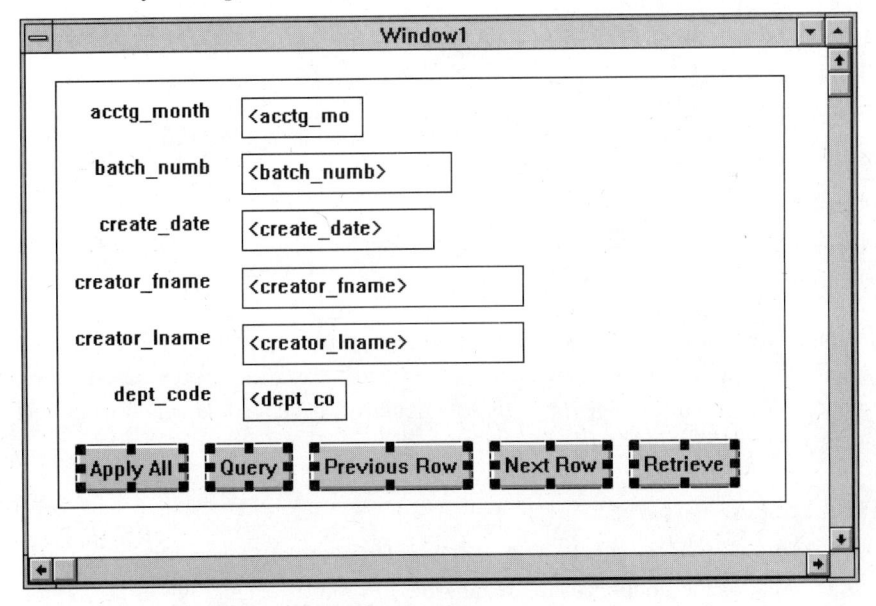

Figure 2-20 - Pasting SuperFields

Once the frame is created, the SuperTable Editor window will be displayed. Several buttons will be displayed representing choices. In the list box displayed to the **left**, an option will be available to choose tables. By using the mouse to click on the word *tables* in this list box, a list of available tables will be displayed in the list box to the right.

Choosing one of these options with a mouse-click will expand the list with a list of available columns for the table. The programmer can then choose from this list of columns and paste SuperField controls for the columns into the window.

Once this step is complete, the user can then paste buttons into the window. The buttons will provide the database-aware component of the SuperTable. Buttons are available to perform the following functions.

SuperTable Buttons

Button	Function
Apply All	Apply all the modified rows in the current SuperTable set to the database. Only new or updated rows will be applied to the database.
Apply Row	Apply the current modified row to the database.
Delete Row	Delete the current row from the SuperTable set.
First Row	Move to the first row in the data set.
Help	Execute Help for the current SuperTable.
Insert Row	Insert a row into the SuperTable set.
Last Row	Move to the last row in the data set.
Next Page	Retrieve the next page of SuperTable rows.
Next Row	Display the next SuperTable row.
Previous Page	Retrieve the previous page of SuperTable rows
Previous Row	Retrieve the previous SuperTable row.
Query	Put the SuperTable into query-by-example mode. The user can entry criteria, and then press the retrieve button when ready.
Retrieve	Retrieve the records for the query criteria entered while in query-by-example mode.
Revert Row	Revert the row to its state before modifications

A simple *browse* window can be created by pasting a set of fields into the SuperTable frame and then pasting the "query", "retrieve", "next" and "previous" buttons into the window. This will provide the basic functionality of the browse window but will not allow the user to update the database.

Field Labels

The field labels pasted into the form are the default field labels for the database columns: the name of the column in the database. In order to change these labels, the SuperField to change must be selected using the mouse and the *properties* window selected. The title for the field and other formatting facilities can then be changed. The field labels inherit their format properties from the containing window. These properties can be overridden using the format properties for the SuperField.

Chapter 2: Using the Window Painter and Application Builder

The tab order for the fields controls the order in which the cursor would move through the window fields using the tab key. The default tab order can be altered by changing the tab order number for the SuperField in the properties window.

Using SuperViews

When pasting fields into a SuperTable, Superviews can be used in place of simple tables. Superviews provide additional information to the Window Painter; information such as validation criteria and input/output formatting characteristics. Using the ViewPoint-Pro program supplied with Informix-NewEra, this information can be input and then shared through a common application database among the developers programming an application. Entering this information in a SuperView provides a means of establishing standard formatting and validation for a database; a standard which is easily shared among programmers.

Note that the SuperView information is not loaded when the application is run, it is loaded when the SuperView is chosen in the Window Painter. The information in the SuperView is then written to the *wif* created by the Window Painter and NewEra code created when the window is saved.

In order to recognize changes in a SuperView, the Window Painter would have to be started, the *wif* would have to be loaded and then saved. At this point, the changes to the SuperView would be recognized in the application code. The application could then be recompiled to create a runnable application.

Establishing Master-Detail Relationships

The current version of NewEra (version 1.0.WE1) does not automatically generate code for master-detail relationships from SuperViews. But the programmer only needs to enter a few lines of code in order to provide this functionality as the code shown below demonstrates.

Assuming there is a window with two SuperTables, the top portion represents the master table data and the bottom portion represents the detail table data. The user will first enter criteria for the master table and then press the "retrieve" button. The "retrieve" button code must first retrieve the data for the master table and then retrieve the data for the detail table, as shown below in the code executed when the retrieve button is pressed for the master table.

```
VARIABLE ok BOOLEAN
VARIABLE superTable   ixSuperTable
variable pk_val       ixValue

    LET superTable = (getVisualContainer() CAST
ixSuperTable)
```

```
-- retrieve data from the master table
LET ok = superTable.retrieve( QBE: TRUE )

-- retrieve detail table data
-- first, get the primary key value
let pk_val = SuperTable.getCellValue( colnum: 1 )

-- use the primary key in the select criteria
call    Window1.items_st.selectFilterPart.setValueStr(
"customer_numb = " || pk_val.getValueStr() )

-- retrieve from the detail table
let ok = Window1.items_st.retrieve( QBE: FALSE )
```

With three lines of code, the corresponding data from the detail table is retrieved and, with the free-form SuperTable, the first row is displayed to the window. The first line of code shown above retrieves the primary key column data from the master table using the `getCellValue` SuperTable member function. This call returns a value stored in an `ixValue` variable, an abstract class that provides a convenient reference to any data type. This value is then used in the next line of code to create the filter string portion of the `select` statement.

The `selectFilterPart` member variable of the SuperTable is an `ixString` data type that represents the filter part (`where` clause) of the query to be executed by the SuperTable to retrieve the data. In this code example, the `ixString setValueStr` member function is used to create the string for the `where` clause by concatenating the primary key name with the primary key value.

Once the `selectFilterPart` for the detail SuperTable has been set with the correct filter criteria for the detail table, the next line of code simply calls the `Retrieve` SuperTable member function to retrieve the detail rows from the database.

This will retrieve detail rows when the retrieve button is pressed. But it is also necessary to retrieve the detail rows as the user browses the master table rows. This requires the "next" and "previous" buttons and the "last row" and "first row" buttons, if they exist in the window, to also execute the code shown above. The example below demonstrates this technique.

```
-- Code executed for the Next row button

VARIABLE ok             BOOLEAN
variable retval         smallint
VARIABLE superTable     ixSuperTable
VARIABLE rowPosition    INTEGER
```

Chapter 2: Using the Window Painter and Application Builder

```
   variable pk_value      ixValue

 LET superTable = (getVisualContainer() CAST
                      ixSuperTable)
 LET rowPosition = SuperTable.getCurrRowNum() + 1

    # get the number of rows for the current displayMode
    IF rowPosition > SuperTable.getNumStoredRows(NULL)
                                                   THEN

       call MessageBox( title: new ixString( "Message"),
             message: new ixString( "No More Rows." ),
             iconstyle: ixExclaimIcon )
         returning retval

       LET rowPosition = ixSuperTable::lastRow
    END IF

   LET ok = superTable.setCurrentCell(rowPosition,
                     ixSuperTable::currentColumn)

-- Retrieve the detail rows for this master table row
-- First, get the primary key value
let pk_val = SuperTable.getCellValue( colnum: 1 )

-- Use the primary key
call Window1.items_st.selectFilterPart.setValueStr(
              "customer_numb = " ||
              pk_val.getValueStr() )

-- Retrieve from the detail table
let ok = Window1.items_st.retrieve( QBE: FALSE )
```

This button handler first executes code to set the current row to the next row in the current set. The `RowPosition` variable is set to the return value of `getCurrRowNum() + 1`, the next row in the set. There are several lines of code to test the validity of the next row position and display a message if the user is attempting to move beyond the end of the current set.

If all is well, then code is executed to set the current row for the master table data to the `RowPostion` row value. The button handler will then retrieve the data for the detail rows. As shown previously, the primary key value is obtained from the SuperTable cell containing the primary key value and stored in an `ixValue` variable. This value is then used to create the filter criteria for the detail SuperTable. And finally, the `Retrieve` SuperTable member function is executed and the detail data is retrieved.

Chapter 3
A Sample Application:
The Accounts Receivable Module

In order to demonstrate the process of application development with NewEra, a sample application is needed, preferably an application that can demonstrate master-detail relationships, has some complexity, and has relevance to Management Information System (MIS) programmers. An accounting application would exhibit all of these properties. More specifically, an accounts receivable application would provide a useful set of examples.

ACCOUNTS RECEIVABLE OVERVIEW

Accounts receivable is an accounting entity used by organizations to track the money owed the organization by its clients. As the company sells its products, it bills its clients for these products. Once a bill is produced, the company must wait for the client to pay the bill. The money owed is considered a *receivable*.

As bills are produced, they are printed and then sent to the customer. These *billing runs* are reports which are run on a regular basis. The criteria for producing these billing runs can vary, making a dynamic query interface for this report useful.

Most companies have an incentive to encourage their clients to pay their bills in a timely fashion. This incentive is usually in the form of a discount if the bill is paid in 30 days or less, known as a *net-30* payment type. There are variations on this which generally alter the number of days and the discount but with the same overall goal: to encourage the client to pay the bill as quickly as possible.

As time progresses, the outstanding accounts receivable *age* and, for various reasons, it becomes important for the organization to collect the money owed it. This time progression and its effect on the billing funds is known as the *accounts receivable aging* process. As accounts remain unpaid, they are aged and flags are set to indicate the condition of the account. After a certain period of time, the account may be flagged as overdue and an overdue billing report run may be used to produce bills for the overdue accounts.

The terms for accounts may vary greatly depending on the characteristics of the customer. Some customers may have generous credit terms; others may be on a *cash only* basis which effectively indicates no credit terms are extended to that customer. The location of the customer may impact the billing process; overseas customers may have different terms than domestic customers. A customer of several years may have terms that are much better than a customer of several months. And there may be some customers that are simply allowed more favorable terms due to some other factor like account size or strategic benefit of the customer.

ACCOUNTS RECEIVABLE DATA FLOW

Accounts receivable data centers around the creation of batches. A batch is an accounting control entity used to group a set of source documents together. These source documents can then be assigned to one individual or group who will take responsibility for them. In the accounts receivable module, these documents are input and then applied to various validations and tests (see Figure 3-1) until finally being applied to the accounting module where the receivable will in turn be applied to the general ledger receivable and income accounts.

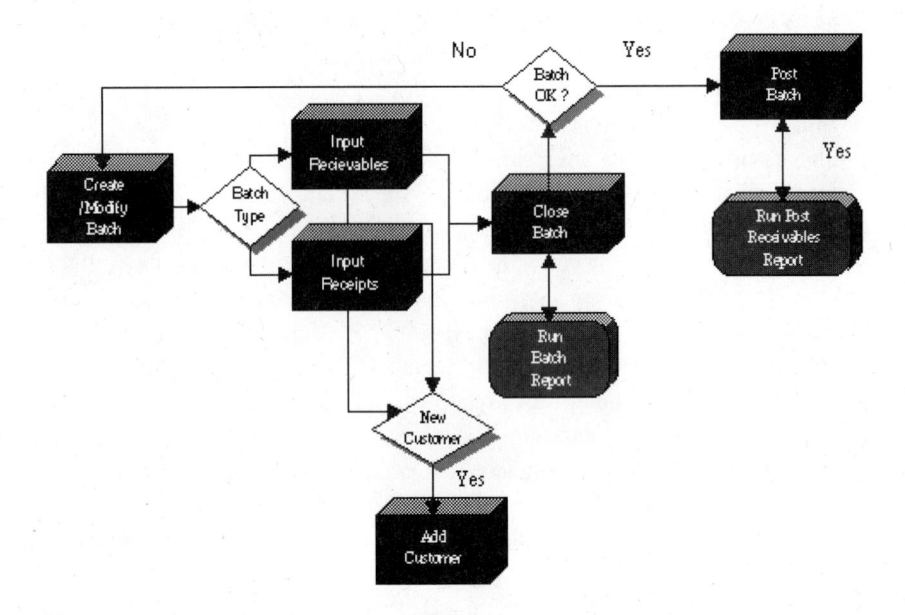

Figure 3-1 - Flow of Accounts Receivable Data

ACCOUNTS RECEIVABLE APPLICATION DEVELOPMENT ISSUES

Terms may vary greatly among different organizations. The accounts receivable system must allow the software to be configured for the company's method of doing business. Configurable links could also be required for links to a *security* module to control the security of the application, or a *customer* module to provide customer marketing features such as mailing list maintenance or customer service applications. The application may also optionally link with a *job cost* module which tracks the cost of producing the goods sold (see Figure 3-2).

Figure 3-2 - Accounts Receivable Module Linkage

As accounts receivable are *posted* to the accounting module, the appropriate accounts receivable account must be posted with the amount of the accounts receivable. This means that a link to the accounting module must be provided. This link would be in the form of an accounts receivable account contained with the billing record.

The stock items listed on the accounts receivable bill require a stock number to reference the stock items. Use of this stock number would require a link to the stock module. Referenced with the stock number would be the stock item description. This description would appear on the bill but would not be stored in the line item table. This is consistent with good relational design.

Security issues would have to be considered in the design of the module. Some users would have the capability to perform certain functions in the module. An accounting clerk would be allowed to enter accounts receivable, generate a receivable report, but would **not** be allowed to post the receivable to the accounting module; an accounting manager would have the capability to post the receivable. Enforcing these rules would require a link to a security module which would contain the user's name, the functions the user would be allowed to perform and other security information.

LOCKING ISSUES AND TRANSACTION MANAGEMENT

When a billing record is entered with its corresponding line items, they represent a transaction. All SQL statements executed within the accounts receivable billing entry operation must be treated as an atomic operation (see Figure 3-3). Since the bill header record contains a total for its constituent line items, all records must be successfully inserted into the database or the transaction is effectively incomplete.

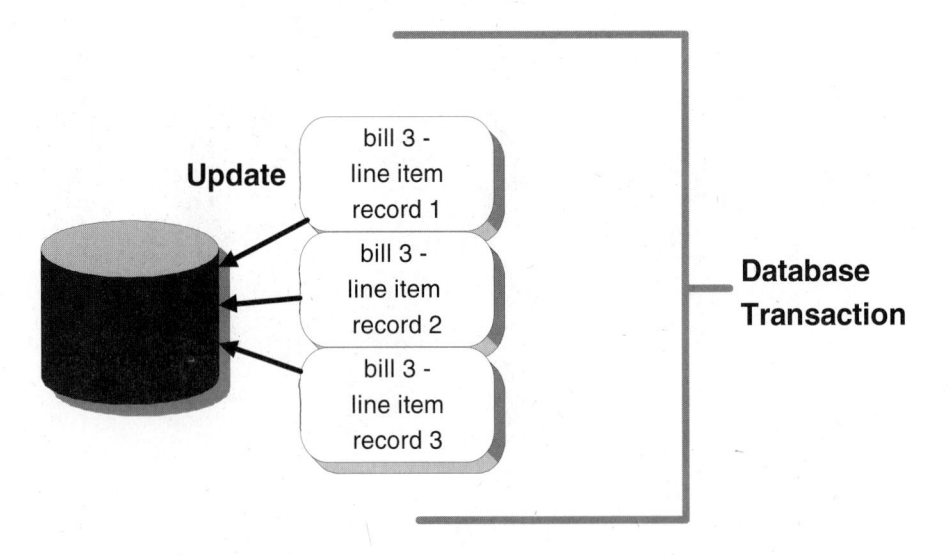

Figure 3-3 - Database Transaction

The accounts receivable posting operation must also be treated as a transaction. The debit and credit entries must both succeed in order for the accounts to remain balanced. If they are not balanced, then the transaction must be rolled back. It will be the responsibility of the posting application to enforce this functionality.

Data Entry Locking Issues

There are also issues about when to lock records during data entry. If the application user were to browse a set of accounts receivable records potentially to update one of the records, should all of the records be locked? Or should only a single record be locked when the user decides to update the record? And there are concurrency issues: If there are two users updating a record, user A and user B, and user A updates the record, when user B attempts to update the record, the data user B is using are now *stale data* since they do not reflect user A's update.

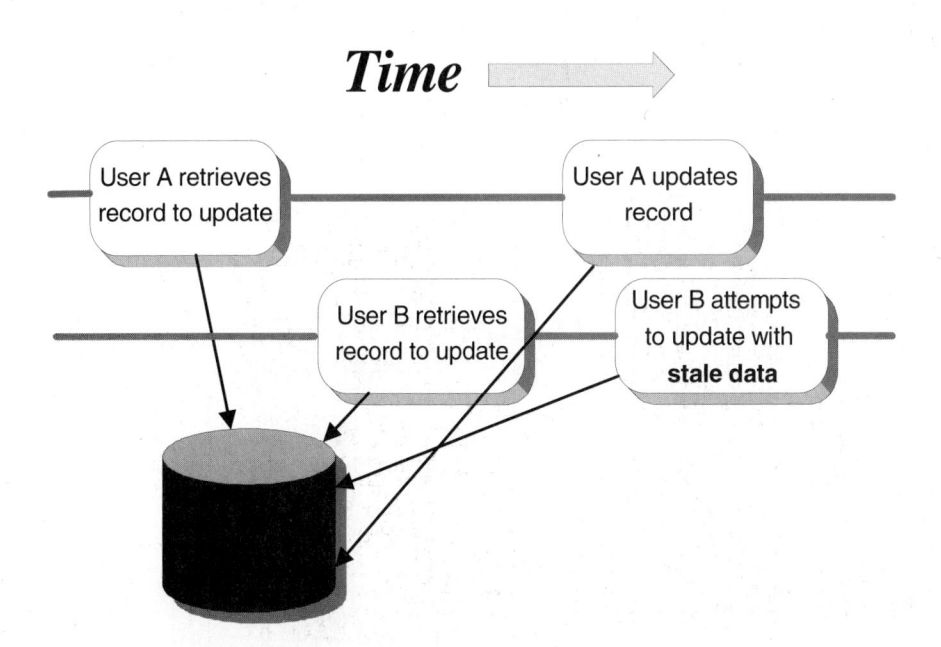

Figure 3-4 - Stale Data

Informix-NewEra provides built-in locking schemes with the SuperTable class library. The *optimistic* locking scheme will lock the records only as the user attempts to update the record to the database. The *pessimistic* locking scheme will lock the records when it detects that the record has been modified by the user. Additionally, NewEra provides a `staleData` event in the SuperTable class (see Figure 3-4). This event detects a stale data situation and allows the programmer to deal with this situation.

APPLICATION WINDOWS

The windows demonstrated in this application will take advantage of the full range of GUI capabilities. Radio buttons, check boxes, list boxes, and drop-down list boxes will be used where appropriate. Some of these intelligent NewEra controls will be extended into a set of *database-aware* controls for use in this (and other) applications. A template window will be developed which provides additional functionality over the NewEra SuperTable.

When a foreign key field must be entered, a *zoom field* list box will be available to allow the user to scroll through the possible values for the field. The functions of the GUI clipboard will be available on a standard menu for cut and paste operations.

Master detail windows will allow master table information to be queried through a *query-by-example* and will automatically display detail table information as each master row is retrieved. When possible, detail screens will reside in detached windows to allow the user the ability to organize their screen better. The following accounts receivable windows will be demonstrated in this application.

Window	A/R Function	NewEra Functions Demonstrated
Customer	Customer table input	Use of Window Painter template. Basic functions of extended SuperTable buttons. Use of NewEra controls - database-aware controls
Customer List	List of A/R customers	Searchable list box using detached search criteria window
Aging report	A/R aging	Report window. Altering window font using detached window. Report printing procedures
Batch entry	Input receivables or cash receipts batch	Master-detail relationships. Use of three detached windows. Use of database-aware list boxes.

Customer Data Entry Window

The customer entry window will provide a basic data entry window for the accounts receivable customer (see Figure 3-5). Information is inserted into the `customer` and `cust_codes` tables. Information such as the customer name, address, and payment terms are input.

The terms code and the district code are validated. If either the term or the district code entered are invalid, then an error message is displayed and the user must re-enter the code until an appropriate code is entered.

A number of standard SuperTable buttons are available on this window. The "query", "retrieve", "update", "delete" and "apply" buttons appear at the bottom of the window. These buttons provide the basic database functionality needed to modify the database tables affected.

When the user enters a zip code, an `afterField` event retrieves the city and state from the zip code table and displays it to the window. A list box is available in the zip code field to provide the user with a list of valid zip codes.

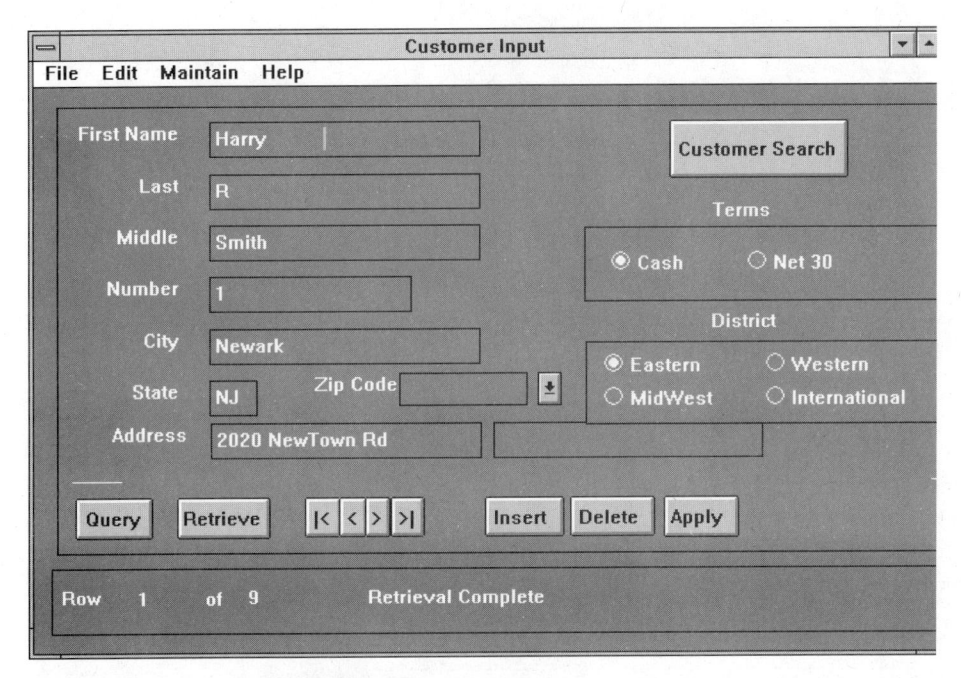

Figure 3-5 - Customer Data Entry Window

The Window Template

A template window (see Figure 3-6) will be used to provide much of the standard functionality desired in the accounts payable application. Within the template, the standard SuperTable data entry buttons are extended to provide additional functionality and information.

The template window contains code to allow the user to retrieve additional rows once the maximum number of rows has been retrieved. If the user attempts to move beyond the active set, an error message is displayed. And a status line is available to display information about the current row relative to the current data set.

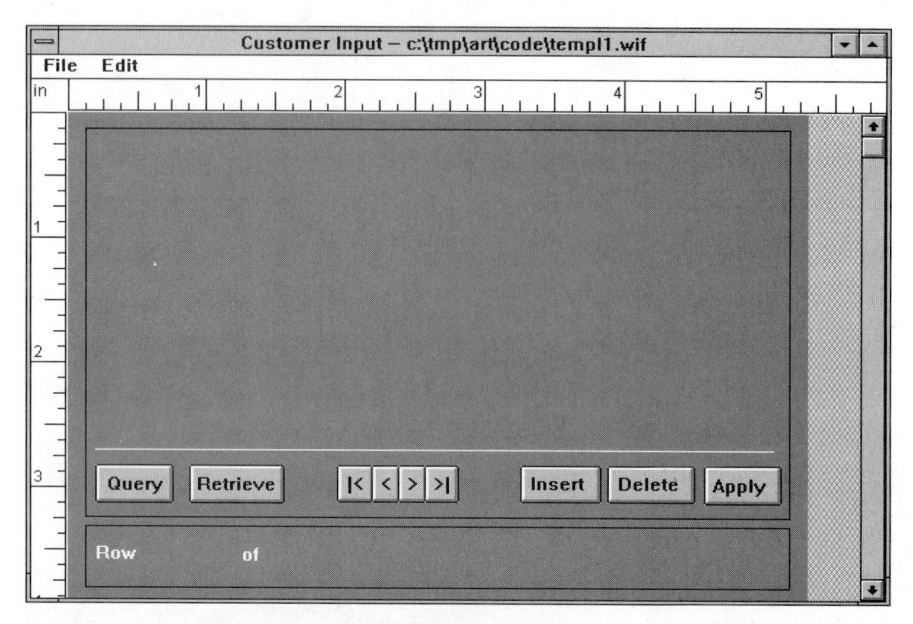

Figure 3-6 - The Template Window

Customer List

The customer list will provide a searchable list of customer names and their corresponding city and state (see Figure 3-7). A separate window will be available to allow the user to enter search criteria and search the list. The *find* and *find next* buttons are available for the user to find the first occurrence of a search value and then find additional occurrences.

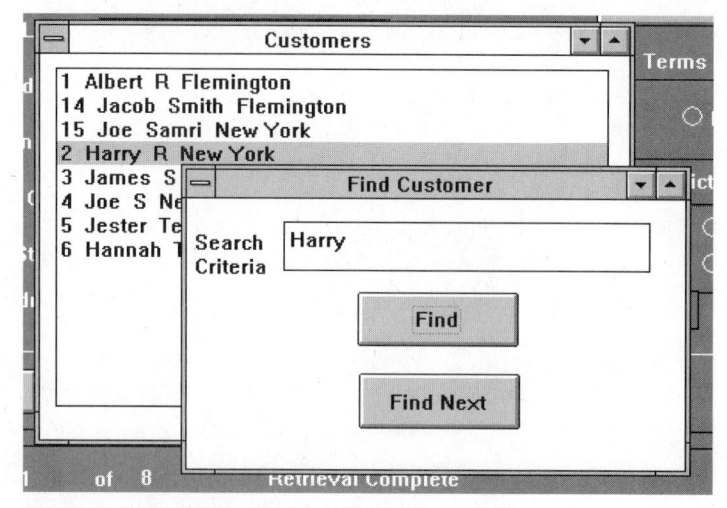

Figure 3-7 - Searchable Customer List

Zip Codes Window

The Zip Codes data entry window (see Figure 3-8) will be a *grid-form* SuperTable that uses a template similar to the template used for the customer window. The same functionality will be provided via a grid-form template, but the presentation of the data will highlight the differences between the *free-form* SuperTable and the grid-form SuperTable.

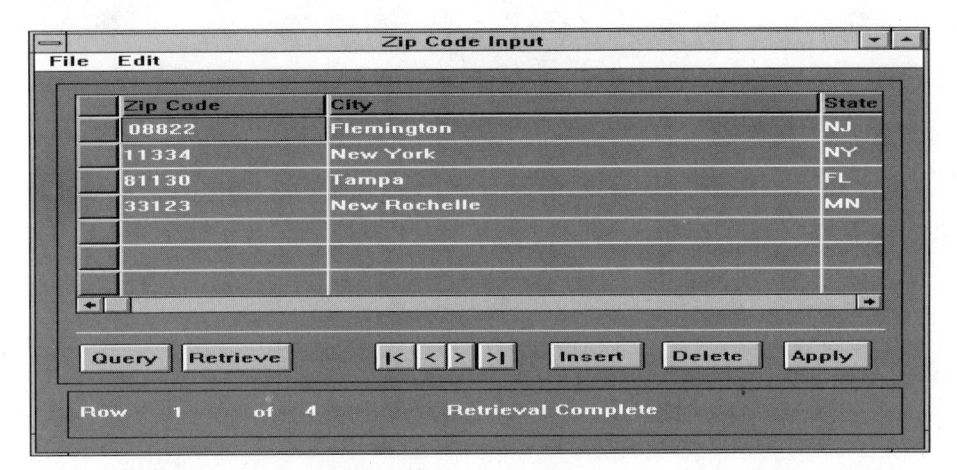

Figure 3-8 - Zip Codes Data Entry Window

Batch Entry Window

The batch entry window (see Figure 3-9) is the starting point for the entry of receivables and payments. This window is used to collect the name of the individual inputting the receives batch. Other information, such as the date the batch was started, and the accounting month for the batch is also input.

This window is the starting point for a set of input windows that will be used to enter the batch data. The batch header window contains a set of radio buttons for receivables or payments. If the "receivables" radio button is pressed and the user presses the enter batch button, the receivables header data entry window is displayed. If the user enters the information for this window and then chooses the *enter detail* button, the line items window will be displayed (the same window is used for payments and receivables input).

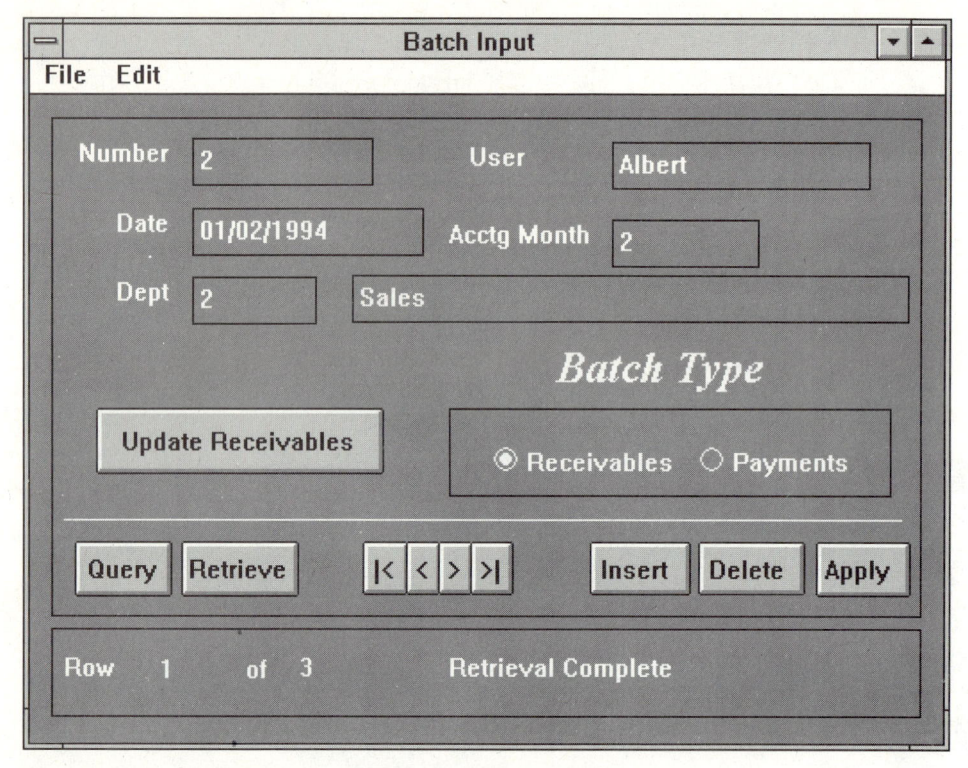

Figure 3-9 - Batch Data Entry Window

If the user chooses to create a new batch, the batch number will be displayed once the batch header record has been placed in the database and the serial field number has been returned to the application by the database engine.

This application will insert and modify data in the batch, bill, and line_items tables. These three windows will be started by the retrieve operation in the batch window. The windows will then work in concert; as data records are traversed in the batch window, the receivables window will be updated as well as the corresponding line items window (see Figure 3-10).

Accounts Receivable Aging Report Window

The aging report generates the Accounts Receivable Aging Report and outputs the report to a window.

Chapter 3: A Sample Application: The Accounts Receivable Module   53

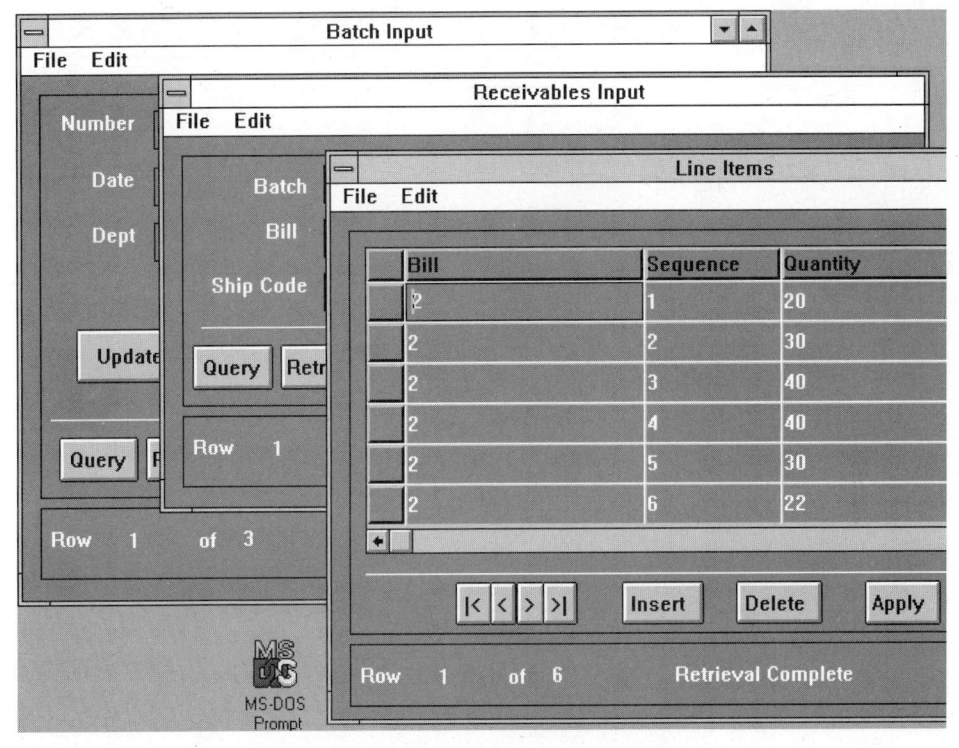

[Screenshot of three cascading windows: Batch Input, Receivables Input, and Line Items, with an MS-DOS Prompt icon.]

Figure 3-10 - Batch Windows Working in Concert

This summary report prints a summary of the number of bills that fall within a certain time period and the total dollar amount of those bills (see Figure 3-11). Aging totals are printed for 30, 60, 90, 120, and over 120 days. At the end of the report, a grand total is printed.

The report will be displayed to a window as shown in Figure 3-11. With this window the user can modify the font size of the report and search the report for a string pattern. Modifying the font size will allow "wide" reports to be shown and printed.

DATABASE DESIGN

The database design must be formulated from the design information presented above. A `customer` table will be needed to store information for the customer, a central data component of this application. This table will contain information about the customer such as the customer name, address, phone, city, state, zip code, and the terms for the customer.

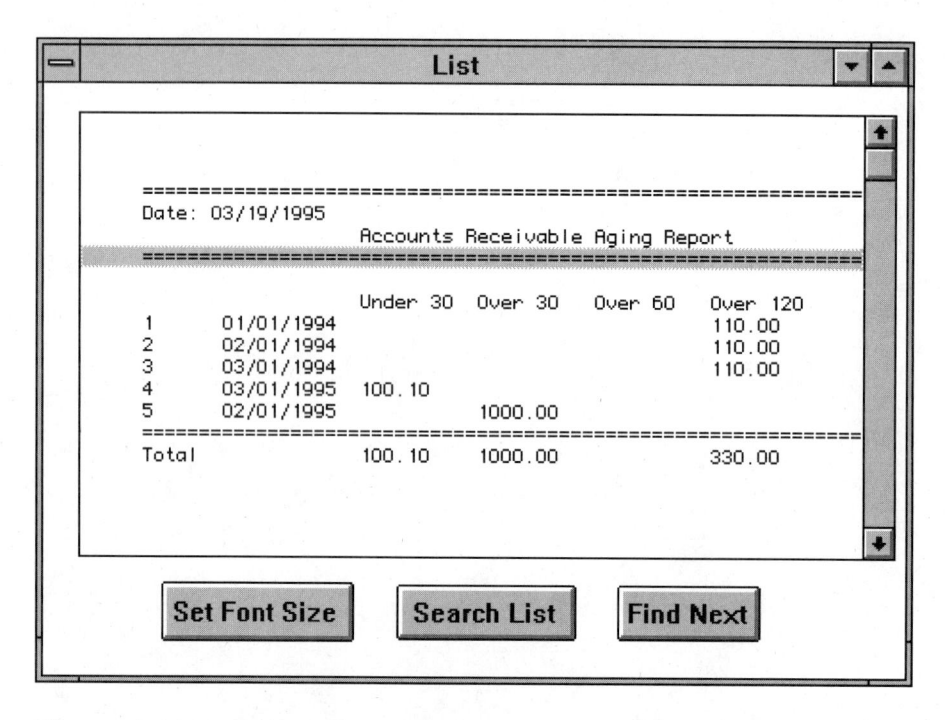

```
                              List
===============================================================
Date: 03/19/1995
                    Accounts Receivable Aging Report
===============================================================
                   Under 30   Over 30   Over 60   Over 120
     1   01/01/1994                                110.00
     2   02/01/1994                                110.00
     3   03/01/1994                                110.00
     4   03/01/1995  100.10
     5   02/01/1995            1000.00
===============================================================
     Total           100.10   1000.00             330.00
```

[Set Font Size]   [Search List]   [Find Next]

Figure 3-11 - A/R Aging Report

To reduce the amount of information contained in this table (to normalize the table), the customer terms will be carried in the customer table as a *terms code*. This terms code will relate to the *terms* table which will contain terms code, a description of the terms, and other information on the credit terms.

As bills are entered for a customer, they will be added to the `bill` table. Related to this table will be the `items` table. The items table will store information for the line items on the customer bill. These line items will reference sales information and reference information in the sales tables.

A shipping table will be used to store the shipping codes used on the accounts receivable bills. The shipping code will be stored in the line items record in the line items table. Stored in the shipping table will be the shipping code, a description of the shipping code, and other related information.

A journal entry table will be used to store any journal entries for accounts receivable. These journal entries will be used to alter receivables that have already been posted to the accounting module. The journal entry will contain entries for the accounts receivable batch, the customer number, the bill number, a description, and an amount to be debited or credited to the customer's account.

Several tables will be present in this version of the database that would not be needed in a more complete version of an accounting system. A stock table will be used to

Chapter 3: A Sample Application: The Accounts Receivable Module

track stock in the absence of a stock module. A security table will be used to indicate the capabilities of system users; this would not be needed if a security module were being used. And a zip code table will be used to provide a lookup capability for zip codes entered in the customer window.

The `batch` Table

The `batch` table is used to store information about the batch being input. This table stores the batch number, the individual who created the batch, the date the batch was created, the department code for the batch, and the accounting month for the batch. The primary key for the table is the batch number which is a serial field.

```
create table batch (
   batch_numb serial,
   acctg_month smallint,
   creator_fname char(15),
   creator_lname  char(15),
   dept_code   char(5),
 department.dept_code
   create_date   date );
```

The `customer` Table

The `customer` table is used to store the header information for the customer. It contains the customer name and address and the unique customer number that is used to reference the customer throughout the accounts receivable module. The customer number (`cust_number`) is the primary key within this table. In the related tables of the accounts receivable module this column will be used as a foreign key to reference the customer.

```
   customer ( cust_number serial,
              cust_fname char(15),
              cust_mi    char(15),
              cust_last  char(15),
              addr1      char(15),
              addr2      char(15),
              city       char(15),
              state      char(2),
              zip        char(5))
```

The `customer_codes` Table

The customer codes table (`cust_codes`) is used to store related information for the customer table. There is a 1:1 relationship between a customer record and a `cust_codes` table record.

```
create table cust_codes ( cust_number  integer,
                          term_code    char(2),
                          district_code integer)
```

The `districts` Table

The `districts` table references the district code (`distr_code`) in the customer codes table. This is a code that indicates the district of the customer. The table contains the district code and a 15-character textual description of the district.

```
districts( distr_code char(5),
           distr_description char(15))
```

The `terms` Table

The `terms` table references the term code stored in the customer codes table. This code indicates the credit terms that will be given to the customer. This table allows flexibility in establishing terms.

Two tables are used to establish the terms. The first table is the `terms` table. This table contains the term code and a description of the term. The next table is the `term_days` table. This table contains the terms code, a sequence number, and a description and a percentage. There is a one-to-many relationship between the terms table and the terms code table.

If the terms to be described with these tables are net 30 (net amount of the bill due within 30 days) with a 10% discount if the bill is paid in less than 30 days, then a single entry will reside in the `term_days` table for this term code. The entry would be the `term code`, a `seq_num` = 1 and a percentage of 10 for 10 percent entered as a -10 to indicate a discount.

If the terms to be described were net 30 with a 10% discount if paid in less than 30 days, and a penalty markup of 20% after 60 days, then there would be two entries in the `term_days` table. One entry would have the term code, a `seq_number` of 1 and a percent field of 10 (entered as a -10 to indicate a discount). The next entry (for the 60 day markup) would have the same term code, a `seq_number` of two, and a percent entry of 20 (entered as a +20 to indicate a markup) for the past due markup.

```
terms ( term_code char(2),
        description char(15))
```

```
term_days( term_code   char(2),
           days        smallint,
           description char(15),
           percent     smallint )
```

The `shipping_codes` Table

The ship codes (`ship_codes`) table references the shipping code stored in the billing record. This code relates to standardized shipping instructions. The table contains a ship code and a character description to store the shipping instructions.

```
ship_codes( ship_code      integer,
            shipping_instr char(40))
```

The `bill` Table

The `bill` table stores the header record for the accounts receivable bill. It contains the bill number, the batch number in which the bill was entered, the shipping code for the order, the date of the bill, and the total amount of the bill. This total amount represents the total of the line items associated with the bill.

```
bill( bill_no      serial,
      batch_number integer,
      ship_code    integer,
      bill_date    date,
      bill_total   decimal(10,2),
      paid_amt     decimal(10,2))
```

The `line_items` Table

The line items (`line_items`) table is used to store the set of items contained in the bill. It contains the bill number, the sequence number of the line item, the stock number of the line item, and the amount or cost of the line item. The bill number references the bill number header record in the bill table and the stock number references the stock number in the stock table.

```
line_items( bill_no  integer,
            seq_no   smallint,
            stock_no integer,
            amount   decimal(10,2))
```

The `stock_items` Table

The stock items (`stock_items`) table stores the stock numbers of the line items on the bill. It contains the stock number, a description of the stock item, the manufacturer number, and the price for the item.

```
stock_items( stock_no     integer,
             description  char(30),
             ship_code    smallint,
             manu_code    integer,
             price        decimal(5,2))
```

The `journal_entries` Table

The journal entries table (`journal_entry`) is used to store the journal entries applied to posted accounts receivable. It contains the batch number of the receivable batch, the customer account number adjusted, and the date of the adjustment.

```
create table journal_entry (
            batch_number   integer,
            customer_numb  integer,
            journal_date   date)
```

The `security` Table

The security table (`security`) is used to store security information about the users of the accounts receivable module. The user's name, department, and permission level is stored in this table.

```
create table security (
            fname          char(15),
            lname          char(15),
            dept           char(10)
            security_code  smallint )
```

The `security_codes` Table

The `security codes` table stores the security code and the appropriate description. It contains two columns: the security code and the security description.

```
create table security_codes (
            security_code  smallint,
            description    char(20) )
```

The `stock` Table

The `stock` table is used to store the stock items referenced in the line items table. This table contains fields for stock number, description, and number on hand.

```
create table stock (
            stock_number    integer,
            description     char(20),
            on_hand         integer )
```

The `zip_code` Table

The zip code (`zip_code`) table is used to store zip code lookup information. Given the zip code, the city and state can be retrieved from this table.

```
create table zip_code (
            zip_code char(8),
            city     char(20),
            state    char(2) )
```

The `control` Table

The `control` table is used to store general information needed by the accounts receivable applications. This table stores the current accounting month and the name of the company using the accounts receivable module.

```
create table ar_control (
            acctg_month    smallint,
            company_name   char(20))
```

Chapter 4
The NewEra Window

The NewEra screen contains a number of window *objects* and controls which map directly to NewEra language objects; they can be instantiated or destroyed at runtime, they have events, and at runtime events can be posted to the objects.

This mapping of screen objects into a language which completely supports object-oriented programming is a powerful feature. The classes for these screen objects can be used to derive custom classes. These custom screen classes can then be selected in the Window Painter. This allows object properties to be customized and then reused throughout the application by simply indicating the class name of your custom class in the Window Painter.

NewEra control classes can be customized to create *database aware* controls. These controls would recognize database columns and bind the columns to SuperFields on the screen. Using the controls would involve little more than painting the control, setting the control *class* property to the class of the custom class, and initializing the control. Examples of creating database aware controls will be shown in chapter 7.

NewEra objects are painted into a window and then become components of that window. In the NewEra generated code, these objects become member objects of the window object. They can therefore be referenced through the window object. If a NewEra window is named `window1`, then referencing a SuperTable object member function in a SuperTable named `SuperTable1` that is contained within the window, the following NewEra language statement could be used.

```
call Window1.SuperTable1.retrieve( QBE: FALSE )
```

These references are also known as containers. They are composed of the object reference and its components as defined in the class definition for the class of the object. In the example shown above, the window named `window1` was defined in its class definition as containing a SuperTable object named `SuperTable1`. The SuperTable class defintion, in turn, defines a member function named `retrieve`, which is the function being called in the code shown above.

An object reference can be resolved at runtime and functions can return an object reference. This is a powerful capability that allows reusable and simplified code to be written. For example, to simplify access with visual objects, the `getVisualContainer` function can be called as follows.

```
variable st ixSuperTable
let st = getVisualContainer() CAST ixSuperTable
call st.retrieve( QBE: FALSE )
```

In this example, a SuperTable reference is needed. To make the code reusable, it is preferable not to use the actual name of the SuperTable but instead make a call to a function to return a reference to the container. This can be accomplished with the NewEra supplied function `getVisualContainer`. The `getVisualContainer` function will return a reference to the visual container (`ixVisualContainer` object) that contains the handler or control where this code is contained. This reference is then used to call the SuperTable `retrieve` member function on the next line. This code could have been combined into a single line of NewEra code as shown below.

```
call (getVisualContainer() cast ixSuperTable).retrieve(
QBE: FALSE )
```

NewEra provides a number of different window objects. The commonly used window objects are listed below. The classes for these objects are in turn derived from other more generalized classes, but the complete class list is omitted here.

The `ixVisualObject`

Almost all NewEra screen objects are derived from `ixVisualObject`. The `ixVisualObject` is a generalized abstract class which embodies some of the more common attributes for a screen object: displaying and hiding the object, availability of the object, and enabling and disabling the object.

A member function exists to return a reference to the current visual container. By casting the results of this function call, a reference to the current window or frame can be obtained as shown below.

```
variable SuperTable ixSuperTable

LET superTable = (getVisualContainer() CAST ixSuperTable)
call SuperTable.retrieve( QBE: FALSE )
```

In this example, a variable is declared to be of type `ixSuperTable`.; since this is generic code that will not necessarily have knowledge of the *name* of the current SuperTable. But the name is not needed, only an object reference for the current

Chapter 4: The NewEra Window   63

SuperTable. Since `ixSuperTable` is a subclass of `ixVisualObject`, an `ixVisualObject` can be cast as an `ixSuperTable` using the NewEra CAST statement.

    A number of other `ixVisualObject` member functions exist and are listed below. These functions can be called for a variety of screen objects that are subclassed from `ixVisualObject`. For example, to hide and then later show a button, the following code would be executed.

```
variable button1 ixButton
if status_flag = button_off  then
   call button1.hide()
end if
...
if status_flag = button_on then
    call button1.show()
end if
```

IxVisualObject Member Functions

Event	Description	Parameters	Return Value
disable	Disable the object. The object will then be displayed in half-intensity.		VOID
displayHelp	Call the help viewer using the help number for this object.		VOID
enable	Enable the object.		VOID
getAnchor	Get the anchor (the upper-left corner) of the object relative to the upper-left corner of the container.		integer, integer
getAvailabilty	Returns a value indicating this visual object is *open*, *unopened*, or *closed*.		smallint
getBackColor	Return the color number of the current background color.		integer
getFont	get the actual names of the font, point size and the flags for bold, underline, and italic attributes for the object.		fontname char(*), size smallint, bold, underline, italic BOOLEAN

Event	Description	Parameters	Return Value
getFontName	Return the name of the current font.		fontname char(*)
getFontSize	Return the point size of the current font.		point_size smallint
getForeColor	Return the color number of the foreground color.		color integer
getHeight	Return the height of the object in PGUs.		integer
getLeft	Return the left location in PGUs.		integer
getSize	Return the size of the object (height and width).		height integer, width integer
getTop	Returned the top location in PGUs.		integer
getVisualContainer	Returns the container of the current control.		ixVisualContainer
getWidth	Returns the width in PGUs.		integer
getWindow	Returns a reference to the current window container.		ixWindow
hide	Hide the current object.		VOID
isEnabled	Returns TRUE if the object is enabled.		BOOLEAN
isFontBold	Returns TRUE if the font BOLD attribute is used.		BOOLEAN
isFontItalic	Returns TRUE if the font Italic attribute is used.		BOOLEAN
isFontUnderline	Returns TRUE if the font underline attribute is used.		BOOLEAN
isShown	Returns TRUE if the object is shown.		BOOLEAN
setAnchor	Set the anchor (the upper-left corner) of the object relative to the upper-left corner of the container.		VOID
setColor	Set the color (foreground and background) of the object and redraw if necessary.	foreground integer, background integer	VOID

Chapter 4: The NewEra Window   65

Event	Description	Parameters	Return Value
setFont	Change the font attributes and repaint the object if it is currently shown.	fontname char(*), fontsize smallint, bold, italic, underline BOOLEAN	VOID
setSize	Set the size of the object (height and width) and redraw if necessary.	height integer, width integer	VOID
show	Show the current object.		VOID

The NewEra SuperTable

The NewEra *SuperTable* is a database-aware object of class `ixSuperTable` that provides a powerful application programmer interface (API) between screen data entry and database manipulation. It contains member functions for displaying, inputting, and validating data and member functions for retrieving and updating the database. It appears in two forms: the *free-form* SuperTable and the *grid-form* SuperTable. Member functions can operate on either form of SuperTable member.

The Free-form SuperTable

The *free-form* SuperTable is a variation of the SuperTable class that allows the SuperTable fields (SuperFields) to be placed anywhere on the screen. It is property of the SuperTable class `ixSuperTable`.

Because the SuperTable is a class, the programmer can easily derive a class from this class and implicitly inherit all of the member functions and data in this class. Programmers can then extend or override capabilities to suit their needs. This allows screen input and validation member functions to be customized and then automatically transferred to all input and validation routines through inheritance.

The SuperTable class contains a number of different member functions that provide for screen and database manipulation. There is a tight binding between the screen fields and the database tables/columns. Data entry functions allow for inserting data into a field, clearing a field, replacing data in a field, and moving keyboard focus to a field. Database member functions allow for *applying, retrieving,* and *deleting* data from the database.

NewEra provides a very complete set of events for SuperTables and SuperFields. Events exist to trap execution before or after a row and can explicitly test for a *stale data* condition.

SuperTable Events

Event	Description	Parameter(s) Received	Return Value(s)
afterApply	Raised after data has been applied to the database.		BOOLEAN
afterRetrieve	Raised immediately after a query has been processed.		BOOLEAN
afterRow	Raised before the current row loses its status as the current row.		VOID
afterRowApplied	Called after changes to the row are applied to the database.		BOOLEAN
beforeApply	Raised before any changes to the row are applied to the database.		BOOLEAN
beforeRetrieve	Raised immediately before a query is processed.		BOOLEAN
beforeRevert	Raised before a modified row is reverted to its previous state.		BOOLEAN
beforeRow	Raised before a row becomes the current row	rowNum integer: currentRow	VOID
beforeRowLocked	Raised before locking to allow the programmer to begin a transaction.	row ixRow	BOOLEAN
dataRowCheck	Raised to allow row validation in displayData mode.	row ixRow	BOOLEAN
maxRowsExceeded	Raised when the number of rows retrieved exceeds `maxRows` value.		VOID

Event	Description	Parameter(s) Received	Return Value(s)
queryRowCheck	Raised to allow row validation in displayQuery mode.	row ixRow	BOOLEAN
rowRetrieved	Raised after each row is retrieved from the database, but before it is added to the current set of rows.	row ixRow	BOOLEAN
SQLDelete	Raised to delete a row from the database.	Row ixRow	Integer
SQLFetch	Raised to fetch a row from the database		Integer, ixrow
SQLFreeSelect	Is Raised to close the database cursor and other resources allocated.	Row ixrow	Integer
SQLInsert	Raised to insert the row into the database when the row is applied to the database.		Integer
SQLPrepSelect	Raised to prepare a select statement before fetching data.		Integer
SQLUpdate	Raised to update the database	row ixRow	Integer
staleData	Raised when the values in the row have changed since they were last fetched.	NewRow ixrow, oldrow ixrow, dbrow ixrow, stalecols ixVector)	BOOLEAN

The Grid-form SuperTable

The *grid-form* SuperTable is identical to the *free-form* SuperTable except that the data entry fields are presented the format of a scrollable region on the window (see Figure 4-1). In this format, each line represents a row of the data set and a scrolling region is available to scroll the rows up, down, and sideways if necessary.

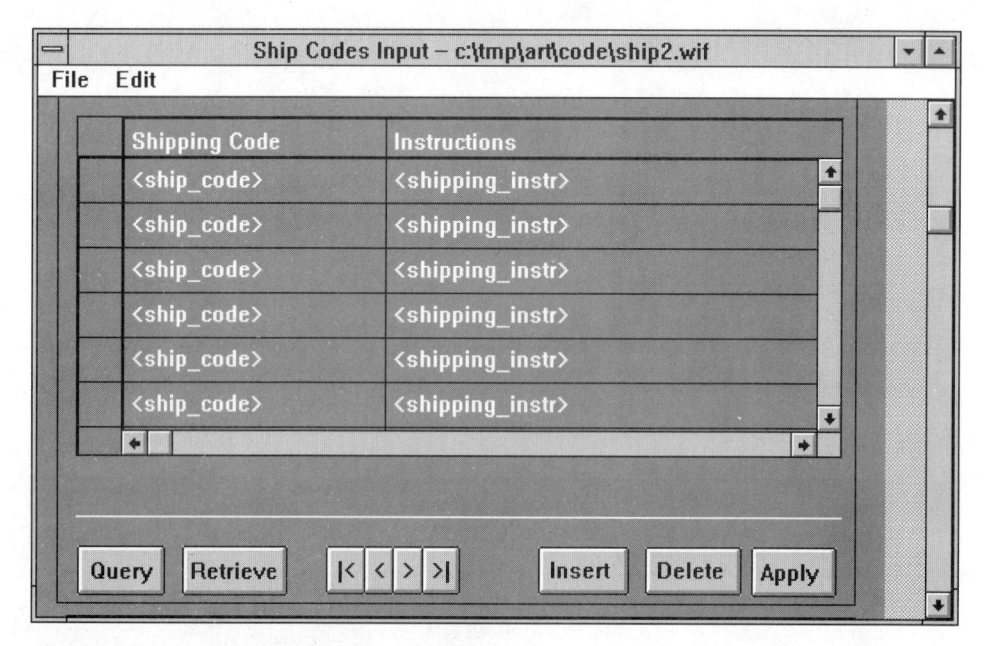

Figure 4-1 - Grid-Form SuperTable

The member functions and events available to the *grid-form* SuperTable are the same as for the *free-form* SuperTable. The major difference between these two SuperTable types is that of presentation rather than functionality since the same member functions can be used on both. The SuperTable is derived from `ixFrame` and can therefore be a container for other controls and can have a border.

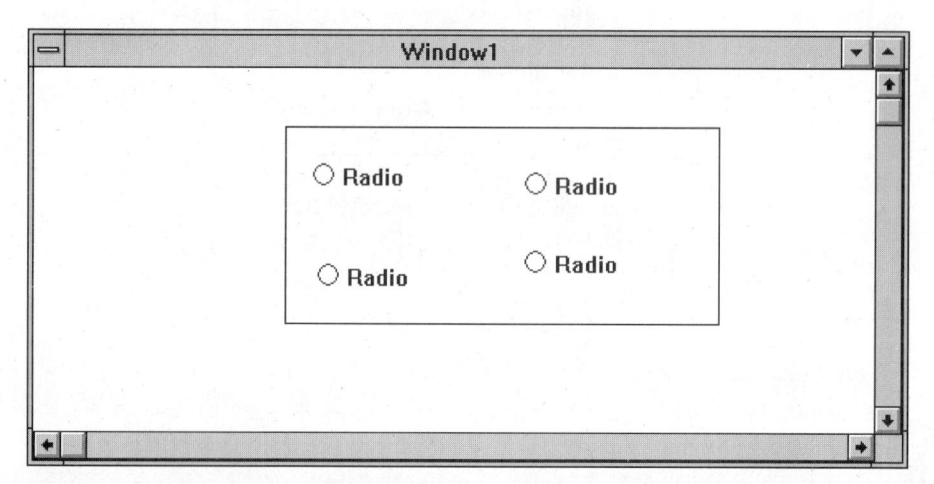

Figure 4-2- Frame Used to Group Radio Buttons

The Visual Frame Object

The *frame* visual object allows the use of a visual frame on the screen. It is an object of class `ixFrame` and can be used to group visual controls such as radio buttons together on the screen (see Figure 4-2). A number of frame events are available and are listed below

Frame Events

Event	Description	Parameters	Return Value
frameFocusIn	Raised when a control within this frame has received keyboard focus		VOID
frameFocusOut	Raised when a control within this frame has lost keyboard focus		VOID

The Text Box Control

The *text box* object is of class `ixTextBox` and is used to display text to the screen. Optionally, only a portion of the text can be shown in the box and the user can use the arrow keys on the right-hand side of the control to scroll through the text (see Figure 4-3).

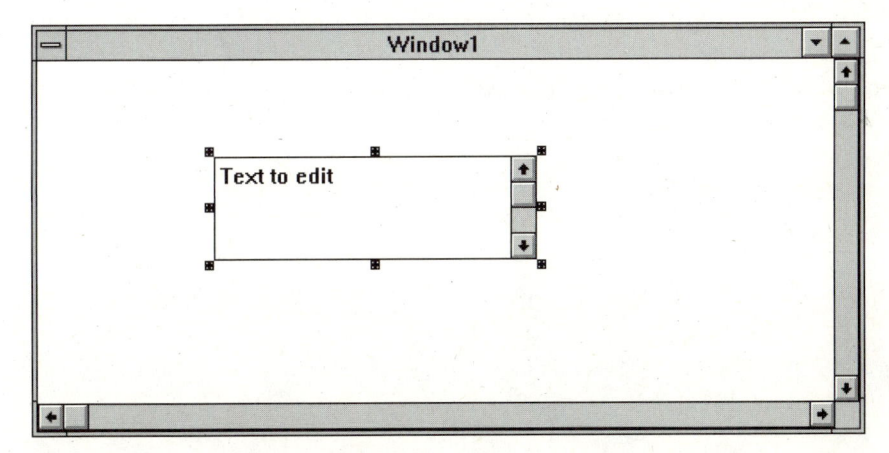

Figure 4-3 - Text Box Control

The text box has several events available as listed below. Note that the `keyPress` event is not triggered by a mouse click. Only a keyboard entry would trigger this event. The `keyPress` event receives an integer code as a parameter. This integer code is the same as the value returned by the built-in `fgl_keyval` function used in Informix-4GL. It is an integer code representing a key or a sequence of keys pressed on the keyboard, including function keys and several control key sequences.

Text Box Events

Event	Description	Parameters	Return Value
click	The pointer was clicked inside a textbox.		VOID
keyPress	A keyboard entry has been made.(a mouse click is **not** a keyboard entry)	key integer	VOID
valueChanged	The box is losing keyboard focus and the text value has changed		VOID

The `valueChanged` event indicates that a window cursor has left the textbox and the value of the textbox has changed. For the programmer, this removes the need to check the contents of a text box before and after the user has left the box. The programmer need only create a handler for the `valueChanged` event of the text box and process the data as needed.

The Label Control

The *label* object is of class `ixLabel` and is used to place text on the screen (see Figure 4-4). Once created, a number of properties such as font and point size can be applied to the text in the label. Since the `ixLabel` object does not provide for input, there are no events associated with a text label. It is possible, however, to programmatically change its contents at runtime using the `setText` member function. The call would be made as follows:

```
variable label1 ixLabel
let label1 = new ixLabel( text: "This value" )

-- now change value of the label
call label1.SetText( "this text " )
```

Chapter 4: The NewEra Window 71

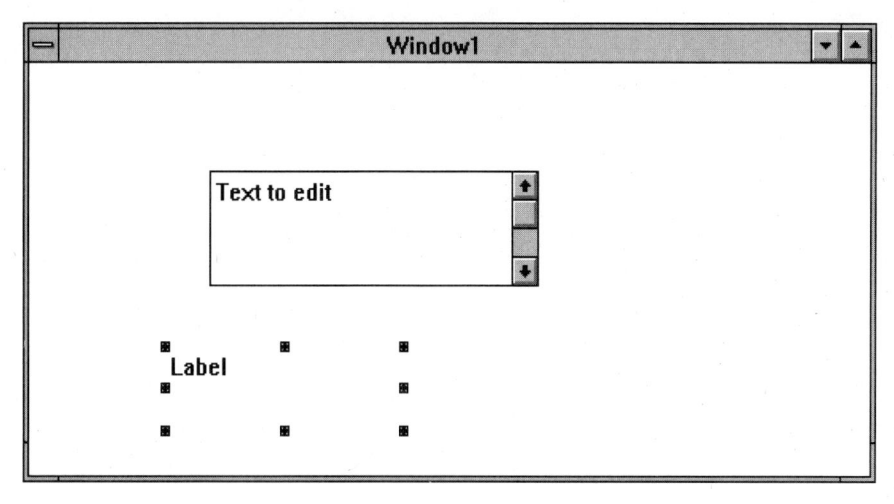

Figure 4-4 - The Text Label Object

The Button Control

The *button* control places a button on the screen; it is of class `ixButton` (see Figure 4-5). The button is used primarily to allow the user to trigger other events in the application. The button has a title which describes its function. The single button control event is listed below.

Button Events

Event	Description	Parameters	Return Value
focusIn	The button is receiving keyboard focus		
focusOut	The button is losing keyboard focus		
activate	The button was pressed by the user.		VOID

The most common use for a button is to display an option and create a handler for the `activate` event triggered by the user's selection of the button. The user selects a button by using the mouse to single-click a button.

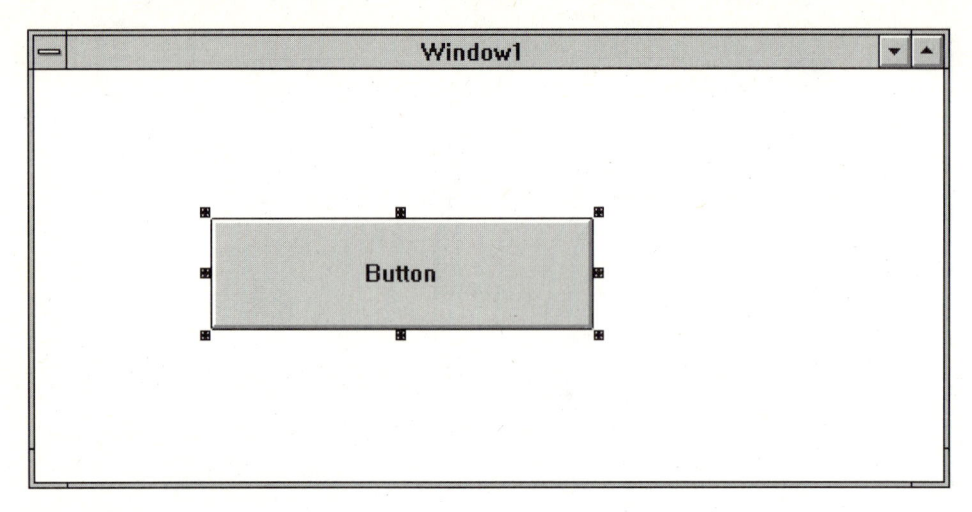

Figure 4-5 - Button Control

The Picture Button

The *picture button* is identical to the button control except that instead of a title, a picture is displayed on the front of this button (see Figure 4-6). It is presumed that this picture would somehow describe the function of this button. This allows the buttons to use less space on the screen and, if an appropriate picture is used, provide a clearer explanation of the function of the button. This control is of class `ixPictureButton` which is derived from class `ixButton`.

The picture button indicates the current state of the button as *enabled*, *disabled*, or *pressed* by displaying three different bitmaps, one for each state respectively.

While the size of the button can be set in the properties for the button, the actual size of the image is dependent on the image and the image format. The image will not be scaled to the size of the button.

Picture buttons are a useful means of adding graphics to an application. To place a graphic into an application, a picture button could be created and set to disable mode. The *disable* picture could then be assigned to the desired graphic.

Picture Button Events

Event	Description	Parameters	Return Value
activate	This button was pressed by the user.		VOID

Chapter 4: The NewEra Window 73

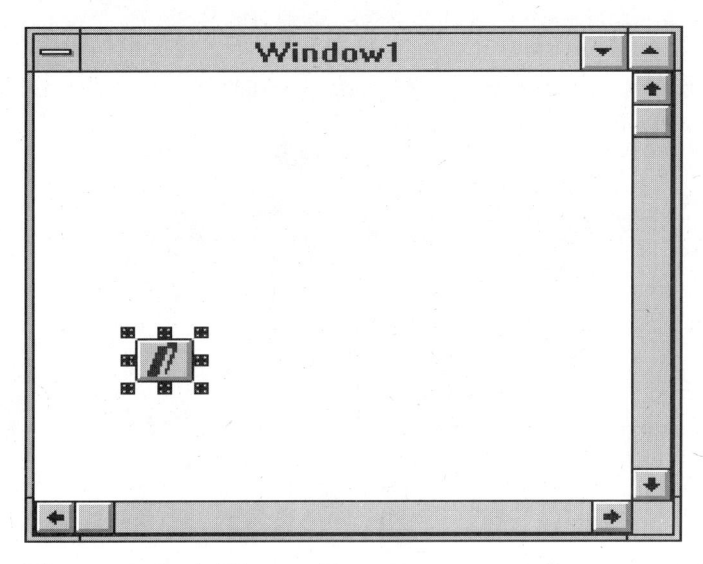

Figure 4-6 - A Picture Button

The `ixPictureButton` class has no events of its own but does inherit the `activate` event from the `ixButton` class. This is the event that would be used to trap the user's selection of the picture button.

The picture button allows the function of the button to be described in a smaller space, thus allowing more buttons to be placed on the screen. The danger is that the user will not understand the picture being used. Careful choice of the picture, or using a picture and a small description, can solve this problem.

The Radio Button

The *radio button* is of class `ixRadiobutton`. This control is used to represent a mutually exclusive choice. In a set of radio buttons, a selection of one button will automatically deselect the other buttons in the same visual container. This control is often placed within a frame as shown in Figure 4-2.

Radio Button Events

Event	Description	Parameters	Return Value
select	This button was pressed by the user.		VOID

The `select` event handler would usually contain code to indicate the user's choice. Since this code could assert the user has made a mutually exclusive choice, a simple status variable may be set to the value logically corresponding to the button.

The Check Box

The *check box* control is similar to the radio button with the exception that the check box does **not** represent mutually exclusive choices. An example is shown below in Figure 4-7.

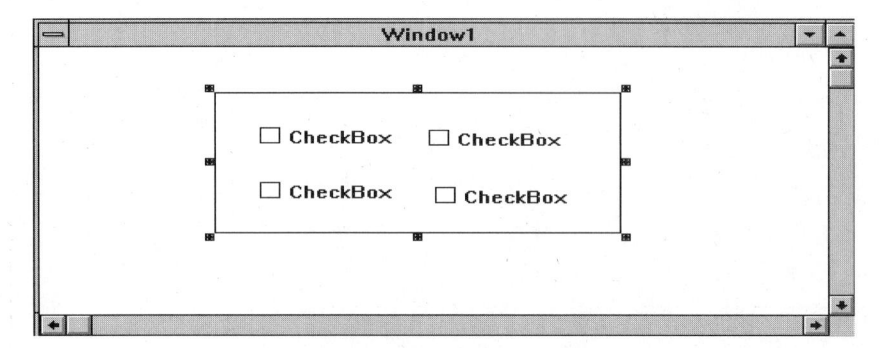

Figure 4-7 - Check Box Controls

A series of check boxes is usually placed within a frame. This set of check boxes represents choices that the user can select. This functionality is similar to a check box on a form where a user can select one or many choices.

Check Box Events

Event	Description	Parameters	Return Value
valueChanged	The value of this button has been changed. A call to the `isChecked` member function will indicate the current setting of the box (returns TRUE if checked, returns FALSE if not).		VOID

A handler is usually written for the check box to handle the `valueChanged` event. A set of variables could be coded for the initial values of the check boxes and when the user changes a box, the `valueChanged` event handler would reset the value of the code based on the return value from the `isChecked` member function for the check box. If the user has checked the box, then the associated value could be assigned to the variable. If the user has not checked the box, the value of the variable could be set to indicate this. This code is demonstrated in the code fragment below.

```
variable cbox1 ixCheckBox
variable cbox1_on  Boolean
```

```
let cbox1 = new ixCheckBox( ... )

-- the valueChanged handler
if cbox1.isChecked() then
   let box1_on = TRUE
else
   let box1_on = FALSE
end if
```

The List Box

The *list box* control provides a series of choices for the user (see Figure 4-8). It is a member of the class `ixListBox`. The user can scroll through the choices using the arrow keys and then select one or, optionally, many choices.

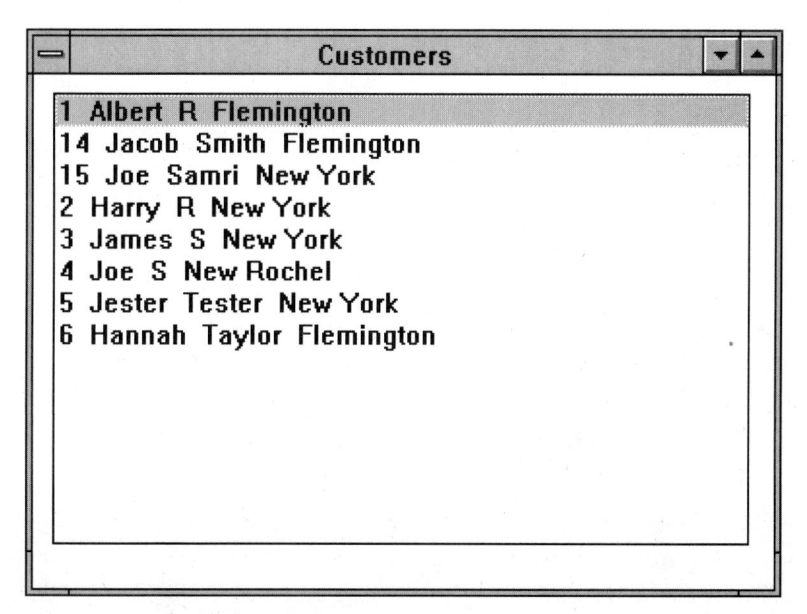

```
┌─────────────────── Customers ───────────▼─▲─┐
│ 1  Albert  R  Flemington                    │
│ 14 Jacob  Smith  Flemington                 │
│ 15 Joe  Samri  New York                     │
│ 2  Harry  R  New York                       │
│ 3  James  S  New York                       │
│ 4  Joe  S  New Rochel                       │
│ 5  Jester  Tester  New York                 │
│ 6  Hannah  Taylor  Flemington               │
│                                             │
│                                             │
└─────────────────────────────────────────────┘
```

Figure 4-8 - The List Box

The list box can be *single-select* or *multi-select* and can be a *drop-down* list box or a *fixed* list box. With the *drop-down* list box, when the user presses the down arrow on the side of the list box, the list portion of the list box is displayed and the user can scroll through the set as a list box. Note that the box must be sized large enough in the Window Painter to support the rows to be displayed on the screen. The drop-down list box only allows a single selected item. The fixed list box supports both a single selection mode and a multiple selections mode.

List Box Events

Event	Description	Parameters	Return Value
select	An item in the list box was activated. This is generally initiated by a double click on a highlighted item.		VOID
activate	An item in the list box was selected. This essentially means an item was highlighted.		VOID

If the list box is a *single select* list box, meaning only a single item from the list can be selected, then only one value will be retrieved from the list box `getSelection` member function. The code below demonstrates the retrieval of the single selected item for a list box.

```
variable list1 ixListBox
variable selection char(*)

let list1 = new ixListBox(...)

-- handler code for the select event for list1
let selection = window1.list1.getItembyNumber(itemnum:
                        window1.list1.getSelectedItem()
)
```

In this example, a list box is named `list1`. A character string for storing the selected item must be declared. The character string value of the selection can be retrieved using the `getItembyNumber` member function. But the `getItembyNumber` member function requires the integer offset in the list for the selected item. This can be retrieved using the `getSelectedItem` member function. The sample code above uses both of these functions combined in a single call.

An `ixvector` object can be used to populate a list box. When this is done, the return value of the `getSelectedItem` member function can be used to provide the offset for the selected element into the `ixVector` set. The following code provides an example of this approach to using list boxes. It assumes the list box allows only a single selected item.

```
global variable Glist1 ixvector = new ixVector()
variable retval smallint
```

Chapter 4: The NewEra Window 77

```
-- load ixVector object
...
call window1.list1.insertlist( Glist1 )
        returning retval

...
-- handle the select event
variable str ixString

let str =  Glist1.get( window1.list1.getselectitem() )
             cast ixString

-- str now contains the ixString value of the selected item
```

In the code above, an `ixVector` object is created and named `Glist1`. This object is then populated with the values to be displayed in the list box. The values inserted need not be `ixString` values, but they must be values that can be converted into `ixString` values.

Next, the code for obtaining the list box selection is written. An `ixString` variable is created and used to capture the return value of the call to the `ixVector` get member function. This call returns a data type `ixObject` which is cast as a data type `ixString` (this is allowed since `ixString` is a subclass of `ixObject`). At this point, the `ixString` data variable contains the selected value from the list.

The Multi-Select List Box

If a multi-select list box has been used, then the potentially multiple return values must be handled by the application. This is done via the one-dimensional dynamic array, `ixVector`. This is the data type returned by the `getAllSelectedItems` member function of the list box class. The following code demonstrates the management of this return value:

```
variable allitems   ixVector
variable retval,n   smallint

call window1.list1.getAllSelecteditems()
        returning allitems

if allitems IS NULL then
    call
 messagebox(title: new ixString( "Message " ),
            message: new ixString( "Nothing Selected" ))
       returning retval
```

```
        else
            -- list return values
            for n = 1 to allitems.getcount()
                        display " Selected value " || n ||   " : " ||
                ( allitems.get( n ) cast ixString ).getvaluestr()
            end for
end if
```

In this example, a multi-select list box named `list1` has been used. The `ixListBox` member function `getAllSelecteditems` is used to retrieve an `ixVector` object (declared and named `allitems`) for all of the selected items. The code above first tests the `ixVector` object (named `allitems`) object to determine whether or not any items were in fact selected. If the object is NULL, then a message is displayed indicating this. If the object is not NULL, then a display window is created with a listing of the selected items using the NewEra `display` statement. To avoid writing additional lines of code, the NewEra ability to resolve object references in `call` statements is used in the `display` statement. The statement

```
display " Selected value " || n ||   " : " ||
    ( allitems.get( n ) cast ixString ).getvaluestr()
```

resolves to

```
variable str ixString
let str = allitems.get(n) cast ixString
display " Selected value " || n ||   " : " ||
str.getValueStr()
```

The combined statement requires fewer lines of code and, when used judiciously, can make code more understandable.

The SuperField Control

The SuperField control provides the input medium for the data entered in the data entry window. The SuperField is *connected* internally to the SuperTable and as data is entered, the SuperTable will update one of its internal `ixRowArray` member object with the changes.

Chapter 4: The NewEra Window

The SuperField control also provides the events for the activity concerning input for the field. The `afterCell`, `beforeCell`, `afterDataChanged` and other field level events are associated with the SuperField.

The `primaryKey` Property

The `primaryKey` property is set to TRUE if the associated SuperField represents the primary key for the table represented by the SuperTable. Otherwise, this parameter is set to FALSE, the default value (see Figure 4-9).

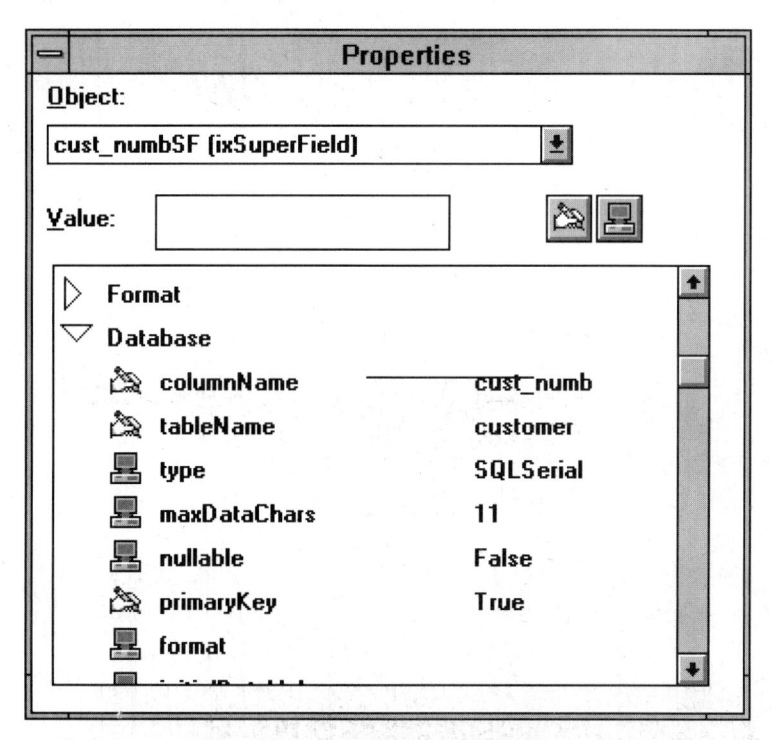

Figure 4-9 - The Primary Key Property

If a SuperTable is to perform database updates, then at least one of the SuperFields must be identified as the primary key. Once the primary key value is identified, then the `updateTable` property will be set for the appropriate SuperTable (see Figure 4-10).

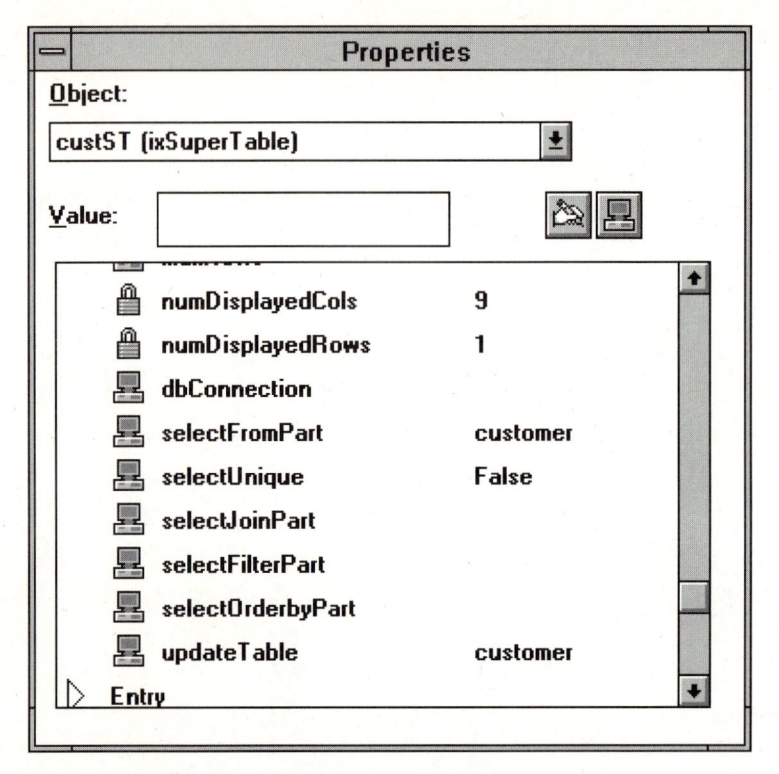

```
┌─────────────────────────────────────────────┐
│ ─              Properties                   │
│ Object:                                     │
│ ┌─────────────────────────────────┐ ┌──┐   │
│ │ custST (ixSuperTable)           │ │ ▼│   │
│ └─────────────────────────────────┘ └──┘   │
│                                             │
│ Value: ┌──────────────────────┐  ┌──┐┌──┐  │
│        │                      │  │🖉 ││🖳 │  │
│        └──────────────────────┘  └──┘└──┘  │
│   ┌──────────────────────────────────────┐ │
│   │  🔒  numDisplayedCols      9       ↑│ │
│   │  🔒  numDisplayedRows      1        │ │
│   │  🖳  dbConnection                    │ │
│   │  🖳  selectFromPart        customer  │ │
│   │  🖳  selectUnique          False     │ │
│   │  🖳  selectJoinPart                  │ │
│   │  🖳  selectFilterPart                │ │
│   │  🖳  selectOrderbyPart               │ │
│   │  🖳  updateTable           customer  │ │
│   │  ▷ Entry                           ↓│ │
│   └──────────────────────────────────────┘ │
└─────────────────────────────────────────────┘
```

Figure 4-10 - The `UpdateTable` Property

The SuperTable Control

The SuperTable control is the workhorse of the data entry process in NewEra. It provides window data entry interaction and database update capabilities. It provides excellent flexibility with numerous events, default handlers, and member functions. Several of the database properties that can optionally be set for the SuperTable (see Figure 4-11) are listed below.

The `updateTable` property is set to the value of the name of the table that will be updated in the database by the SuperTable. This value is set based on the table associated with the SuperTable used to paint the window. This value is locked for user update and can only be set programmatically by the Window Painter.

Chapter 4: The NewEra Window 81

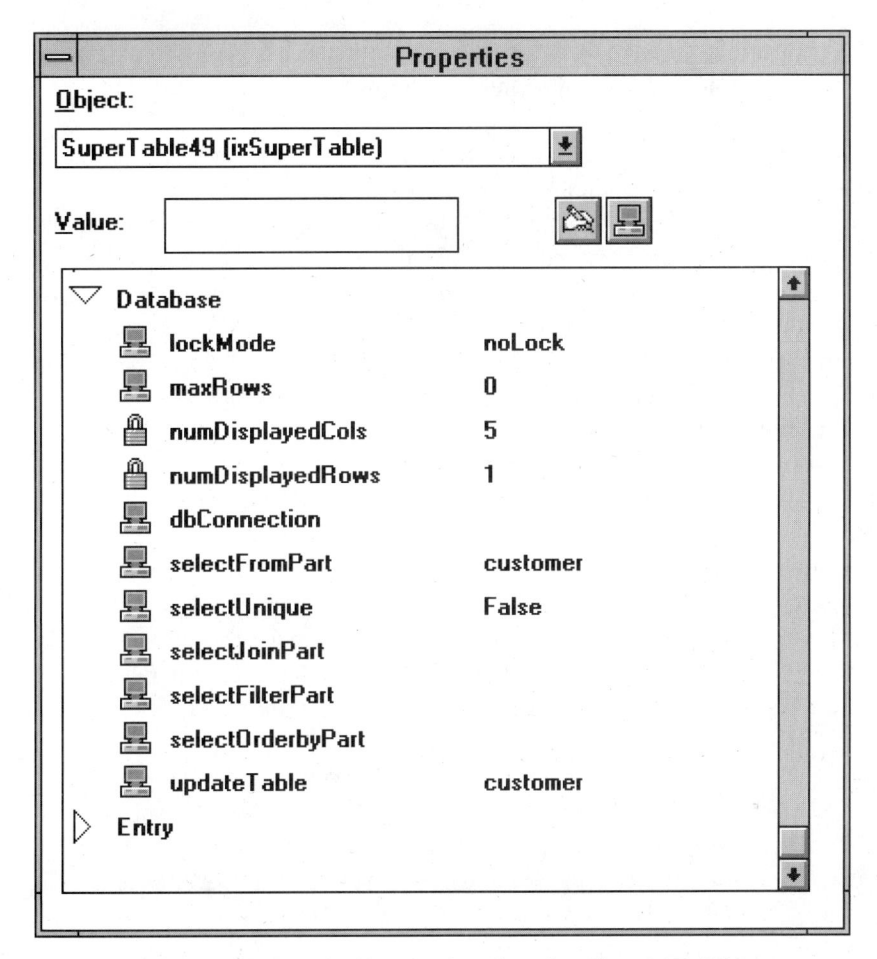

```
┌─────────────────────────────────────────────────┐
│ ─                    Properties                 │
│ Object:                                         │
│ ┌─────────────────────────────────┐ ┌─┐         │
│ │SuperTable49 (ixSuperTable)      │ │▼│         │
│ └─────────────────────────────────┘ └─┘         │
│ Value: ┌──────────────────────┐  ┌──┐ ┌──┐      │
│        │                      │  │🖉 │ │🖥 │     │
│        └──────────────────────┘  └──┘ └──┘      │
│  ┌───────────────────────────────────────────┐  │
│  │  ▽  Database                              │  │
│  │     🖥  lockMode              noLock       │  │
│  │     🖥  maxRows               0            │  │
│  │     🔒  numDisplayedCols      5            │  │
│  │     🔒  numDisplayedRows      1            │  │
│  │     🖥  dbConnection                       │  │
│  │     🖥  selectFromPart        customer     │  │
│  │     🖥  selectUnique          False        │  │
│  │     🖥  selectJoinPart                     │  │
│  │     🖥  selectFilterPart                   │  │
│  │     🖥  selectOrderbyPart                  │  │
│  │     🖥  updateTable           customer     │  │
│  │  ▷  Entry                                 │  │
│  └───────────────────────────────────────────┘  │
└─────────────────────────────────────────────────┘
```

Figure 4-11 - Database Properties for the SuperTable

The `lockMode` Property

The database `lockmode` allows the locking mode for the SuperTable to be set to either *nolocking, pessimistic,* or *optimistic* locking. These properties directly impact how and when the SuperTable will lock the rows retrieved by the user.

With *pessimistic* locking, the database row is locked once the SuperTable detects a change to the contents of one of the SuperFields. The database row will remain locked until the `applyRowSQL` SuperTable function is called.

With *optimistic* locking, rows are not locked until the rows are written to the database. The rows are locked one row at a time with singleton locks. Once the rows are updated, the lock is freed.

If the data rows in the database table have changed since the rows were retrieved, the SuperTable will detect this condition and raise a `staleData` event. It is then up to the programmer to reconcile the condition. Possible solutions would be to apply the old record (the record originally retrieved from the database and available within the SuperTable using the `revert` member function) or to simply indicate to the user that stale data was found and their changes were applied.

The programmer also has the option of setting the locking mode to *nolocking* and then controlling locks manually through SuperTable events. Various approaches are available to the programmer.

One possible approach would be to attempt to lock the row in the `beforeRow` event and if the lock fails, not allow the user to edit that row. The user could be kept in the current row by setting the current row to the previous row using the `setCurrentCell` member function.

Another possible approach would be to lock all of the rows retrieved by the user before the user begins editing. This could be accomplished within the `afterRetrieve` event which is raised once all of the rows have been retrieved from the database. The handler for the `beforeApply` event would then have to release the locks before the data could be applied to the database.

Locks could also be acquired in the `rowRetrieved` event handler. The `rowRetrieved` event handler receives the currently retrieved row as a parameter. The primary key value for the row could be retrieved from the parameter and a cursor used to lock the row. The `beforeApply` or `beforeRowApplied` event could then be used to remove the lock and allow the row to be applied to the database.

Transaction Management

Transaction management could be used with various retrieval schemes. Note that standard transaction logic may not apply when using SuperTables. By default, SuperTables will retrieve all rows that apply to a query and then close the cursor used to retrieve the rows. Therefore, if the isolation mode were set to `repeatable read` and rows retrieved from the database by the SuperTable, closing the cursor would release all of the locks held by the cursor and would remove any of the concurrency restrictions the programmer was attempting to enforce.

The `maxRows` Property

The `maxRows` parameter defines the number of rows to be retrieved from the database by the `retrieve` member function. There is currently no automatic contingency for retrieving an additional set of rows once the `maxrows` value has been reached. Logic to do this must be coded into the application (an example of doing this will be shown in chapter 6).

Setting the value of `maxrows` correctly is important. If the value is set too high, then the initial retrieval of data could take a long time. For example, if the `maxRows` parameter were set to 200, the user could be forced to wait a minute or two while data rows are being retrieved; a retrieval time that would most likely leave the user complaining about the application being too slow. It would be better, instead, to retrieve 50 rows and indicate to the user that the maximum number of rows had been reached and they must enter another query to retrieve more rows.

The `number of displayed rows` and columns concerns the data that will be displayed on the screen. In the case of the *free-form* SuperTable, this value will always be one. In the case of the grid-form SuperTable, the value will reflect the number of rows displayed within a grid SuperTable.

The `selectfromPart`, the `selectUnique`, and the `selectJoinPart` all concern the portions of the SQL statement that will be created by the SuperTable. The `updateTable` parameter indicates the name of the table that will be updated by this SuperTable. These are public variables that are a critical part of the SuperTable. Changing the values of these variables can alter the amount of data being retrieved from the database by the SuperTable.

Chapter 5
The Structure of NewEra Applications

The NewEra application program is composed of a `main` program block and optionally, functions, objects, events and reports. The program execution usually involves a window or set of windows and the objects that reside in those windows. The understanding of this program execution and the underlying application structure is an important part of learning the NewEra language. This chapter will describe the NewEra program structure and the code behind that structure.

STRUCTURE OF A NEWERA PROGRAM

The `main` program block is the main entry point for a NewEra application just as in an Informix-4GL application. The program operation starts there. Where NewEra differs from Informix-4GL is in its interaction with the window environment. If a NewEra `return` statement exists in the NewEra `main` program block, NewEra will, at that point, pass control to the window manager (in what is sometimes called the "window manager event loop") and wait for an event to be posted to one of its objects.

If, however, an `end main` statement is encountered before a `return` statement in the `main` program block, then the program will exit at that point and the NewEra application will **not** wait for events from the window manager

The Window Object

The NewEra window is the *container* for all visual components within the window. This container is an object of the Informix-supplied class `ixWindow`. Within this object are contained the controls that reside in the window.

Visual objects, such as windows and the controls within a window, are based on the class `ixVisualObject`. This class is the mediator between the native window environment (such as Windows) and the NewEra application. As the user interacts with the NewEra application, the window environment *manager* will translate their actions into events and ultimately post these events to the NewEra application. It is the objects of the `ixVisualObject` class and its subclasses that will receive these events and, by executing NewEra code in event handlers, perform actions based on the events.

The code shown in this chapter is the Window Painter generated code for the customer data entry window shown in Figure 5-1. This is a complete data entry screen with facilities for querying, inserting, updating and deleting records from the database. It interacts with a single database table, a table which contains data for an accounts receivable customer.

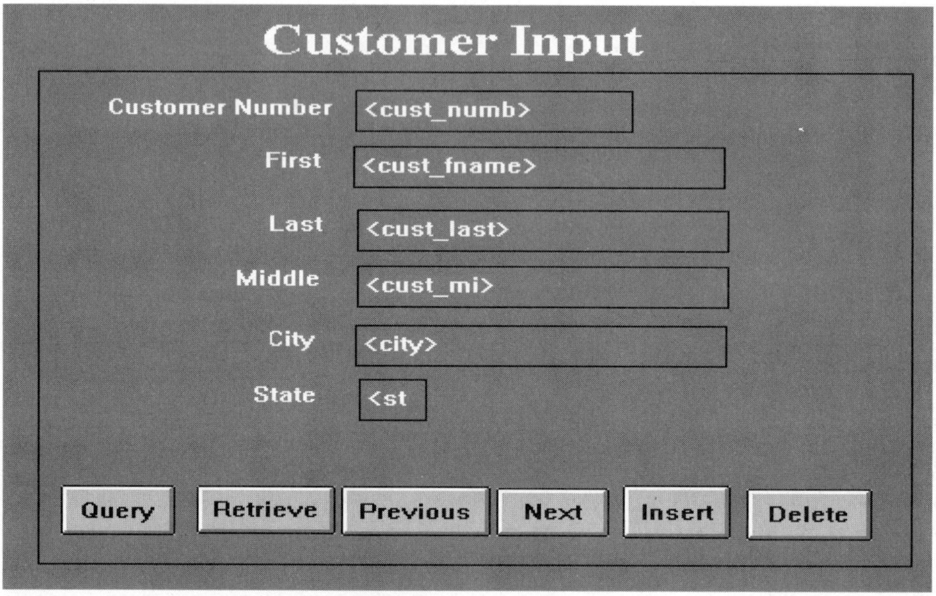

Figure 5-1 - Customer Data Entry Window

In order to make the application code more readable, some of the default names supplied by the Window Painter are changed with the properties dialog box to provide clearer names; others that are not accessed directly in NewEra code to be written, are left with their default names. An example of this is changing the name of the main window from the default name of `Window1` to `custWindow` a name which more clearly identifies the purpose of the window.

The Pre-Header Section

The first few lines of this application are used to load the *header* files (usually identified by the `4gh`, extension but not required) for the program. The Window Painter will always create a header file for the class definitions to be used in the program. As additional screen objects are added and identified, their corresponding header files will be included in this header file.

Any of the code that has been inserted in the pre-header code window for the window in the Window Painter will be placed at the start of this header file immediately following the `include` statements generated by the Window Painter. The Window Painter will add a number of header files to this section automatically as visual objects are pasted into the window, though they are not shown when the code window for the preheader section is displayed in the Window Painter.

If the programmer has added additional code to the application that requires a header file, it would be included here. If an Informix-supplied class has been added *manually* to the application code, then it may also be necessary to include the header file in this code block. If the header file is for an Informix class definition or header file contained in the Informix system "include" directory, then the `include` statement can use the `system` clause and may be entered as

```
include system "ixApp.4gh"
```

In the example below, the `cust.4gh` and the `ixconn.4gh` files are included in the Window Painter generated code. The `cust.4gh` file was automatically created by the Window Painter. The `ixconn.4gh` file is included because the NewEra Window Painter defaults to using the ODBC compatible Connectivity Class Library Statements of NewEra which make use of the `ixConnect` class defined in the `ixconn.4gh` header file.

```
INCLUDE "cust.4gh"
INCLUDE SYSTEM "ixconn.4gh"
```

Global Variables

Global variables are then declared. A global variable is declared for the Window object used in this application. This makes referencing the object easier.

```
GLOBAL VARIABLE Window1 Window1
```

The `main` Program Block

The `main` program block calls the `ixSQLConnect` member function to make a connection to the database. In this case, the database name is `ar` for an accounts receivable database.

Next, the window object is instantiated or created by using the `New` operator. Note that the constructor call following the `new` verb does not include any parameters. The default parameters that have been assigned in the class definition for the window class (in `cust.4gh`) will be used to create the window.

Once the window has been created, the `open` member function is called to open and display the window. The `return` statement is then called to return the application to the window manager event loop that will continually examine the system state to determine what action the user has taken.

```
MAIN
  CALL
ixSQLConnect::getImplicitConnection().connect("ar")
  LET Window1 = NEW Window1()
  CALL Window1.open()
  RETURN
END MAIN
```

Event Handlers

Next, code for the event handlers is inserted for the various events handled by the application. Many of these are handlers for buttons contained in the window. These buttons are named using the default naming convention of the Window Painter. These names can be changed by entering a new name in the Window Painter property window for the button object. The handlers for the various buttons in the window are listed below. Note that the button handler name are assigned by default by the Window Painter.

The Query Button Code

The handler for the *activate* event of the *query* button is shown below. The default name generated by the Window Painter is `Button18`. (This name would most likely be changed to a more meaningful name.) The handler statement references a handler for the `ixButton` class and specifies the handler for the specific SuperTable button.

The code for this button must set the SuperTable into *query* mode. This requires that the `setDisplayMode` member function of the SuperTable class be called and passed the `ixSuperTable` constant `displayQuery`. In order to make this call, a reference for the current SuperTable must first be identified. Since the button code generated is generic and does not necessarily *know* the name of the current SuperTable or the current window, the function `getVisualContainer` must be called and the result is *cast* as an object of class `ixSuperTable`. (This requires that the *container* property for the button be the SuperTable.)

This object is then referenced to call the `ixSuperTable` member function `setDisplayMode` and passed the parameter `displayQuery`. The `displayQuery` constant is a public variable of the `ixSuperTable` class. The result of entering this mode would be the clearing of the screen fields, the insertion of the any default values for the fields, and the placement of the cursor in the first field in the window as set by the tab order property for the SuperField.

Chapter 5: The Structure of NewEra Applications

```
HANDLER ixButton::Window1_Button18_activate()
    RETURNING VOID
VARIABLE SuperTable ixSuperTable
   LET SuperTable =
       (getVisualContainer() CAST ixSuperTable)
   CALL
  SuperTable.setDisplayMode (ixSuperTable::displayQuery)

END HANDLER -- ixButton::Window1_Button18_activate
```

The Retrieve Button Code

The code below is for the *retrieve* button in the `customer` SuperTable. The only code required to perform a SuperTable retrieve operation is a call to the SuperTable `retrieve` member function with the correct parameters, which in this case is to set the QBE (query by example) named parameter to TRUE. But as with the above handler, a reference to the current SuperTable must be obtained. To do this generically, a call to `getVisualContainer` member function (part of the `ixVisualContainer` class and inherited by the `ixWindow` class) is cast as an `ixSuperTable` object. This object reference is then used to call the `ixSuperTable retrieve` member function for the current SuperTable, which is the `customer_st` SuperTable.

```
HANDLER ixButton::Window1_Button19_activate()
   RETURNING VOID
VARIABLE ok BOOLEAN
VARIABLE SuperTable ixSuperTable
    LET SuperTable =
    (getVisualContainer() CAST ixSuperTable)
    LET ok = SuperTable.retrieve( QBE: TRUE )

END HANDLER -- ixButton::Window1_Button19_activate
```

The Previous Button Code

The handler code below is for the *previous* button. To move back a row in a SuperTable requires only one call, a call to the `setCurrentCell` member function passing the new row number and the `currentColumn` variable value for the current SuperTable. But since we are moving back one row, we must decrement the current row by one. The value returned must be validated to determine whether or not it is positive; if it is not positive, then there has been an attempt to move to an invalid row. It would be convenient to indicate an error at this point (such code is demonstrated in a later chapter).

If the value is not positive, then it is simply set to the value one. This row position value is then passed to the `setCurrentCell` ixSuperTable member function to move the current row to that row position.

```
HANDLER ixButton::Window1_Button20_activate()
    RETURNING VOID
VARIABLE ok BOOLEAN
VARIABLE SuperTable ixSuperTable
VARIABLE rowPosition INTEGER

    LET SuperTable = (getVisualContainer() CAST ixSuperTable)
    LET rowPosition = SuperTable.getCurrRowNum() - 1
    IF rowPosition < 1 THEN
        LET rowPosition = 1
    END IF
    LET ok =
  SuperTable.setCurrentCell(rowPosition,
                            ixSuperTable::currentColumn)

END HANDLER -- ixButton::Window1_Button20_activate
```

The Next Button

The handler code below is for the *next* button. This requires a call to the `setCurrentCell` member function shown above passing the new row number and the `currentColumn` variable value for the current SuperTable. Since we are moving forward one row, we must increment the current row by one. The value returned is then validated to determine whether or not it is beyond the current number of stored rows. If the row position is beyond this value, the row position is set to the `lastRow` value in the SuperTable. This row position value is then passed to the `setCurrentCell` ixSuperTable member function to move the current row to that row position. Once again, an error could be indicated at this point using a pop-up window or a message to the screen. Code to perform this error checking will be demonstrated in chapter 7.

```
HANDLER ixButton::Window1_Button21_activate()
    RETURNING VOID
VARIABLE ok BOOLEAN
VARIABLE SuperTable ixSuperTable
VARIABLE rowPosition INTEGER
```

```
    LET SuperTable =
      (getVisualContainer() CAST ixSuperTable)
    LET rowPosition =
      SuperTable.getCurrRowNum() + 1

    # get the number of rows for the current displayMode
    IF rowPosition > SuperTable.getNumStoredRows(NULL)
                                                              THEN
        LET rowPosition = ixSuperTable::lastRow
    END IF
    LET ok =
        SuperTable.setCurrentCell(rowPosition,
                ixSuperTable::currentColumn)

END HANDLER -- ixButton::Window1_Button21_activate
```

The Insert Button

The following code is for the *insert* button. This button is used to allow the user to insert a row into the current active set. This row is **not** inserted in the database; it is instead inserted into the active set on the client (internally into an `ixRowArray` element); the `apply` SuperTable member function is used to later insert the row into the database.

The insert process using the SuperTable is simple; it is only necessary to call the `insert` member function. But first a reference to the current SuperTable must be obtained. This is accomplished using the `getVisualContainer` function which will return a reference to the current visual container. This reference is then CAST as a SuperTable and is then used to the access the SuperTable and call its constituent `insert` member function .

```
HANDLER ixButton::Window1_Button22_activate()
    RETURNING VOID
VARIABLE rowNum INTEGER
VARIABLE SuperTable ixSuperTable

    LET SuperTable =
           (getVisualContainer() CAST ixSuperTable)
    LET rownum =  SuperTable.insert()

END HANDLER -- ixButton::Window1_Button22_activate
```

The Delete Button

The *delete* button is used to delete the current row from the active set; it does **not** delete the row from the database. The *apply* SuperTable member function is used to later delete the row from the database. As with the other handlers, the `getVisualContainer` is first used to get a reference to the SuperTable. The SuperTable reference will then be used to call the *delete* member function to delete the rows. The value returned by the `delete` member function can be used to indicate an error, but in this code sample it is ignored. The deleted row is returned in the `deleteRow` `ixRow` variable.

```
HANDLER ixButton::Window1_Button23_activate()
      RETURNING VOID
VARIABLE deletedRow ixRow
VARIABLE SuperTable ixSuperTable

   LET SuperTable =
        (getVisualContainer() CAST ixSuperTable)
   #just use default rowNum = currentRow
   #need not do anything w/ deletedRow

   LET deletedRow = SuperTable.delete()

END HANDLER -- ixButton::Window1_Button23_activate
```

The Window Constructor

The following section of code defines the window class constructor. Since every window in NewEra represents a new class, a constructor is needed for the new window class. If the class is a subclass of `ixWindow`, then the constructor for the new class must include a call to the constructor of the inherited class.

The section of code which follows uses the initial function header. It is uses the syntax

```
          ...) : classname ( parameter1: value1,
parameter2: value2 )
```

where the class name is the inherited class of the new class for which the constructor is being written.

Chapter 5: The Structure of NewEra Applications

```
FUNCTION Window1::Window1(
  geometry ixGeometry,
  appearance ixAppearance,
  windowStyle SMALLINT,
  title CHAR(*),
  containingWindow ixWindow,
  enabled BOOLEAN,
  icon CHAR(*),
  shown BOOLEAN,
  helpFile CHAR(*),
  helpNum INTEGER,
  name CHAR(*)
)
  : ixWindow(
    containingWindow : containingWindow,
    name : name,
    enabled : enabled,
    shown : shown,
    helpNum : helpNum,
    geometry : geometry,
    appearance : appearance,
    helpFile : helpFile,
    title : title,
    icon : icon,
    windowStyle : windowStyle
  )
```

Within the body of the window constructor, several member variables are declared. Since the window includes a SuperTable, it is instantiated here and given the name assigned the SuperTable within the Window Painter; in this case it is the default Window Painter name of `SuperTable2`.

The SuperTable Constructor

The parameters passed into the constructor for the SuperTable virtually match the parameters assigned to the SuperTable in the Properties window of the Window Painter. Since NewEra will resolve the value of parameters if possible, objects can be instantiated while being passed as parameters. This is a useful capability that is used often in NewEra generated code. An example of this is in the "appearance" parameter for `SuperTable2` shown below. The *appearance* parameter requires an object of type `ixAppearance`. This object is created in the parameter list as follows:

```
    appearance : NEW ixAppearance(
         fontName : NULL,
         fontSize : NULL,
         fontBold : NULL,
         fontItalic : NULL,
         fontUnderline : NULL,
         foreColor : NULL,
         backColor : NULL
    ),
```

This creates an `ixAppearance` object and passes NULL values for the various parameters (which are, in fact, the default and thus could have been omitted). These NULL values will force the window object to use the values of these parameters for the visual container of the object when created. The same process of object instantiation in parameter passing is used for the *geometry* parameter below.

```
VARIABLE itemList ixVector
VARIABLE includeTable ixRow
VARIABLE result INTEGER

LET result = 0

LET SuperTable2 = NEW ixSuperTable(
   geometry : NEW ixGeometry(
         top : 720,
         left : 390,
         height : 4770,
         width : 6780
   ),
   appearance : NEW ixAppearance(
         fontName : NULL,
         fontSize : NULL,
         fontBold : NULL,
         fontItalic : NULL,
         fontUnderline : NULL,
         foreColor : NULL,
         backColor : NULL
   ),
```

Chapter 5: The Structure of NewEra Applications

```
    updateTable : "customer",
    enabled : TRUE,
    selectUnique : FALSE,
    numDisplayedCols : 6,
    selectFromPart : "customer",
    selectJoinPart : NULL,
    selectOrderbyPart : NULL,
    borderWidth : 20,
    shown : TRUE,
    helpNum : 0,
    name : "SuperTable2",
    lockMode : ixSuperTable::noLock,
    layout : ixSuperTable::freeForm,
    numDisplayedRows : 1,
    dbConnection : NULL,
    selectFilterPart : NULL,
    displayMode : ixSuperTable::displayData,
    maxRows : 50,
    container : SELF
)
```

The SuperField Constructor

After the creation of the SuperTable, the SuperFields contained in the window are created. These SuperFields are *bound* to the SuperTable through the `SuperTable` parameter in the SuperField constructor. This parameter is passed the reference to the SuperTable (a member variable of the window class) as shown below.

```
    queryState : ixSuperField::enabledState,
      titleJustify : ixSuperField::rightJustify,
      primaryKey : FALSE,
      SuperTable : SuperTable2
)

LET includeTable = NEW ixRow()
LET cust_fname = NEW ixSuperField(
    geometry : NEW ixGeometry(
         top : 700,
         left : 2445,
         height : 400,
         width : 2860
    ),
```

```
    appearance : NEW ixAppearance(
        fontName : NULL,
        fontSize : NULL,
        fontBold : NULL,
        fontItalic : NULL,
        fontUnderline : NULL,
        foreColor : NULL,
        backColor : NULL
    ),
    titleGeometry : NEW ixGeometry(
        top : 715,
        left : 1060,
        height : 400,
        width : 1125
    ),
    titleAppearance : NEW ixAppearance(
        fontName : NULL,
        fontSize : NULL,
        fontBold : NULL,
        fontItalic : NULL,
        fontUnderline : NULL,
        foreColor : NULL,
        backColor : NULL
    ),
    colInfo : NEW ixColumn(
        type : 0,
        encLength : 15,
        nullable : TRUE,
        tableName : "customer",
        columnName : "cust_fname"
    ),
    SQLRole : ixSuperField::updateRole,
    colNum : 1,
    title : "First",
    tabIndex : NULL,
    tabEnabled : TRUE,
    shown : TRUE,
    helpNum : 0,
    name : "cust_fname",
    pictureString : NULL,
    initialDataValue : NULL,
    maxDataChars : 15,
    dataState : ixSuperField::enabledState,
```

Chapter 5: The Structure of NewEra Applications

```
            multiLine : FALSE,
            initialQueryValue : NULL,
            queryState : ixSuperField::enabledState,
            titleJustify : ixSuperField::rightJustify,
            primaryKey : FALSE,
            SuperTable : SuperTable2
        )
```

Once the constructor is called for the column, various SuperField member functions are called to establish the SuperField. These are member functions that can be called again at runtime to change the properties of the SuperField as needed. The "includetable" parameter below uses an `ixRow` data type variable to store validation parameters for the row. This is only used if the `useIncludes` SuperField parameter is set to TRUE. For the column below, it is set to FALSE so this parameter is not used.

```
    CALL cust_fname.setFormat(NULL)
    CALL cust_fname.setDataJustify(ixSuperField::leftJustify)
    CALL cust_fname.setShiftPolicy(ixSuperField::noShift)
    LET cust_fname.required = FALSE
    LET cust_fname.verify = FALSE
    LET cust_fname.includeTable = includeTable
    LET cust_fname.useIncludes = FALSE
    LET cust_fname.autoNextOn = FALSE
    LET cust_fname.blobEditor = NULL
    LET includeTable = NEW ixRow()
```

The remaining SuperFields are established in the same manner. The constructor for the SuperField is called and various SuperField parameters are set in the constructor. Then several SuperField member functions are called to set the appearance and behavior of the SuperField. The only exception to this process is for the *includeTable* SuperField parameter shown above; this parameter is only included in the **first** SuperField column.

The `ixLabel` Constructor

Finally, the window class constructor contains a constructor for the `ixLabel` class. This constructor is used to create a window text label. A scalable font is chosen to allow the text to be scaled to a large point size making it easier to read on the screen. The text is set in the constructor and could be changed at runtime with a call to the `setText` member function as follows:

```
    call window1.title.setText("New Title")
```

The code for the `ixLabel` constructor is shown below.

```
LET Title = NEW ixLabel(
   geometry : NEW ixGeometry(
         top : 165,
         left : 1950,
         height : 450,
         width : 3330
   ),
   appearance : NEW ixAppearance(
         fontName : "Times New Roman",
         fontSize : 22,
         fontBold : NULL,
         fontItalic : NULL,
         fontUnderline : NULL,
         foreColor : NULL,
         backColor : NULL
   ),
   shown : TRUE,
   name : "Title",
   labelJustify : ixLabel::centerJustify,
   text : "Customer Input",
   container : SELF
)
END FUNCTION -- Window1::Window1
```

The Window Header File `include` File

The `4gh` file contains a number of `include` statements that have been placed in the pre-header code window within the Window Painter. It contains the class definition for the window around which the application is being developed. Within this class definition, public variables are declared for the various screen objects painted within the window.

In this example, the SuperTable named `SuperTable2` is declared as a public variable within the class definition for the window `Window1`. The SuperFields are also declared within this class definition as well as the button objects used within the window.

Chapter 5: The Structure of NewEra Applications

```
INCLUDE SYSTEM "ixrow.4gh"
INCLUDE SYSTEM "ixwindow.4gh"
INCLUDE SYSTEM "ixsuptbl.4gh"
INCLUDE SYSTEM "ixsupfld.4gh"
INCLUDE SYSTEM "ixbutton.4gh"
INCLUDE SYSTEM "ixlabel.4gh"

CLASS Window1 DERIVED FROM ixWindow
  FUNCTION Window1(
    geometry ixGeometry : NEW ixGeometry(
        top : 0,
        left : 0,
        height : 6585,
        width : 8160
    ),
    appearance ixAppearance : NEW ixAppearance(
        fontName : NULL,
        fontSize : NULL,
        fontBold : NULL,
        fontItalic : NULL,
        fontUnderline : NULL,
        foreColor : 16777215,
        backColor : 8421504
    ),
    windowStyle SMALLINT : ixWindow::mainTop,
    title CHAR(*) : "cust_wind",
    containingWindow ixWindow : NULL,
    enabled BOOLEAN : TRUE,
    icon CHAR(*) : NULL,
    shown BOOLEAN : TRUE,
    helpFile CHAR(*) : NULL,
    helpNum INTEGER : 0,
    name CHAR(*) : "Window1"
  )
  PUBLIC VARIABLE
    SuperTable2 ixSuperTable,
    cust_fname ixSuperField,
    cust_lname ixSuperField,
    cust_mi ixSuperField,
    city ixSuperField,
    state ixSuperField,
    Button18 ixButton,
    Button19 ixButton,
```

```
    Button20 ixButton,
    Button21 ixButton,
    Button22 ixButton,
    Button23 ixButton,
    cust_numb ixSuperField,
    Title ixLabel
END CLASS -- Window1
```

Chapter 6
Creating NewEra Applications

The NewEra Window Painter performs a variety of functions. It is a screen painter, a code generator, and an application code organizer. Whereas Informix-4GL depended on structured code to organize an application, the NewEra Window Painter performs part of this function by providing a visual interface to the underlying code of the application. When a programmer needs to see a list of available event handlers for a window object, the programmer can simply double-click on the window object using the mouse and the Window Painter will display the list of available event handlers.

The NewEra Window Painter therefore becomes the focal point of application development. The user will trigger events by activating controls. These controls are painted onto the screen using the Window Painter tool bar. And since the user is allowed to control the flow of an application in a GUI environment, the programmer must develop code to handle the events triggered by the user. This code is entered in the *code windows* for the event handlers.

THE PROCESS OF CREATING A NEWERA APPLICATION

As always, an orderly, pragmatic approach to programming yields better results than a haphazard approach. The following section outlines such an approach to NewEra programming. Each of the steps listed below (see Figure 6-1) depend, to a certain extent, on the preceding steps.

In some cases the steps may be taken out of sequence, as when a class library is needed to complete an application, but for reasons that will become clearer, they are usually performed in sequence.

These steps suggest a transition from database design to window design. With a database design complete, windows can then be designed around the data that must be captured to populate the database tables. Once the windows have been designed, the process of data entry can then be further defined through the development of the menu structure. Other controls that direct the execution of the program can also be used to supplement the menu design and pull parts of the application together. User-friendly controls such as radio buttons, check-boxes and list boxes can be used to make the application thoroughly user-friendly.

Often parts of the application must be linked using additional code segments in handlers. Once the screens are complete and the programmer has some confidence in their structure, this additional code to link parts of the application together should be written.

Reports are listed as one of the final steps in the application development process, but they could be developed in parallel with the development windows. They are usually launched from a menu handler or a button handler.

Cosmetic changes are the last to be programmed into the application. Once the complete structure of the windows is known, the cosmetic aspects of the window can be refined. It is best not to spend too much time on cosmetic issues early in the application development effort.

- Create Database Schema
- Identify Functionality and Interaction of Windows
- Create Class Libraries
- Create Windows
- Create Menus
- Add Code to Glue Application Objects
- Create Reports
- Make Cosmetic Changes

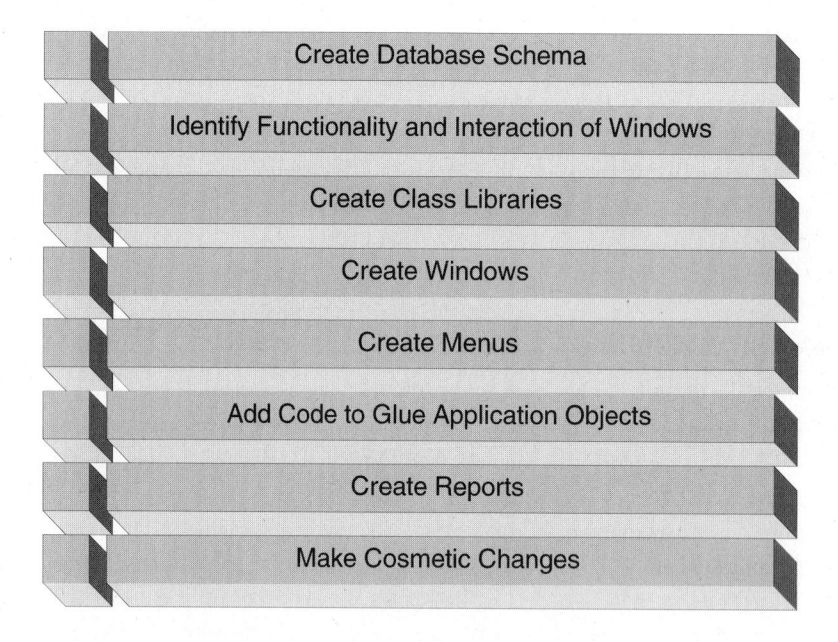

Figure 6-1 - Steps in Creating a NewEra Application

CREATE DATABASE SCHEMA

The database schema is the foundation upon which the application will be built. It is imperative that this be solid before proceeding with the development process. This is even more true in a GUI environment where the structure of the database can directly impact the design of the application.

IDENTIFY FUNCTIONALITY AND INTERACTION OF WINDOWS

The interaction of a window with other windows must be considered early in the design process. A window that contains the fields for the master table in a master-detail table relationship may be designed to spawn the window for the detail table based on this function. The window used for input of the master table data could be designated as a NewEra *normal top* window. The window that is spawned to provide data entry for the detail data could be designated as a *normal pop-up* based on its function. Thus, how the tables contained in the windows will function in a master-detail relationship impact the design of windows and their connectivity.

The functionality of the windows with other windows will also impact design decisions. A window that requires input before an application can continue should be designated as a *modal pop-up* window. A modal pop-up window requires a containing window, and thus the *connectivity* and interaction of the window must be known before this window can be created.

CREATE CLASS LIBRARIES

As the application, is being designed it will become clear that certain procedures are performed over and over. These repetitious procedures could be reduced to a set of functions which would become part of a class library.

It may become clear that some of the basic features of the class libraries provided by NewEra are inadequate. Or it may simply be desirable to extend these classes. With NewEra, this can be accomplished with relative ease. A new class can then be created which inherits all of the properties of the Informix class library class. The new class then overrides **only** those functions or properties that the programmer wants to change. The programmer would then reference this new class in the Window Painter. Several examples of this process are presented later in this book.

CREATE WINDOWS

The creation of the NewEra windows for an application draws upon the previous steps. The relationship of the data displayed in a window and the function of the window directly impact the design of the window. The various decisions necessary to complete the window have been made by this point.

The Process of Creating NewEra Windows

There are several common steps to creating a window in NewEra. These steps are outlined in Figure 6-2. The overall goal of these steps is to create an application with a consistent "look and feel." A good start towards this effort is to create a *template* window as shown below. (The design of the template window will be discussed in more detail later in this chapter.)

Once the template window has been developed, several other steps can make the creation of the NewEra application windows easier. These steps involve capitalizing on the NewEra Window Painter facilities. They are discussed in greater detail below.

> Create Template Window with Common Attributes
>
> Open Template Window and Set Window Properties
>
> Paste SuperTable Fields, Buttons and Properties
>
> Add Additional Controls and Code
>
> Format Screen
>
> Add Code Where Needed

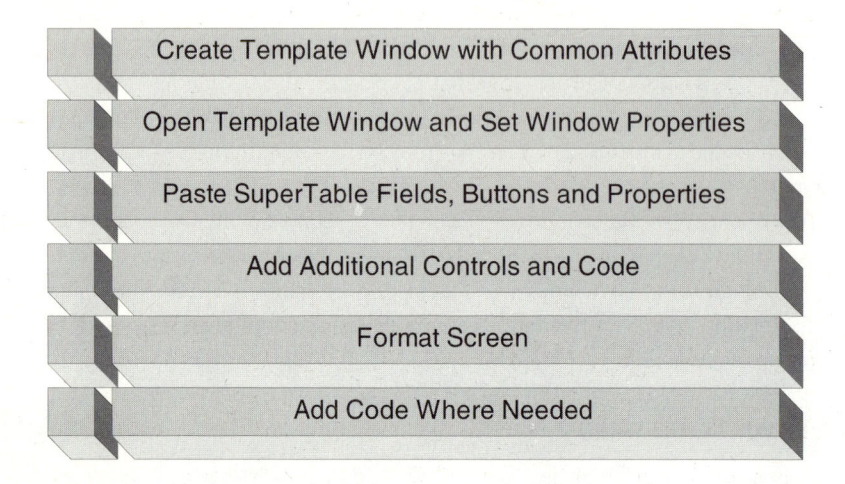

Figure 6-2 - Steps in NewEra Screen Development

Create Template Window

Creating a template window can help a programming group keep the look and feel of the application consistent. This window is essentially a NewEra window with various properties pre-set and optionally several programmed event handlers and menu items (see Figure 6-3).

The development of a template window is detailed later in this chapter. A development approach which demonstrates the use of templates plus NewEra extended classes, thus tapping the power of both the Window Painter and object-oriented programming is shown in chapter 11.

Open Template Window and Set Window Properties

The programmer would first load the template window and change the screen name and title to a meaningful name and title for the window. Changing both the *Name* and *Title* properties in the Window Painter *Properties* dialogue box will make this possible.

The programmer would then change the general properties for the window to values appropriate for the window's function. If the window will be a main window and will be used to start an application, then the *startup* property should be set to TRUE and the window *type* should be set to `maintop`. This will cause the Window Painter to generate code which will instantiate the window object for the window and open and display the window.

Chapter 6: Creating NewEra Applications 105

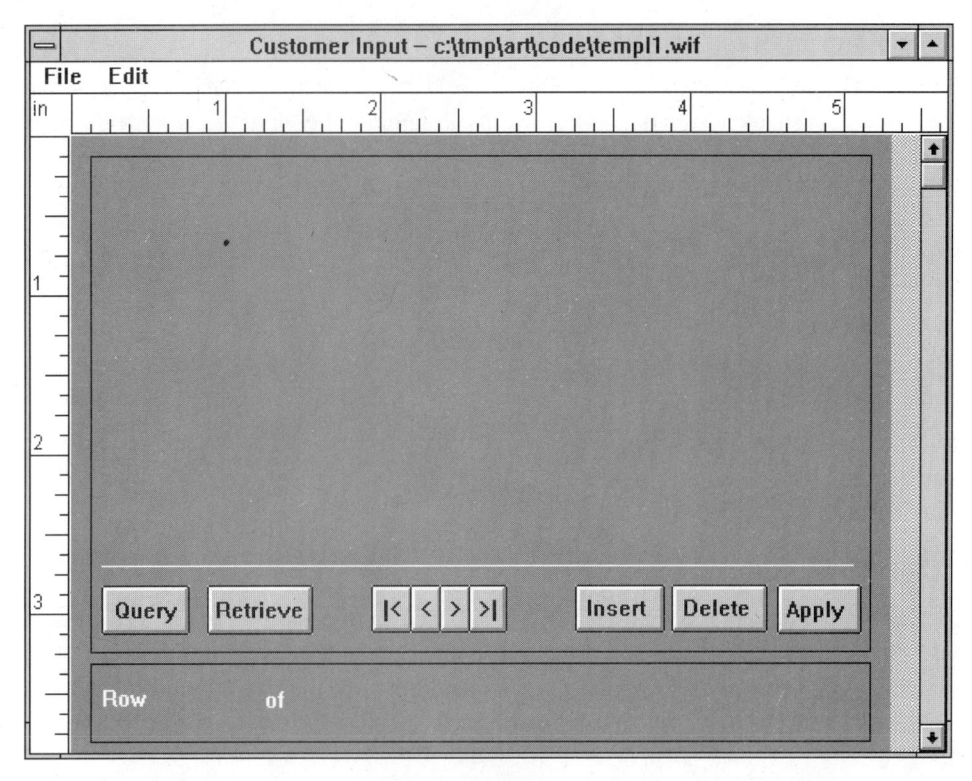

Figure 6-3 - A NewEra Template Screen

Once these changes have been made, the window should be saved using the "save-as" option. The *wif* should be given a meaningful name at this point.

Paste SuperTable Fields and Buttons for Table(s) and Set SuperTable Properties

The programmer would then use the cursor to select the frame for the SuperTable and then paste the SuperFields into the SuperTable frame. Various properties for the SuperTable would then have to be set correctly.

The SuperField *primary key* would have to be identified and a locking mode would have to be selected for the SuperTable. This would make the "update" buttons in the window operational. If these buttons are not needed, then they could be deleted from the window.

Add Additional Controls and Code

If any additional controls are needed in the application, they should be added at this point. Drop-down list boxes, radio buttons, and check boxes all add to the user friendliness of an application and are easily pasted and integrated into a window.

Format Screen

Next, the screen should be formatted. Field labels should be sized if needed and screen objects should be aligned. If the *select-all* option is chosen in the Window Painter, the selected fields can then be aligned using the alignment buttons in the upper right-hand corner of the Window Painter menu bar.

If the screen is not large enough, altering the *location* property of the window will create additional room.

Add Code Where Needed

As a final step, any code needed to *glue* screen objects should be added. If there is a master-detail relationship, a few lines of code are needed to retrieve the detail records when the master records are retrieved. This code would be added to the handler for the "retrieve" buttons and for the "next row" and "previous row" buttons if they are placed on the screen.

CREATE MENUS

Once all of the procedures and interconnections of the application and its windows are known, the menus can be completed. While some basic menu items may be included in the previous step (the exit option and clipboard functions), the menu items that spawn additional windows or provide an alternative to the window buttons may be added in this step.

ADD CODE TO GLUE APPLICATIONS

Some additional code may need to be added to bring certain sections of the application together. If pressing a button on a NewEra window is to spawn another window, then the code to perform this function must be entered in the *activate* event for the button. The same would be true for menu items and their corresponding *activate* events. The code to perform these functions would be entered in this step.

CREATE REPORTS

Generally, the reports required for a particular application are well known when the application is being developed (in fact, they often drive the design of an application). They could be developed in parallel with any of the previous steps with the exception of the database design step.

The reports will usually be run from a menu item. Some pop-up windows may be necessary to allow the user to enter report criteria. Many of the lookup windows developed for the application may be used to help the user choose the correct report criteria. (For instance, the user can use a query-by-example screen to browse a list of customers. These same query criteria could then be used to generate a customer report.)

MAKE COSMETIC CHANGES

As a final step, cosmetic changes could be made to make the application more attractive. Picture buttons could be used to replace normal buttons and drawing objects and graphics could be inserted into windows to make the windows more interesting. This is recommended as a last step with the belief that it is best not to focus on this aspect of the application early in the development process.

These steps, or some close variation of them, combine to make GUI development with NewEra easier and more focused. They will help add consistency and speed the development process. An important component of this process is the use of templates discussed in the next section.

CREATING THE TEMPLATE WINDOW

A template window can embody any number of features. In practice, several template windows should be developed for several different window types. Some of the features that may be desirable are listed in the table below.

Feature	Programming Required
"no rows found" message	Entered in the handler code for the activate event of the *retrieve* button.
"no more rows" message	Entered in the handler code for the activate event of the *next* and *previous* buttons
Prompt for retrieval of more rows if `maxrows` number of rows has been reached	Code entered in the event handler for the *rowretrieved* event of the SuperTable
File menu option with *exit* choice	Use menu editor to create menu and enter code for the *exit* option
Edit menu option with clipboard options	Use menu editor to create menu and enter code for the *edit* options
"VCR" type buttons for SuperTable set traversal	Insert buttons and modify button 'title' parameter
Browse status information	Indicates the position in the current data set ("Row 1 of 20")
Message/mode information	Indicates current mode of operation ("Query", "Insert" ...)
Color and font of window	Enter window properties

A great many of the data entry operations of a NewEra application are performed using the SuperTable class library. The SuperTable class library supports both the database interaction and the screen interaction. When it is necessary to alter or manipulate the data contained in the SuperTable, it can usually be accomplished with very few lines of code.

Any attempt to customize the data entry operation for use in a template window would therefore require some modification to the default SuperTable operations. The following section details some of these changes.

So that the template screen requires very few changes for the programmer, the code entered to implement the various features should be as *generic* as possible. Since this code will be placed in windows with different window objects, it should not contain specific names of window objects. For example, the event handler code for the `rowRetrieved` event used the specific name of the SuperTable as shown below.

```
if wind1.custST.getNumStoredRows() =
           (wind1.custST.maxRows - 1 ) then
....
```

A more generic reference is needed if this code is to be inserted into other applications. This generic reference can be provided with the `self` identifier. The `self` identifier references the container object for the member function or handler, so that in the case of the rowRetrieved event, the `self` identifier would reference the SuperTable being used (this connection to the SuperTable is made by the Window Painter in the code generated for the SuperTable handler). Thus the code below would be used for the `rowRetrieved` event handler.

```
variable retval smallint
variable str char(10)
variable st ixSuperTable

if self.getnumstoredrows() = (self.maxrows - 1 ) then

    call messagebox( title: new ixString( "Message" ),
                        message: new ixString(
            "Maxrows reached. Retrieve 25 More Rows ?" ),
                        iconstyle: ixQueryicon,
                        buttonstyle: ixYesNo )
            returning retval

    if retval = ixYesButton then
       let self.maxrows = self.maxrows + 25
    end if

end if

return TRUE
```

This code checks the number of rows retrieved by the SuperTable and displays a message if the number of rows is one less than the value of the SuperTable `maxRows` member variable. The user is then allowed to indicate whether or not they would like to continue retrieving rows. This code is explained in more detail later in this text. The use of the `self` identifier allows this code to be used without modification in other applications where the name of the SuperTable object is unknown.

Menu Options for the Template Window

The template should provide a standard menu on every window. Options may be added to the menu as needed by the programmer. The standard template window menu shown in this text provides for a File option, which allows the user to exit the screen, and an Edit option, which allows the user access to the GUI clipboard. The code for these menu options is shown in the table below.

Menu Option	Code Inserted
Exit	exit program
Copy to Clipboard	call ixApp::copySelectedText()
Cut to Clipboard	call ixApp::cutSelectedText()
Paste from Clipboard	call ixApp::pasteText()

The "Copy to Clipboard" and "Cut to Clipboard" menu options both allow the selected text to be *copied* or *cut* to the clipboard. The Informix-supplied `ixApp` class provides functions for interacting with the GUI clipboard. The functions `copySelectedText` and `cutSelectedText` are used to perform these functions. If there is no selected text to copy, the function will fail quietly (the function returns `void` and there is no global error variable set).

The `pasteText` `ixApp` member function is used to paste the text from the clipboard into the current SuperField. The text will be inserted into the field at the current cursor position; it may prepend or append any data in the field at that time.

To use these functions on a particular SuperField, the application must currently have keyboard focus into that SuperField. If the user is in insert mode and the user has used the mouse to select the current field, or the user has used the tab key to move to a field, then they will automatically have keyboard focus into that field. If necessary, a `focus` function, part of the `ixVisualObject` class, is also available to perform this function programmatically.

The Exit option executes the NewEra statement 'exit program'. If the window were being used as a popup window, then this option should either be eliminated or changed to a call to an `ixWindow close` or `hide` member function call. Alternatively, the `ixApp exit` member function could be called to exit the program.

Customizing SuperTable Functionality in the Template Window

The NewEra SuperTable provides the programmer with both database manipulation and screen input and output capabilities. And through the use of object-oriented and event-driven programming features, it allows the programmer significant flexibility in customizing the functionality of the SuperTable. How the SuperTable retrieves rows from the database may be one area where customization is desirable.

SuperTable Row Retrieval Modifications

When rows are retrieved by NewEra using the SuperTable `retrieve` member function, NewEra will attempt to retrieve **all** of the rows that qualify for the query up to the `maxRows` SuperTable parameter value. The number of rows retrieved is controlled by the SuperTable `maxRows` parameter. By default, the `maxrows` parameter is set to zero which will allow **all** rows to be retrieved. If there are a large number of rows that qualify for the query, the NewEra application may use all available disk space to retrieve the rows, something that would wreak havoc on a PC running Windows.

One alternative is to set the `maxRows` parameter to a value that will limit the number of rows retrieved. This would eliminate the problem of using all available disk resources to support the application, but it could also be constraining for the user. It would be preferable to allow the user to retrieve up to the `maxrows` number of rows and then optionally choose to retrieve some additional records, but still limit the total number of records retrieved.

One solution to this problem would be to attach the `rowRetrieved` event to a handler that would attempt to detect the number of rows that have been retrieved. The handler can then display a prompt when the `maxrows` number of rows has been retrieved and allow the user to retrieve more records.

Desired Functionality

The functionality desired would allow the user to enter query criteria in the usual manner. The user could then press the *retrieve* button and begin retrieving rows. When the rows retrieved matched the `maxrows` parameter, a prompt would be displayed indicating that the `maxrows` parameter had been reached and giving the user the option of retrieving more rows. The user could press the "yes" button to retrieve more rows, or press the "no" button to quit retrieving rows (see Figure 6-4).

Chapter 6: Creating NewEra Applications

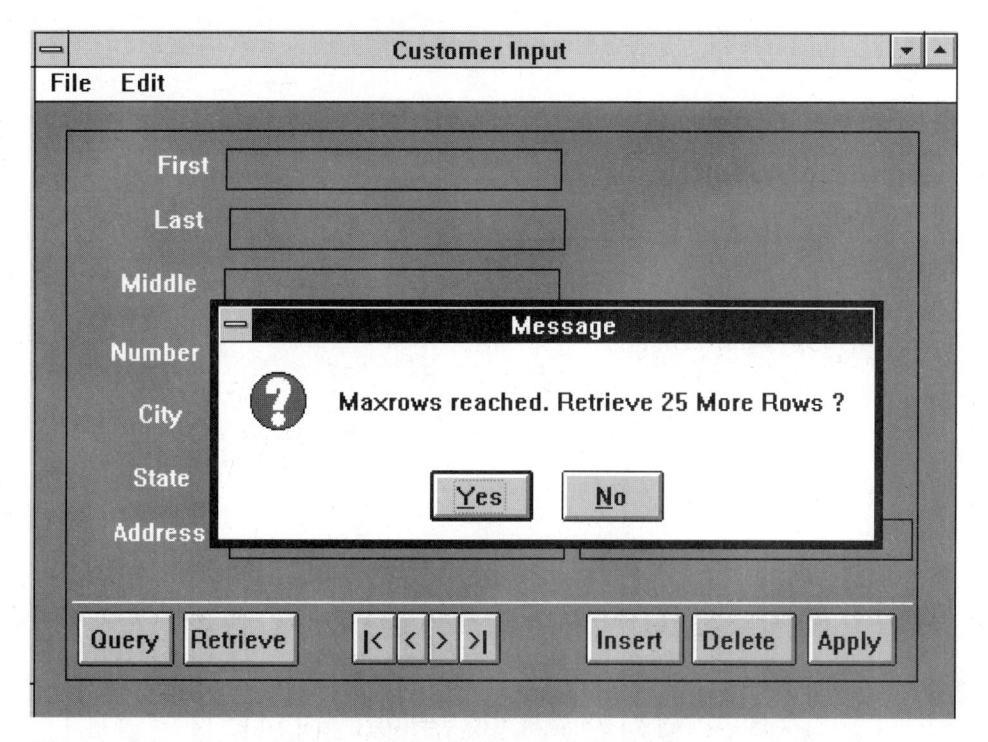

[Screenshot of "Customer Input" window with a Message dialog: "Maxrows reached. Retrieve 25 More Rows ?" with Yes and No buttons]

Figure 6-4 - SuperTable `rowRetrieved` Prompt

The `maxRowsExceeded` event is raised when the number of rows retrieved matches the value of the `maxRows` parameter. This event does not return a value. It is intended to allow the programmer to display a message to the user indicating that more rows exist to fulfill the query than have been retrieved.

It would be preferable to use this event handler to prompt the user to retrieve additional rows, but when this event handler is called, the SuperTable facilities have **finished** retrieving rows from the database. There is no simple way to allow the SuperTable to retrieve more rows at this point. It is for this reason, the `rowRetrieved` event is used instead.

The rowretrieved Event

The SuperTable `rowRetrieved` event is executed after each row is retrieved from the database. It is called from within the retrieval loop that brings rows back to the client from the database server. Since this is called after each row is retrieved, it is possible to determine how many rows have been retrieved and, when necessary, alter the `maxrows` parameter to suit the user's needs. The code used to provide this functionality from within the `rowRetrieved` event is shown below.

```
HANDLER ixSuperTable::wind1_cust_st_rowRetrieved(
     theRow ixRow)
          RETURNING BOOLEAN
variable retval smallint
variable str char(10)

-- must look at maxrows - 1,
-- else maxRowsExceeded event is raised

if wind1.cust_st.getNumStoredRows() =
                (wind1.cust_st.maxrows - 1 )      then

  call messageBox( title:   new ixString( "Message" ),
                   message: new ixString(
"Maxrows reached. Retrieve 25 More Rows ?" ),
                   iconstyle:   ixQueryicon,
                   buttonstyle: ixYesNo )
                                          returning retval

   if retval = ixYesButton then   --increment maxrows
      let wind1.cust_st.maxrows =
              wind1.cust_st.maxrows + 25
   end if

end if
return TRUE

END HANDLER    --ixSuperTable::wind1_cust_st_rowRetrieved
```

In the code above, the value of the total number of rows currently retrieved is tested. This value is retrieved using the `getNumstoredRows` SuperTable member function. This value must be tested for a value one less than the `maxRows` parameter. A test for the exact value of the `maxRows` parameter could not be used because when this value is reached, the SuperTable will stop retrieving rows and execute the `maxRowsExceeded` event. This would preclude the possibility of retrieving more rows for the current data set. For our purposes, we do not want row retrieval to stop and therefore test for a value one less than `maxRows`.

If the user does not request more rows retrieved, then this code does not interfere with the normal SuperTable functionality. If the user replies with a "no" button press to the prompt to retrieve more rows, the SuperTable will still retrieve **exactly** maxrows number of rows. In this case, the event handler will merely allow the SuperTable to continue retrieving rows until the number of rows retrieved matches the maxrows parameter.

Chapter 6: Creating NewEra Applications

If the number of stored rows (as returned by the `getNumStoredRows` SuperTable member function) is one less than the value of the `maxRows` parameter, a message box is displayed to prompt the user to continue. There are two buttons on the message box, a "yes" button and a "no" button. (This style of buttons is provided by using the `ixYesNoButton` style with the NewEra `messageBox` function.) The return value that we care about is the return value indicating that the user has pressed the 'yes' button. This is indicated by the return value of `ixYesButton`, an integer constant value contained in the `ix4gl.4gh` include file.

If the user has pressed the "yes" button, then the value of `maxRows` contained in the SuperTable object is changed. This value is incremented by 25. If the user has pressed the "no" button, then nothing will be done and control will pass to the return statement at the end of the handler. In this case, the SuperTable will simply continue retrieving rows till the `maxRows` number of rows is retrieved or until no more rows can be retrieved.

The final line of code in the handler returns a BOOLEAN value as required by the handler signature. In all cases, this handler will return TRUE, allowing the SuperTable to continue processing the row just retrieved. Returning a value of FALSE would have rejected the row which was just retrieved, which is not the goal of this modification.

Adding Additional Functionality

These minor changes to the `rowRetrieved` handler significantly alter the behavior of the SuperTable. The user can now retrieve additional rows for their query rather than having to try to create a query to retrieve a smaller number of rows that will fit within the `maxRows` value.

But it may still be desirable to set a total limit on the number of rows retrieved. This maximum value could be entered into the code shown above to limit the total number of rows retrieved. An example of this approach is shown below.

```
HANDLER ixSuperTable::wind1_cust_st_rowRetrieved(
         theRow ixRow)
                 RETURNING BOOLEAN
variable retval smallint
variable str char(10)
if wind1.cust_st.getnumstoredrows() = 200  then
   call messagebox( title: new ixString( "Message" ),
                    message: new ixString(
"Maximum Number of Rows Total Retrieved.")
                         returning retval

    let wind1.cust_st.maxrows = 200
    return TRUE
end if
```

```
          -- Must look at maxrows - 1,
          -- Else maxrowsexceeded event is tripped
          if wind1.cust_st.getNumStoredRows() =
                         (wind1.cust_st.maxrows - 1 ) then

              call messagebox( title:   new ixString( "Message" ),
                               message: new ixString(
                   "Maxrows reached. Retrieve 25 More Rows ?" ),
                               iconstyle:   ixQueryicon,
                               buttonstyle: ixYesNo )
                                       returning retval

              if retval = ixYesButton then  --increment maxrows
                 let wind1.cust_st.maxrows =
                            wind1.cust_st.maxrows + 25
              end if

          end if

          return TRUE

          END HANDLER    --ixSuperTable::wind1_cust_st_rowRetrieved
```

In this example, a specific value (200) is tested against the number of rows currently retrieved. If this value has been reached, then a message box is displayed to the user (see Figure 6-5). Once the user confirms reading the message, the handler will return immediately. This prevents the remaining code from being executed and limits the SuperTable retrieval to the fixed number of rows. The remainder of the code is identical to the example shown previously.

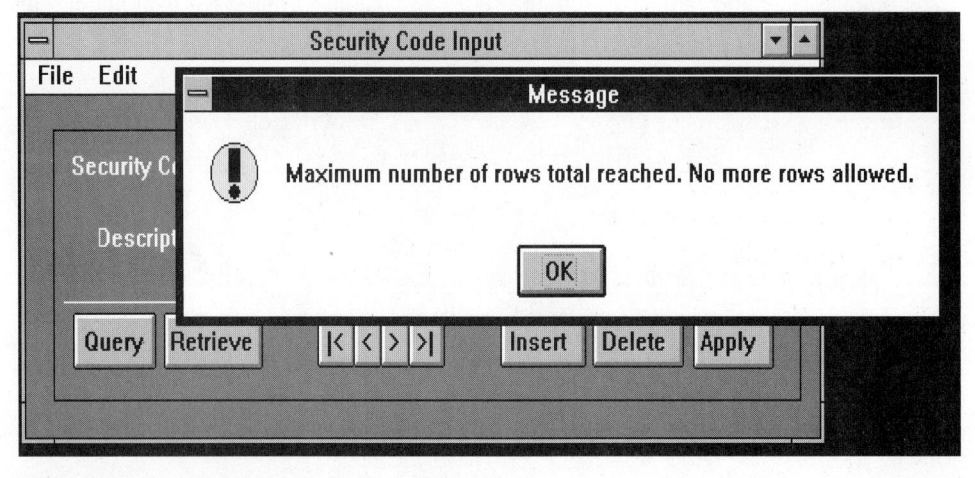

Figure 6-5 - Total Rows Limit Message

Chapter 6: Creating NewEra Applications

Adding Informational Messages

A user-friendly interface should provide informational messages for the user at various points during the retrieval and browsing of data. For instance, when the user has reached the end of the current set and is attempting to move past the end of the set, a message could be displayed indicating that there are 'no more rows' available (see Figure 6-5). Another message could be displayed when the user has entered a query and no rows were found.

By default, the NewEra SuperTable does not provide this functionality. And there are no handlers where code can be entered to provide these features. To implement these functions, the default code for the various SuperTable buttons must be changed as shown below.

Template SuperTable Button Handlers

Query Button Activate Handler Code

The "query" button puts the screen in input (insert) mode and allows the user to enter query criteria. The data entered by the user is entered into the query *data set* for the SuperTable. The query criteria is processed when the user activates the "retrieve" button.

```
VARIABLE superTable ixSuperTable
LET superTable = (getVisualContainer()
                  CAST ixSuperTable)

CALL superTable.setDisplayMode(
            ixSuperTable::displayQuery)
CALL message( message: "Query", window: getWindow() )
```

In this code example, a variable is declared to be of the class `ixSuperTable`. This variable is then initialized using the `let` statement. The `getVisualContainer` function is a member function of the class `ixVisualContainer`. Since the query button was derived from `ixVisualObject` which contains this function, this function is available to return the *container* of the current control, which in this case is an `ixButton` object contained by the SuperTable. The `getVisualContainer` function is declared to return an `ixVisualContainer` object. Since the `ixSuperTable` class is derived from `ixVisualContainer`, the return results of this function can be cast as an `ixSuperTable` class.

Once this reference has been obtained, the `setDisplayMode` member function is called and passed parameters to set the SuperTable into "query" mode. This will allow the user to enter query criteria. The `message` function is called to display a message to the bottom of the screen indicating to the user that the application is in "query" mode. This is a custom function that will be explained in chapter 9.

Retrieve Button Activate Handler Code

The "retrieve" button "activate" event handler will take the query parameters that have been input while the SuperTable was in Query mode, and process the query. It simply calls the SuperTable retrieve member function to retrieve the data. Before the data is retrieved, the SuperTable reference must be obtained. The `getVisualContainer` function is used again to get the `ixSuperTable` object reference. The code for the "retrieve" button "activate" handler is shown below.

```
VARIABLE ok BOOLEAN
VARIABLE superTable ixSuperTable
variable cust_numbIV ixValue

 LET superTable = (getVisualContainer() CAST ixSuperTable)

    call message( message: "Retrieving", window: getWindow() )
-- make the font italic
    call setMessageFont( font_italic: TRUE, window: getWindow() )


    LET ok = superTable.retrieve( QBE: TRUE )

call cust_codes_retrieve()

    -- make the font normal
    call setMessageFont( window: getWindow() )

    call message( message: "Retrieval Complete",
                window: getWindow() )

    if SuperTable.getNumStoredRows() = 0  then

           call msgbox( title: getWindow().getTitle(),
                    message: "No Rows Retrieved." )
        return

    end if

    call browse_status( row: 1,
            totalRows: SuperTable.getNumStoredRows(),
            window: getWindow() )
```

In the code above, the `message` function displays a message to the screen indicating that the SuperTable is retrieving rows from the database. Since the retrieval operation may take some time, the message is first displayed in italic font. The message text label is set to this font using the `setMessageFont` function which will be discussed in chapter 9. This change of fonts is meant to draw the user's attention to the message.

When the retrieval operation is complete, the message font will be set back to normal font using the default settings of the `setMessageFont` function call. If no rows are found during the retrieval operation, then a message is displayed to the window using the `msgbox` function (see Figure 6-6).

Figure 6-6 - No Rows Found Error Message

Next and Previous Buttons Activate Handler Code

The "next" and "previous" buttons retrieve the data that has currently been selected in the retrieval process. The SuperTable reference is obtained using the `getVisualContainer` function. The row position is then set to the current row (as obtained by adding or subtracting one to the value returned by `getCurrRowNum` function). If the calculated row position is greater than the number of stored rows in the SuperTable (as returned by the `getNumStoredRows` member function), then the row position is set to the `lastrow` member variable value.

This row position is then used as a parameter to the `setCurrentCell` SuperTable member function to advance to the next row. This member function is passed the row position as calculated above and the current cell as stored in the `ixSuperTable::currentColumn` member variable. This will have the effect of moving the SuperTable forward one row, if possible, and redisplaying all shown fields of the SuperTable with the values for the next row.

```
VARIABLE ok BOOLEAN
VARIABLE superTable ixSuperTable
VARIABLE rowPosition INTEGER

    LET superTable = (getVisualContainer() CAST ixSuperTable)
    LET rowPosition = superTable.getCurrRowNum() + 1

    # get the number of rows for the current displayMode
    IF rowPosition > superTable.getNumStoredRows(NULL) THEN

        call msgbox( title: getWindow().getTitle(),
                     message: "No More Rows." )

        LET rowPosition = ixSuperTable::lastRow
    END IF
  LET ok = superTable.setCurrentCell(rowPosition,
ixSuperTable::currentColumn)
call cust_codes_retrieve()

    call message( message: "Browse",
                  window: getWindow() )

    call browse_status( row: rowPosition,
                        totalRows:
                            superTable.getNumStoredRows(),
                        window: getWindow() )
```

The message function is used to display a message to the window indicating that the application is in browse mode. The browse_status function will display the current row position and the total number of rows to the pre-set labels on the template screen. If the user has attempted to move beyond the end of the current set, then a message indicating there are "no more rows" is displayed using the msgbox function as shown in Figure 6-7.

Figure 6-7 - No More Rows Error Message

Apply Button Activate Handler Code

The "apply" button is used to take the data that has been modified by the user and insert that data into the database. As with the other buttons, it uses a generic reference to the SuperTable and retrieves this reference using the `getVisualContainer` function.

The `apply` member SuperTable member function is then called to apply all modified rows to the database. The function returns an error value, but this value is not checked.

```
VARIABLE ok BOOLEAN
VARIABLE superTable ixSuperTable

    LET superTable = (getVisualContainer() CAST
ixSuperTable)

    call message( message: "Applying",
                window: getWindow() )
    call browse_status( row: 0,
                    totalRows: 0,
                    window: getWindow() )

    -- make the font italic
    call setMessageFont( font_italic: TRUE,
                    window: getWindow() )

    LET ok = superTable.apply()

    -- make the font normal
    call setMessageFont( window: getWindow() )

    LET ok = superTable.retrieve( QBE: TRUE )

    call message( message: "Apply Complete",
                window: getWindow() )
```

The `message` function is used to display a message indicating that the SuperTable is applying rows to the database. Since the apply operation may take some time, the message is displayed in italic font to let the user know the operation is taking place and has not yet completed. When the apply operation is complete, the message is changed to indicate the apply operation is complete and the font is set to normal font. The `browse_status` function is called to set the current row and total number of rows values displayed in the window to zero.

Delete Button Activate Handler Code

The "delete" button allows the user to delete the currently displayed row from the data set. It does not delete data from the database; the `apply` or `applyRowSql` SuperTable member functions must be called to perform this function.

The "delete" button retrieves a reference to the current SuperTable (the SuperTable of the current container) and then calls the SuperTable `delete` member function. The default code generated by the Window Painter does not check for error conditions. The deleted row is stored in the `ixRow` variable declared in the handler. In the event the programmer wanted to retrieve this value elsewhere in the application, the value in this local variable would have to be preserved.

```
VARIABLE deletedRow ixRow
VARIABLE superTable ixSuperTable

    LET superTable = (getVisualContainer() CAST
ixSuperTable)
    #just use default rowNum = currentRow
    #need not do anything w/ deletedRow
    LET deletedRow = superTable.delete()

    call message( message: "Delete",
                  window: getWindow() )
    call browse_status( row: 0,
                        totalRows: 0,
                        window: getWindow() )
```

A `message` indicating the application is in delete mode is displayed to the window using the message function. The `browse_status` function is called to indicate the current row and total number of rows is zero.

Insert Button Activate Handler Code

The code generated for the "Insert" button simply obtains a reference for the current SuperTable and then calls the insert member function to insert a new row into the SuperTable. Note that this does **not** insert data into the database; the row must be inserted into the current set in the application and then applied to the database using the `applyRowSql` SuperTable member function.

```
variable   cust_numbIV   ixValue

    LET superTable = (getVisualContainer() CAST
ixSuperTable)
```

```
    LET rownum = superTable.insert()

    call message( message: "Insert",
                  window: getWindow() )
    call browse_status( row: 0,
                        totalrows: 0,
                        window: getWindow() )
```

In the code above, the `message` function is used to display a message indicating the window is in insert mode and the `browse_status` function is called to set the current row and total number of rows to zero.

Using the Template Windows

An example of a template window is shown in Figure 6-3. This window contains all of the features listed in the table above. To use the template, the programmer would simply open this window (a Window Painter file named `template10.wif`), select the SuperTable object, and then paste the table or SuperView columns desired into the SuperTable frame.

Once the database columns have been pasted into the SuperTable frame, several database properties would have to be set. These properties are specific to each SuperTable instance and are not part of the template window. The *primary key* would have to be identified and a locking mode would have to be selected. This would make the update buttons (insert, delete, apply) operational. If these buttons are not needed, then they could be deleted from the window. The type of the window should be identified and the *startup* property may have to be changed.

Once these changes have been made, the window should be saved using the 'save-as' option. The name of the window should be changed at this point.

Free-form and Grid-form SuperTable Templates

The *grid-form* and *free-form* SuperTables retrieve data using the same member function, but the presentation of the data is different. With the grid-form SuperTable, traversal of the current set can be accomplished using the scroll buttons on the grid box. The "next" and "previous" buttons are also available to move the user through the data on the screen.

When a SuperTable is inserted into a window, its layout parameter is set to the type of SuperTable being used. This parameter is locked by the Window Painter and cannot be changed. For that reason, when using template windows, a separate template window must be provided for both grid-form and free-form SuperTables.

Chapter 7
Creating Application Windows with NewEra

The benefits of using template windows with Informix-NewEra have already been detailed in the previous chapters. This chapter discusses the creation of application windows with NewEra and demonstrates the process of using template windows with the development of a data entry window for the accounts receivable customer. A step-by-step approach for the creation of similar windows is shown.

CREATING SIMPLE WINDOWS WITH TEMPLATES

The first example presented is for a customer data entry window. This window will provide simple data entry into a single table, the accounts receivable customer table, and demonstrates the use of a *database-aware* list box.

The database-aware list box allows the user to select from a list of zip codes. When the user has selected a zip code from the list box, the zip code is inserted into the zip code field and the city and state for the zip code is displayed to the city and state fields. This example will later be expanded to include a customer search window, two sets of radio buttons, and data entry into two tables.

```
Create Template Window with Common Attributes
Open Template Window and Set Window Properties
Paste SuperTable Fields, Buttons and Properties
Add Additional Controls and Code
Format Screen
Add Code Where Needed
```

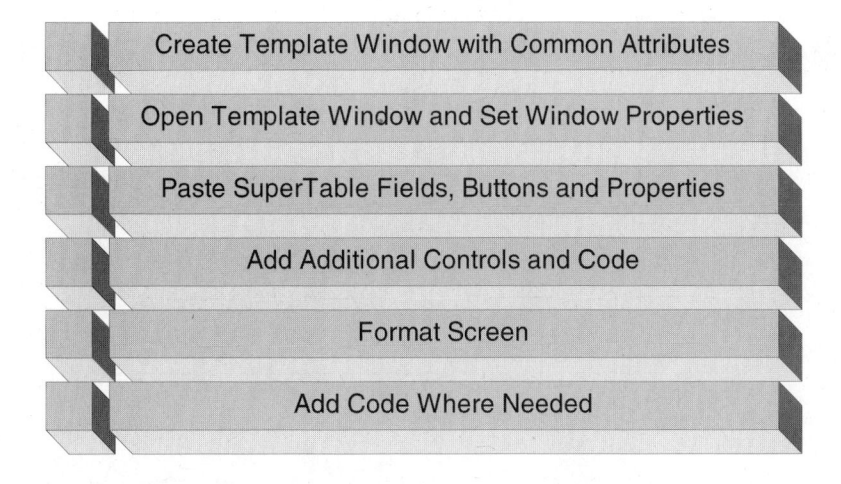

Figure 7-1 - Steps in Creating a NewEra Window

Open Template Window and Set Window Properties

The process of creating the window template was discussed in chapter 6. At this point, we are creating a window based on the template for a free-form SuperTable. Once the template is selected, various properties must be set.

The "File" menu option for the Window Painter is selected and the "Open" option is used to open the window file (wif) for the template window. If necessary, the properties for the window must then be set correctly. For the purposes of the customer data entry window, the majority of the window properties are set correctly. The window is to be a *mainTop* window and will be the startup window. Other properties such as window background and foreground color and window font have been set in the template and need not be changed here. The window title will be changed to a meaningful title for the application.

Pasting SuperTable Fields and Buttons; Setting SuperTable Properties

The SuperTable frame is then selected and the SuperTable editor is displayed (see Figure 7-2). The appropriate SuperTable fields are then pasted into the frame (see Figure 7-3).

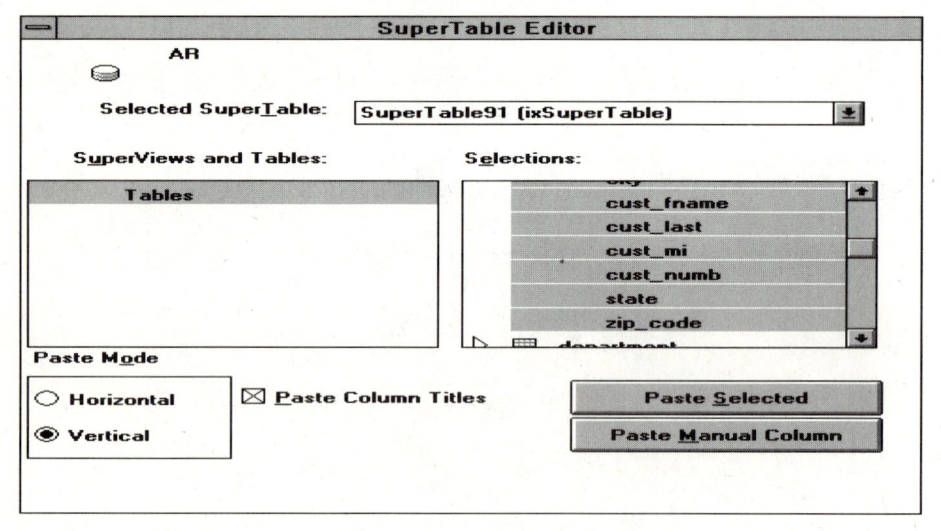

Figure 7-2 -Selecting SuperTable Fields

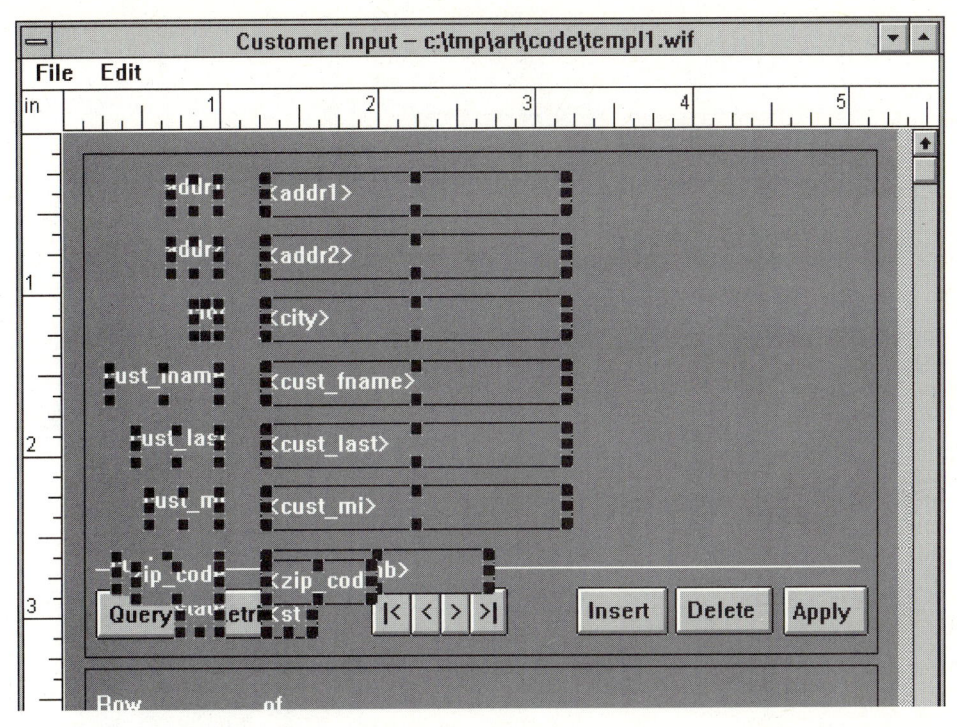

Figure 7-3 - Pasting SuperTable Fields

If the SuperTable update capabilities are to be used, then the primary key for the customer table must be identified. The primary key for the customer table is the customer number (`cust_numb` database table field). The customer number SuperField property for primary key must therefore be set to TRUE (see Figure 7-4).

Only one database table is being represented in this example. If additional tables were being used, they would be pasted into the form in this step and the SuperTable "SelectJoinPart" property would have to be set correctly.

Adding Additional Controls and Code

To add the database aware list box, a list box control is pasted over the zip code field. This must be done in such a way as to hide the zip code field and provide the best possible visible presentation. This may require the field box itself be resized for the list box and/or the zip code field.

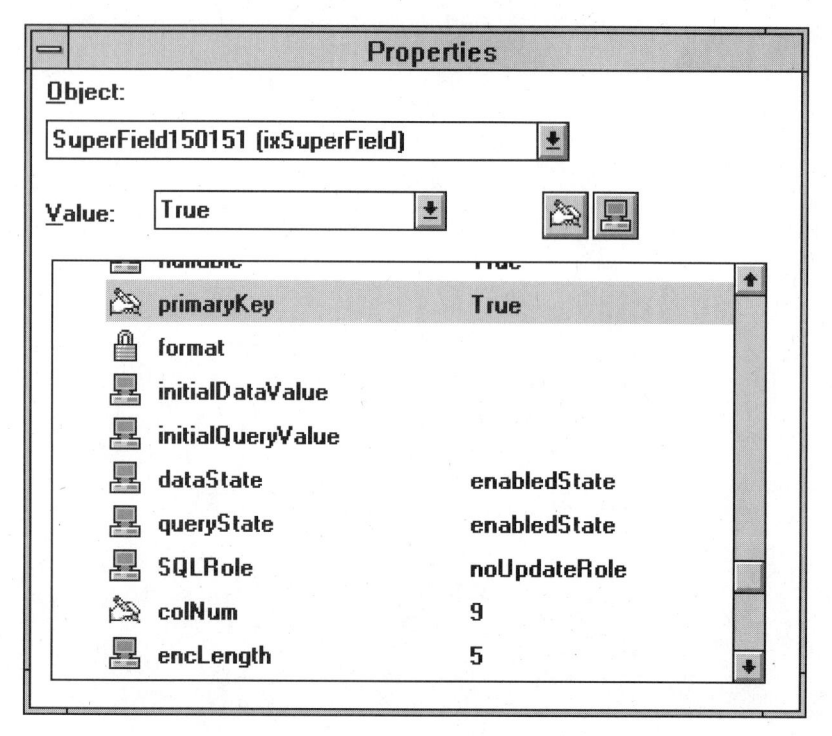

Figure 7-4 - Setting the Primary Key Property

The general property for the list box class must be changed to the `dbelist` class. The pre-header section of the window code section must include the list file for the `dbelist.4gh` include file. This file contains the class definition for the `dbelist` class which is explained in detail in chapter 9.

Format Window

The formatting of a window depends to a certain extent on the aesthetic tastes of the programmer and the target users. The same functionality can be achieved in a variety of ways with a variety of formats. The basics of formatting are discussed below.

Text Formatting

Text within the window should generally use a consistent font for the same controls. The exception would be where the font or font attributes are changed for emphasis. For instance, the title of a frame for radio buttons may use a bold, italic font to emphasize the existence of the frame to the user (Figure 7-6).

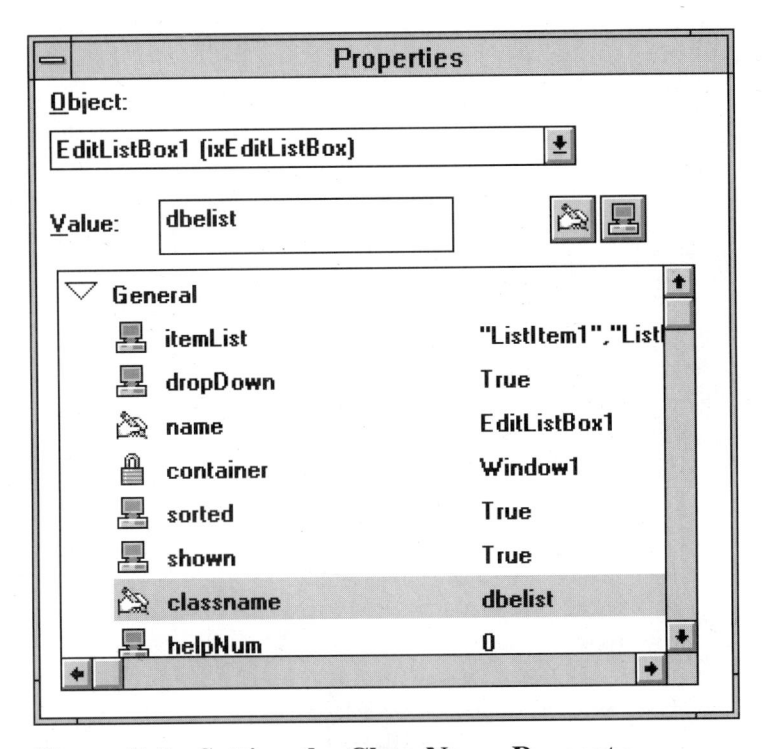

Chapter 7: Creating Application Windows with NewEra

Figure 7-5 - Setting the Class Name Property

Figure 7-6 - Using Text Formatting

The text for field names should be a consistent font. Once again, the exception would be when a field or set of fields needs to be emphasized. The name for these fields could be set to a bold or italic font style.

It is also common for field names to use "initial case" capitalization where the first letter of the name is capitalized.

Control Formatting

Buttons should be aligned and grouped logically. The VCR buttons used to traverse the retrieved SuperTable data set in the template window are grouped together. The buttons to the left of these buttons are used to *query* and *retrieve* data, and the buttons to the right of these buttons are used to perform update operations: *insert*, *delete*, and *apply* changes.

Frames are usually used to group button controls. (The objects for the controls will still be part of the window class, but the visual container for the controls will be the frame object.) The frame will provide a clean visual presentation for controls and screen objects. They will help to focus the user's attention.

In this example, the text labels used to output the informational messages for the SuperTable are contained within a frame.

Controls can also be aligned using the alignment buttons in the window painter. Once the buttons have been selected, they can be centered, right justified, or left justified using the alignment buttons. An option is also available to allow specify the distance separating the fields and then align those fields using that setting.

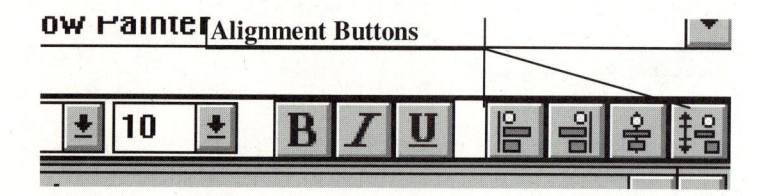

Figure 7-7 - Window Painter Alignment Buttons

Adding Code to *Glue* NewEra Controls

At certain points in the application, code may need to be inserted to manage the controls within the window. The *bound* SuperTable field and select table, columns, and `where` clause must be identified for the database-aware box.

Screen fields may need code for *trapping* events before or after the user has entered the cell. In this example, once a zip code is selected and placed in the zip code cell, the city and state for the zip code must be displayed to the city and state cell. Code is required to perform these operations. Where to place the code, in which event handlers, is critical.

USING THE DBELIST BOX CLASS

This section describes the use of the `dbelist` class in the customer window. Through this class definition the list box control will be bound to the database table and columns and to a SuperField on the window. The control will respond to user interaction and retrieve data from the database and display the data to a list box. When the user has selected an item from the list box, the selected item will be displayed to the bound SuperField.

The section will demonstrate the use of the `dbelist` class. The code for the `dbelist` class will be examined in detail in chapter 9.

Registering the `dbelist` Box

In order for the zip code list box to operate correctly, it must be *registered*. This will establish the connections between the SuperTable, SuperField, list box control, and the database table or tables used. A call to the `init_list` function establishes these relationships as shown below.

```
-- register the zip code list box
call CustWN.zipLst.init_list(
bind_SuperTable: CustST,
bind_SuperField: zip_codeSF,
list_table:    "zip_code",
list_column:   "zip_code"  )
```

The `bind_SuperTable` parameter is supplied a reference for the SuperTable that contains the cell for which the `dbelist` list box is bound. The `bind_SuperField` parameter is supplied a reference for the SuperField that will receive the data. The `list_table` is passed the name of the table or tables that will be used to retrieve the data for the list box. The `list_column` parameter is used to pass the names of the column or columns to be displayed in the list box. An optional `where_clause` parameter is available to specify where clause criteria for the data retrieval operation; the default for this parameter is NULL which indicates that no where clause criteria is to be used.

The `focus` Event for the `zip_code` Field

The functionality for the zip code cell requires that when the zip code is entered, the city and state associated with the zip code be displayed to the screen. The `afterDataChanged` event will **not** indicate that data items were entered into the cell programatically as demonstrated in this example. The `focus` event for the SuperField will be used to provide this functionality.

The database aware list box will take the selected item from the list box and insert the value into the bound SuperTable cell. When this step is complete, the `focus` event for the SuperField will be called to set the focus to the bound SuperField. This allows the `focus` event for the SuperField to be trapped and a handler written to use this event to trigger some action. In this example, the `focus` event for the SuperField is used to take the value of zip code as inserted by the `dbelist` list box and retrieve the city and state for the zip code. The city and state are then displayed to the city and state cells in the SuperTable. The code for the `focus` event for the zip code SuperField is shown below.

```
variable ival ixValue
variable zip_str char(*)
variable lcity, lstate char(10)
variable retval smallint
variable retOK Boolean

let ival = CustWN.CustST.getCellvalue(
              colnum: CustWN.zip_codeSF.getColNum() )
let zip_str = ival.getValueStr()

-- get the city,state values
select city,state
into   lcity, lstate
from   zip_code
where  zip_code = zip_str

-- display to the appropriate fields
call custWN.custST.setCellvalue( newstrVal: lcity,
              colnum: CustWN.citySF.getColNum() )
              returning retOK

call custWN.custST.setCellValue( newstrVal: lstate,
              colnum:
              CustWN.stateSF.getColNum() )
              returning retOK
```

In this example, the value of the zip code cell in the `custST` SuperTable is retrieved into an `ixValue` object using the `getCellValue` function call. This value is then stored in a string variable which is used in an SQL statement to retrieve the city and state for the zip code from the zip code table. (This asserts that the zip code is a primary key for this table and that only one row will be retrieved.) The city and state values returned are then written to the appropriate cells using the `setCellValue` SuperTable member function call.

ADDING ADDITIONAL FUNCTIONALITY TO THE CUSTOMER INPUT WINDOW

The expanded version of the customer window (see Figure 7-8) adds a number of user-friendly features and controls to the application. Data entry into the related `cust_codes` table is provided to allow the data entry into both of these tables to be handled in a single window. Buttons are provided and effectively bound to the cells in the `cust_codes` table. And a customer search facility is added to allow the user to search

Chapter 7: Creating Application Windows with NewEra   131

through a list of customer entries in a pop-up list box. These features and their implementation are discussed below.

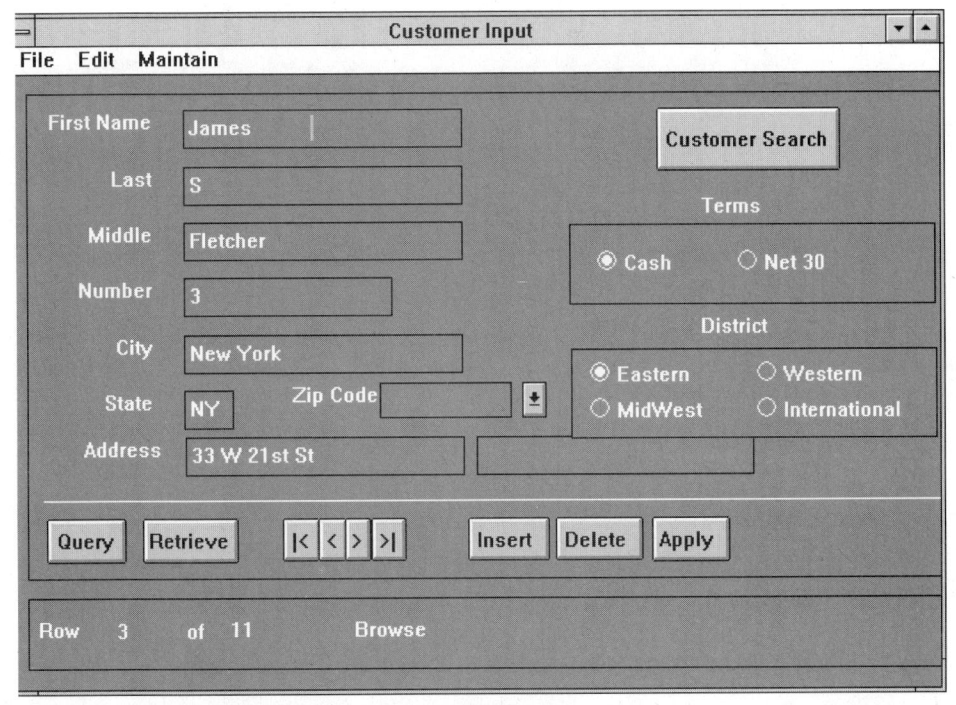

Figure 7-8 - Expanded Customer Window

Use of a Hidden SuperTable

The `cust_codes` table is used to store information that is related to the customer. It would be convenient to provide update capabilities for both of these tables in a single window. Since a single SuperTable can only update a single table, the `cust_codes` table would have to be added to the window in its own SuperTable.

Since the SuperTable data elements are part of the window, the `cust_codesST` SuperTable can be pasted into the `custST` SuperTable without interfering with the operation of that SuperTable.

And since radio buttons will be used to allow the user to provide input for the `cust_codesST` SuperTable cells, the actual SuperTable will be hidden from the user by setting the `shown` property to FALSE (see Figure 7-8 and Figure 7-10).

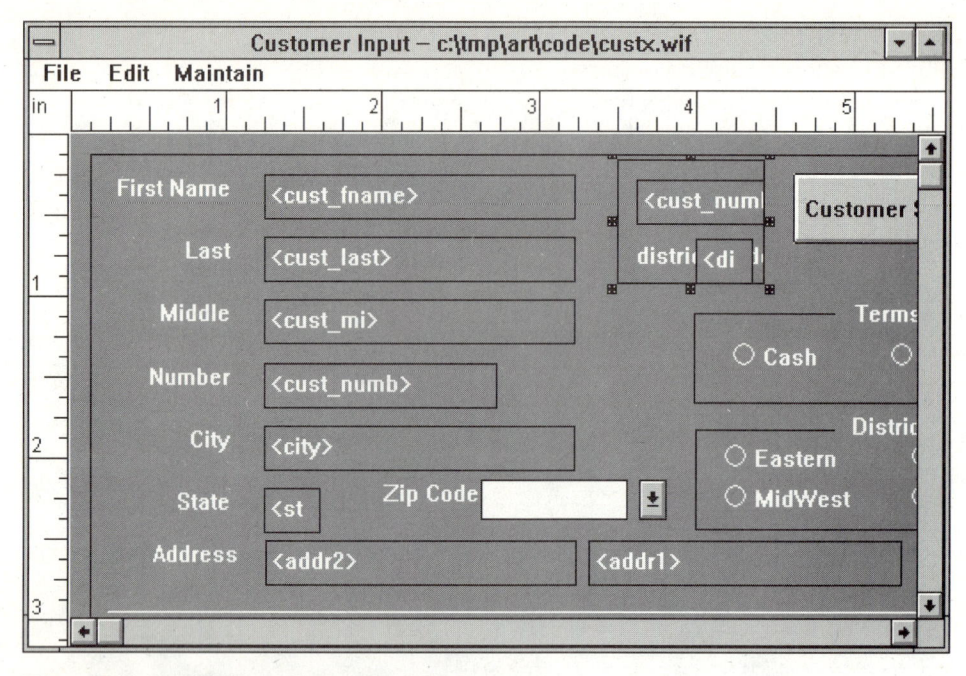

[Figure 7-9 - Hidden SuperTable]

Figure 7-9 - Hidden SuperTable

Inserting Data with Related SuperTables

The use of two updatable tables in the same window creates a problem when an insert is being performed using a `serial` field. Preferably, when an insert is performed using the `custST` SuperTable for the customer master table, an insert would also be performed into the `cust_codesST` SuperTable; both tables would use the same primary key produced with a serial field in the customer table. This can be accomplished by retrieving the serial value of the insert operation in the `afterRowApplied` event as shown below.

```
variable retval smallint

    -- set the cust_codes primary key for
    -- the inserted row
    call CustWN.cust_codesST.setCellValue(
              NewStrVal: sqlca.sqlerrd[2],
              colnum: CustWN.cnSF.getColNum() )
                     returning retval

return TRUE
```

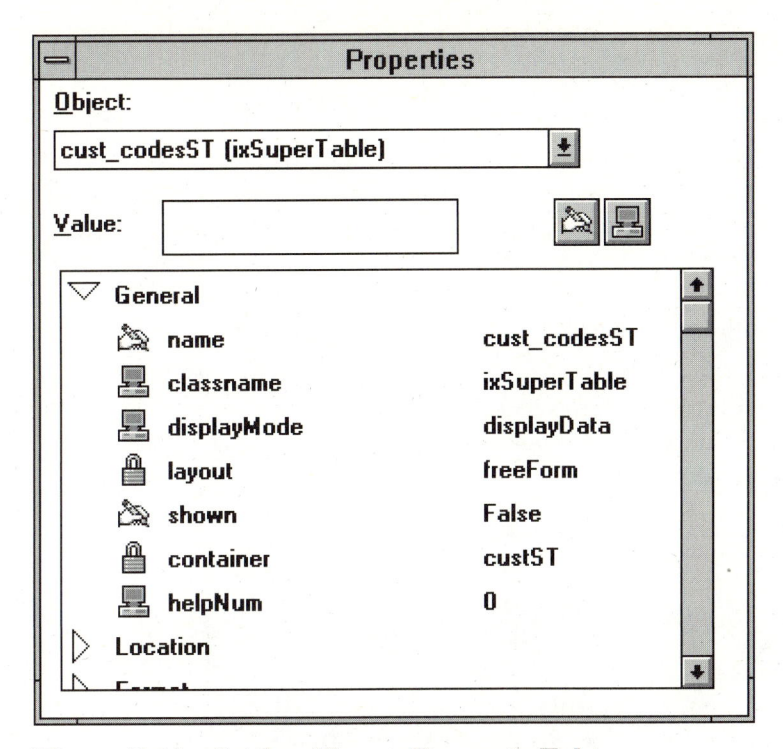

Chapter 7: Creating Application Windows with NewEra

[Properties dialog showing:
Object: cust_codesST (ixSuperTable)
Value:
General
- name: cust_codesST
- classname: ixSuperTable
- displayMode: displayData
- layout: freeForm
- shown: False
- container: custST
- helpNum: 0
Location]

Figure 7-10 - Setting Shown Property False

In this handler, the value of the `cust_codesST` primary key cell is set equal to the value of the `serial` field customer number (`cust_numb`) that has just been inserted into the database. This value is stored in the Informix `sqlca` structure in the `sqlerrd[2]` element. (The CCL/ODBC has no equivalent for this value since serial fields are not part of the ODBC standard.) This value is placed into the `cust_codesST` SuperTable in the `cust_numb` cell. Insert operations for this SuperTable will now contain the correct value in this foreign key cell.

The SuperTable apply button for the `custST` SuperTable must be appended to perform the apply for the `cust_codesST` SuperTable. This apply **must** take place **after** the apply operation for the `custST` SuperTable since the `cust_codesST` requires the primary key information from the results of the customer database insert operation. The code for these apply operations is shown below.

```
LET ok = superTable.apply()
LET ok = CustWN.cust_codesST.apply()
```

In this code, the insert operation is first called for the containing SuperTable, which would be the `custST` SuperTable for the customer table. This apply operation will trigger the `afterRowApplied` event for the `custST` SuperTable. This will execute the code that will place the customer number for the inserted customer row (`cust_numb`) into the customer number cell in the `cust_codesST` SuperTable. The apply operation is then called for the `cust_codesST` SuperTable to insert that data into the database.

Binding Radio Buttons to SuperTable Cells

Radio buttons are used to allow the user to enter the terms codes and the district for the customer. Radio buttons provide a very clear presentation for mutually exclusive user choices, but have the drawback of limiting the amount of information that can be presented and making it difficult to adjust the number of choices dynamically.

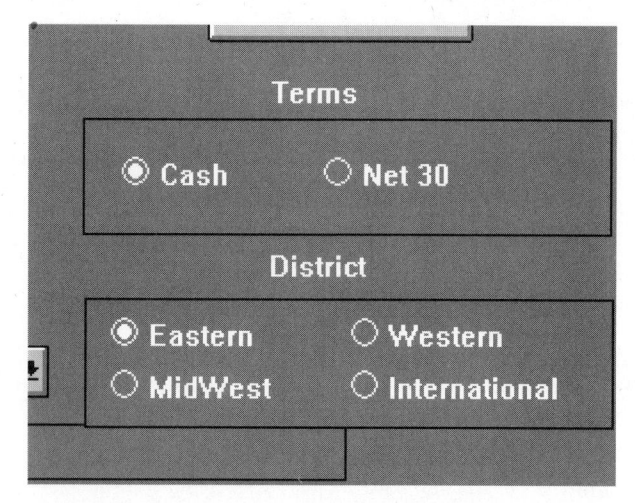

Figure 7-11 - Customer Window Radio Buttons

In this case, the number of choices is limited to two choices for the terms codes and four choices for the district. The use of radio buttons will force the user to choose from a correct set of choices and will provide a default for the user (see Figure 7-11).

The results of the user's radio button choice is automatically stored in the `cust_codesST` by creating handlers for the `select` event for the radio button. The code for the select event for one of these buttons is shown below.

```
HANDLER ixRadioButton::CustWN_CashRB_select()
        RETURNING VOID
variable retok boolean
```

Chapter 7: Creating Application Windows with NewEra

```
let retok = CustWN.cust_codesST.setCellValue(
                colnum: CustWN.termsSF.getColnum(),
                newStrVal: "1" )

END HANDLER -- ixRadioButton::CustWN_CashRB_select
```

In this example, the select event handler executes code that automatically inserts a value into the `cust_codesST` SuperTable terms cell (in the hidden SuperTable). This value is a fixed character value. (This is also true for the other radio buttons that are fixed on the window and will not change dynamically at runtime. Contrast this functionality with that of the list box that uses data items that are loaded each time the list box is used.)

By default, these radio buttons will not change value as the data set is traversed using the "next row"/ "previous row" buttons. This behavior is not desireable; their value should reflect the values of the `cust_codes` table row for the `customer` table row being displayed. This behavior can be accomplished using the code shown below.

```
function cust_codes_retrieve()
variable cust_numbIV, termsIV, districtIV ixvalue
variable retval smallint

-- retrieve the data for the cust_codes table
-- SuperTable
-- get serial value from master table SuperTable
let cust_numbIV = CustWN.custST.getCellValue(
                colnum: CustWN.cust_numbSF.getColNum() )

call custWN.cust_codesST.SelectFilterPart.setValueStr(
                " cust_numb = " ||
                cust_numbIV.getValueStr() )

call CustWN.cust_codesST.retrieve( QBE: FALSE )
        returning retval

-- push the radio buttons
let termsIV = CustWN.cust_codesST.getCellValue(
                colnum: CustWN.termsSF.getColNum( ) )

let districtIV = CustWN.cust_codesST.getCellValue(
                colnum: CustWN.districtSF.getColNum() )

if termsIV IS NOT NULL then

   case termsIV.getValueStr()
```

```
         when "1"     call CustWN.cashRB.push()
         when "2"     call CustWN.net30RB.push()

   end case

end if

if districtIV IS NOT NULL then

   case districtIV.getValueStr()

         when "E"     call CustWN.easternRB.push()
         when "M"     call CustWN.midwestRB.push()
         when "W"     call CustWN.westernRB.push()
         when "I"     call CustWN.internationalRB.push()

   end case

end if

end function
```

This function will first get the value of the `cust_numb` primary key cell from the `custST` SuperTable. This value is then used to create the SQL select filter for the `cust_codesST` SuperTable. Once the `cust_codesST` SuperTable data have been retrieved using the SuperTable `retrieve` member function, the value of the `terms_codes` and `district_codes` cells are retrieved and tested. The values returned in the `ixValue` object are evaluated using the NewEra `case` statement. Depending on the value being evaluated, one of the radio buttons in the frame is set *on* using the `push` member function call; this will automatically set all of the other buttons in the frame to an *off* position. There are two separate `case` statements - one for the terms code and one for the district code. This function is called following the `custST` SuperTable `retrieve` member function as shown below.

```
      ...
        LET ok = superTable.retrieve( QBE: TRUE )

        call cust_codes_retrieve()
      ...
```

Popup Searchable List Box Window

If the user presses the customer search button, a list box is displayed with a list of all of the customers available (see Figure 7-12). The user can enter search criteria and search the list box contents for a particular customer.

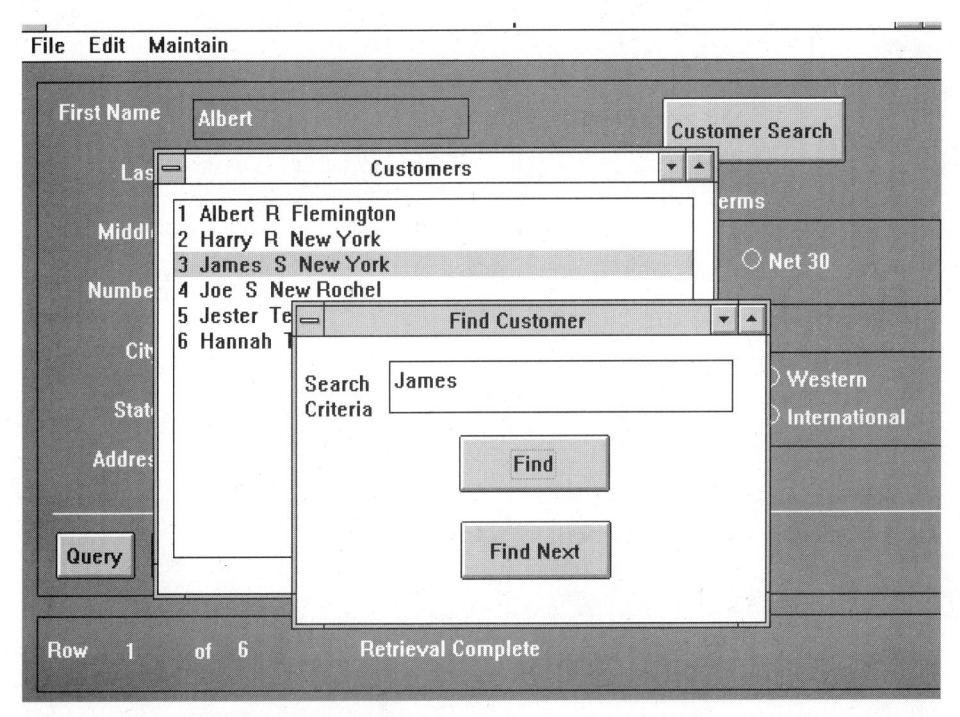

Figure 7-12 - The Searchable List Box

Loading the Searchable List Box

The customer list box is loaded when the "Customer Search" button is pressed. While list boxes are often loaded in the `start` event for the window, the strategy of loading the list box when the user has elected to use the list avoids the overhead of loading the list if the user is not going to use it. It does, however, have the limitation of making the user wait while the list is loaded when the list option has been selected.

A global flag is kept to indicate whether or not the list has been loaded. If the list has been loaded, then the list box is not reloaded every time the user activates the customer list search button. If the list has not been loaded, then the `LoadCustList` function is called to load the list as shown below.

```
if Not CustListLoaded then
```

```
    call LoadCustList()
    let CustListLoaded = TRUE
end if
```

The `LoadCustList` function is used to load the customer data into the list box. This function declares several variables to be used as host variables for the data retrieval operation. In this example, the customer first name, last name, company, city, and state will be retrieved for the list.

A statement is prepared and then a cursor is created for the prepared statement. This cursor is then used in a NewEra `foreach` loop to select the desired columns from the database.

The data retrieved from the database is stored in an `ixString` variable. Rather than incur the overhead of creating a new `ixString` variable on each pass, the `setValuestr` member function of the `ixString` class is called to overwrite or reallocate string memory. This `ixString` object is then passed to the `ixListBox` class `insert` member function to insert the data into the list box.

```
function   LoadCustList()
variable fname, lname, company, city, state, cust_numb
char(20)
variable clist ixVector = new ixVector()
variable istr  ixString = new ixString( " " )
variable retval smallint
variable lstr char(20)

-- load the customer list

prepare s3 from
"select cust_numb, cust_fname, cust_last, city, state
from customer "

declare c3 cursor for s3

foreach c3 into cust_numb, fname, lname, city, state

        call istr.setValueStr( cust_numb clipped ||
                      "  " ||
                      fname clipped || " " ||
                      lname clipped || " " ||
                      city clipped )

    call CustListWN.cust_list.insert(  istr )
```

Chapter 7: Creating Application Windows with NewEra   139

```
                     returning retval
```

```
end foreach

end function
```

Searching the List Box

When the "Search Customer" button is pressed, the `activate` event for the button is called. This code (as shown below) will first make an attempt to determine whether or not the window is currently open. Since the `CustListWN` window has been created in the `start` event for the customer window, we can assert that the object exists the first time the user presses this button. If the user has subsequently closed the window using the GUI system interface, we can still be sure the window is opened because we have entered handler code for the `finish` event for the customer list window which merely hides the window using the `ixVisualContainer hide` member function rather than allowing the window manager to close the window. The code for this handler is shown later in this chapter.

The `activate` handler for the customer search button will call the `getAvailability` member function to determine the current state of the windows used in the customer search option. If the windows are closed or unopened, the `open` member function is called to open the window. Otherwise, it can be asserted that the window is still visible or has been hidden by the user pressing the "Exit" option of the "File" menu, or choosing the "Close" option of the window system menu; in this case, the `show` member function is called.

If the `CustListLoaded` variable is false (as would be the case the first time the button is pressed), then the `LoadCustList` function is called to load the customer list box. Once the `LoadCustList` function has completed, the `CustListLoaded` variable is set to TRUE. This will prevent the list from being loaded on subsequent calls.

The `LoadCustList` function is called from the button handler for the "customer search" button to avoid the overhead of loading the list box if the user does not use the list box. Had the list box simply been loaded within the window `start` event or in the constructor extension for the window object, and then the user decided not to use the list box, then the list box would have been loaded for no purpose.

```
HANDLER ixButton::CustWN_Button111_activate() RETURNING
VOID

if CustListWN.getAvailability() =
         ixVisualObject::closed   or
   CustListWN.getAvailability() =
         ixVisualObject::unopened    then
```

```
      call CustListWN.open()
   else
      call CustListWN.show()
   end if

   if FindWN.getAvailability() = ixVisualObject::closed or
      FindWN.getAvailability() = ixVisualObject::unopened
   then
      call FindWN.open()
   else
      call FindWN.show()
   end if

   if Not CustListLoaded  then
      call LoadCustList()
      let CustListLoaded = TRUE
   end if

   END HANDLER -- ixButton::CustWN_Button111_activate
```

The Search Function

The searchable customer list uses two windows: One window displays the list of customers and the other provides an input window for search criteria and buttons for "Find" and "Find Next". The code for the `activate` event of the "Find" button is shown below.

The code behind the "Find" button expects data to have been entered in the text box but does not explicitly check for that after making the `getText` member function call. The `getText` call returns a character pointer (char (*)).

Ultimately the `ixString find` member function will be used to search each line of the list box for a string pattern. The string pattern parameter required by the `ixString find` member function requires an `ixString` parameter. For that reason, the value returned by the `getText` function call is converted into an `ixString` data type.

A `for` loop is then started from the start of the list box to the value of `FindStartPos` variable. The `FindStartPos` variable is a module scope variable that contains the starting position for the search. If the "Find" button has been pressed, then this variable is set to 1. If the "`find next"` button has been pressed, then this value is set to the current list search position (as stored in the module scope variable `CurrListPos`) to allow the search to continue from the present position.

Chapter 7: Creating Application Windows with NewEra

A Boolean data type variable is evaluated at the end of the loop to determine whether or not the value was found. Before the start of the loop, this variable, appropriately named `found`, is set to the value of FALSE.

As the "for" loop is executed, for each iteration of the loop a call is made to the `ixList` box member function `getItemByNumber`. This function is passed a position parameter and returns a character string value for the list box row at that position. This character string pointer is converted to an `ixString` data type so that the `ixString` `find` member function can be used to search the string.

The `find ixString` member function is then passed the `searchString` value obtained earlier and the string is searched. If this function call returns TRUE, it is an indication that the string was found and the `found` flag is set to TRUE and the `for` loop is exited. If it returns FALSE, then the loop continues. If no matches are found, then the loop will terminate with the `found` flag still set to FALSE.

If the value was found, then the current list search position is stored in the `CurrListPos` module scope variable. This will be used if the user wishes to execute a "Find Next" search. The positional number of the found list box entry is then set as the selected list box item by calling the list box `selectItem` call. If the entry was not found, then a message box is displayed indicating that the item was not found and the `CurrListPos` variable is set to one to start the next search at the start of the list. At the end of the handler, the `findNext` flag is set to FALSE.

```
HANDLER ixButton::findWN_findBN_activate() RETURNING VOID
variable listentr char(*)
variable istr    ixString = new ixstring( " " )
variable retval, itemnum, n smallint
variable found Boolean

-- get the search criteria
let searchString = new ixString(
               findWN.search_criteria.getText() )

let found = FALSE

if FindStartPos = 0  then
   let FindStartPos = 1
end if

for n = FindStartPos to
             CustListWN.cust_list.getnumitems()

   call istr.setvaluestr(
          CustListWN.cust_list.getitembyNumber( n ) )
```

```
           if istr.find( searchString )   then
              let found = TRUE
              exit for
           end if

    end for

    if  found  then
          let CurrListPos = n
          call CustListWN.cust_list.selectitem( n )
          let listentr =
                 CustListWN.cust_list.getitembynumber( n )
    else
            call messagebox( title: new ixstring( "Message"),
                       message:  new ixstring( "Not Found" ) )
                   returning retval
           let CurrListPos = 1
    end if

    let FindNext = FALSE

    END HANDLER -- ixButton::findWN_findBN_activate
```

The List Box select Event

The functionality of the searchable list box requires that the `select` event retrieve the customer number and place that value in the customer number field in the `custST` SuperTable. This is accomplished with the code below.

First, the value of the selected item is retrieved from the list box. (This is a handler for the list box, so a full container reference is not needed.) This is accomplished with a call the `getItembyNumber` member function call using the `getSelectedItem` call to get the position of the selected item. These calls retrieve a character string pointer that is converted into an `ixString` object.

This is required to use the `getSubstring ixString` member function call to retrieve a substring starting from the start of the string until the first blank is encountered. This will effectively retrieve the customer number which is a contiguous string starting at the first byte of the list entry. This substring is stored in an `ixString` data type that is then placed in the `cust_numb` field in the `custST` SuperTable.

```
    HANDLER ixListBox::CustListWN_cust_list_select()
    RETURNING VOID
    variable retok boolean
    variable cust_num char(10)
```

Chapter 7: Creating Application Windows with NewEra 143

```
    variable lstr ixString

    let CustListWN.SelectStr = new ixString(
                 getItembyNumber( getSelectedItem() ) )

    -- cust number is the first set of characters
    -- in the selected string from the list
    let lstr =
           CustListWN.SelectStr.getSubString(pos: 1,
                                             len:
                 CustListWN.SelectStr.findChar( " " ) )

    let cust_num = lstr.getValueStr()

    -- update the customer window with the selected customer
    call CustWN.CustST.setCellValue(
             colnum: CustWN.Cust_numbSF.getColNum(),
             newStrVal: cust_num )
         returning retok

    END HANDLER -- ixListBox::CustListWN_cust_list_select
```

The preheader Section

The "preheader" section for the customer list window of the customer module is used to declare certain variables used throughout the application. The `CustListWN` and `findWN` object references reference window objects opened in the customer module. They are therefore declared as external variables.

The `FindStartPos`, `CurrListPos` and `FindNext`, variables are all declared with module scope, meaning they will be visible only throughout this source code module. These variables are used to store values that must be retained on repeated function calls, so a local variable would not be appropriate since it would be reset on each function call. And a global variable is not needed since the values of these parameters are only needed in this module.

```
    INCLUDE "custlst2.4gh"

    external variable CustListWN CustListWindow
    external variable findWN findWindow

    variable FindStartPos smallint = 1,
             CurrListPos  smallint = 1,
             FindNext     boolean  = FALSE
```

```
variable searchString ixstring
variable FoundString  char(*)
```

The Find Next Button Handler

When the user chooses the "Find Next" parameter, the following code is executed. The `FindStartPos` module scope variable is set to the current list position (as stored in `CurrListPos`) plus one to start the search at the next item past the current item.

This value is then tested for sanity. If the value is greater than or equal to the total number of items in the list as returned by the `getNumItems` member function, then it is set to the value of one.

The `findNext flag` is set to TRUE. The activate handler for the find button is then called to execute the find operation. Since the `FindStartPos` value has been set correctly, the search will begin from the present position and proceed to the end of the list.

```
HANDLER ixButton::findWN_findNextBN_activate()
    RETURNING VOID

let FindStartPos = CurrListPos + 1

if FindStartPos >= CustListWN.cust_list.getNumItems()
then
    let FindStartPos = 1
end if

let FindNext = TRUE
call findWN.findBN.activate()

END HANDLER -- ixButton::findWN_findNextBN_activate
```

The finish Event

The `finish` event code for the windows used in the customer search function is shown below. The finish event is passed an integer parameter indicating how the window was closed. In our case, we only care that the user has chosen to close the window from the system menu. If this is the case, then the window is hidden with a call to the `hide` `ixWindow` member function. We must then return FALSE to indicate that the window should not be closed. Otherwise, we return TRUE indicating that the window has been closed by some other means and it is OK to close the window.

Chapter 7: Creating Application Windows with NewEra 145

```
HANDLER CustListWindow::CustListWN_finish(
                  byWhom smallint)
   RETURNING BOOLEAN

if byWhom = ixWindow::ClosedbySysMenu  then
  call self.hide()
  return FALSE
else
  return TRUE
end if

END HANDLER -- CustListWindow::CustListWN_finish
```

Using a Grid-Form SuperTable Template: The Zip Code Window

The zip code input window is used to perform simple data entry into the zip code table using a grid-form SuperTable. It uses a template similar to the template used for the customer table, but the visual presentation of the data is different.

The zip code window is created by opening the grid-form SuperTable template with the Window Painter and then selecting the SuperTable frame (see Figure 7-13). The fields for the zip code table are then pasted into the form and the SuperTable window is closed.

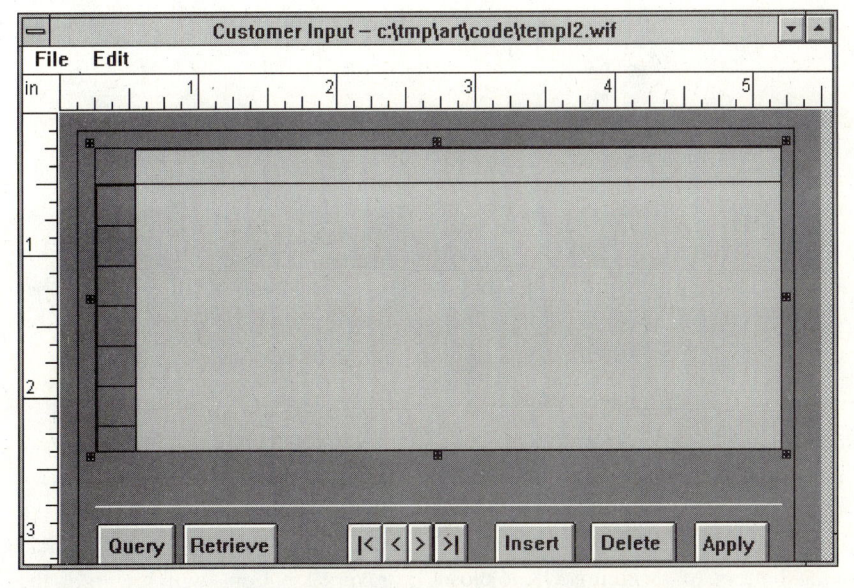

Figure 7-13 - SuperTable Frame Selected in Template

The next step is to modify the field names of the SuperTable fields from the sometimes cryptic column names that are the window painter defaults. In this example, the field names are placed in title case using the default window font. Note that selecting a field with the grid-form SuperTable requires the entire column to be selected (see Figure 7-14).

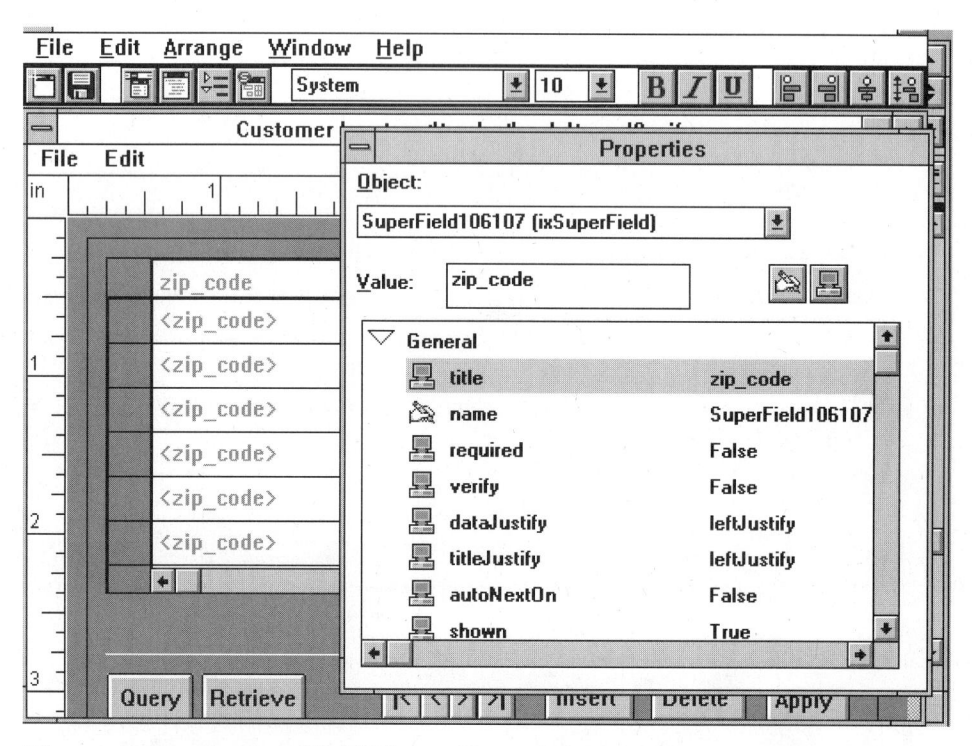

Figure 7-14 - Setting Field Name Properties

As a final step in preparing the zip code window, database properties must be set correctly. The zip code field is selected as a primary key field. The locking mode is set to pessimistic locking. This will allow the update buttons to be used with the zip code table.

The data traversal buttons on the zip code input window behave slightly different than they do with the free-form SuperTable. The entire retrieved data set is available in the scrolling region of the grid-form SuperTable. This data set can be traversed using the scrolling bar on the side of the SuperTable grid frame, or by using the VCR traversal buttons at the bottom of the window. The VCR traversal buttons will highlight the current row and display messages to the message frame as with the free-form SuperTable. As the user moves through the data set, the first cell of the current row is "selected".

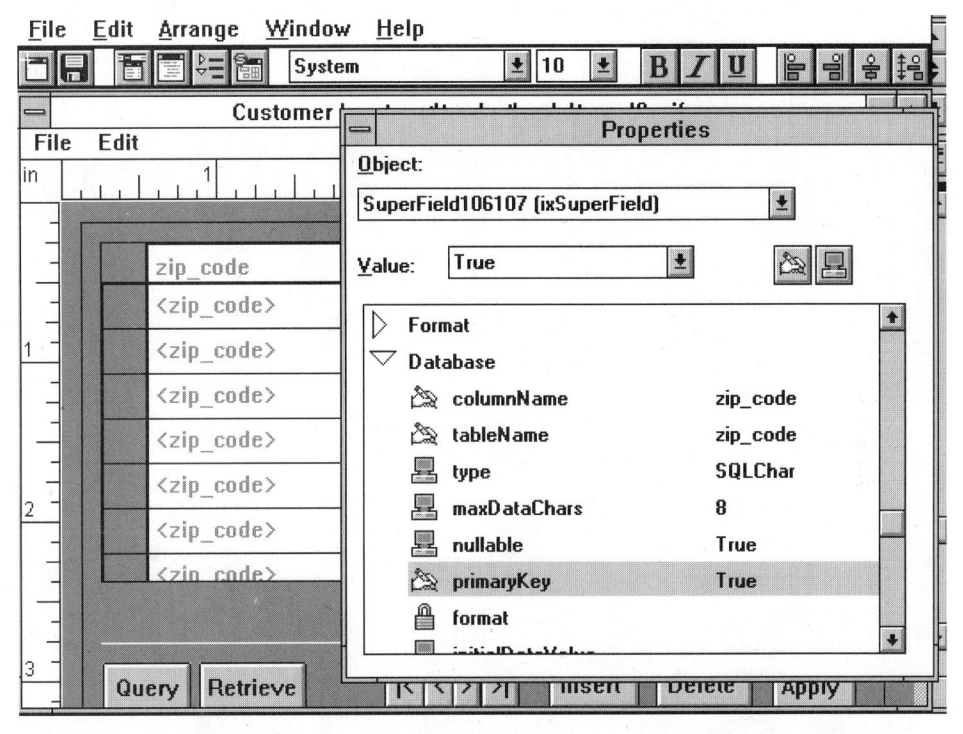

Chapter 7: Creating Application Windows with NewEra 147

Figure 7-15 - Setting Database Properties for SuperTable

The grid-form column widths can be adjusted at runtime by using the cursor to select the column separators in the window and then dragging the separator to the desired width (see Figure 7-16). They cannot be adjusted in this manner in the Window Painter.

With the zip code window, rows can be inserted using the insert button. A number of rows can be inserted and modified at the same time. When the user is ready to apply the changes to the database, the apply button can be selected to apply the data to the database.

No extra coding is needed for this window. All of the functionality needed is provided with the template used to create the window.

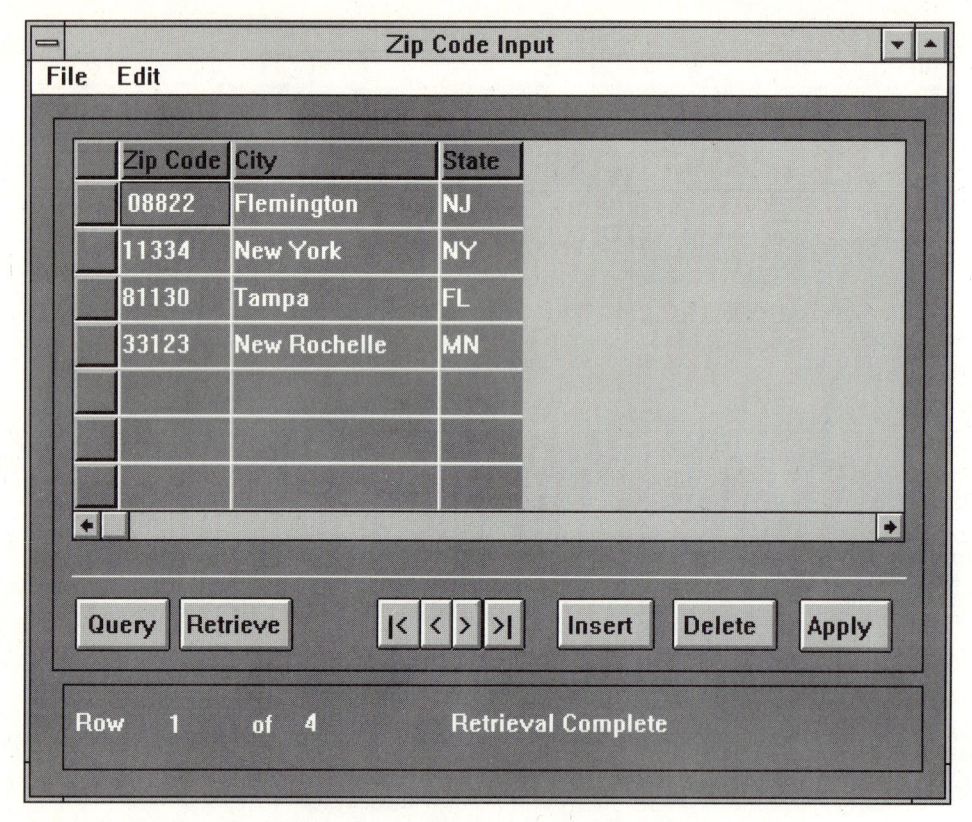

Figure 7-16 - User Resizing Grid Form SuperTable Columns

Interacting Windows

The customer data entry window and the zip code window are part of the same accounts receivable application. It would be reasonable to place these and other windows together in the same application. With Informix-NewEra, this requires that window references be established correctly. This example will demonstrate how to piece together the customer and zip code windows into the same application.

Creating the Main Menu Window

A menu window is first developed. This will encompass a menu that can be used to call different components of the application, as well as buttons that will execute many of the same options.

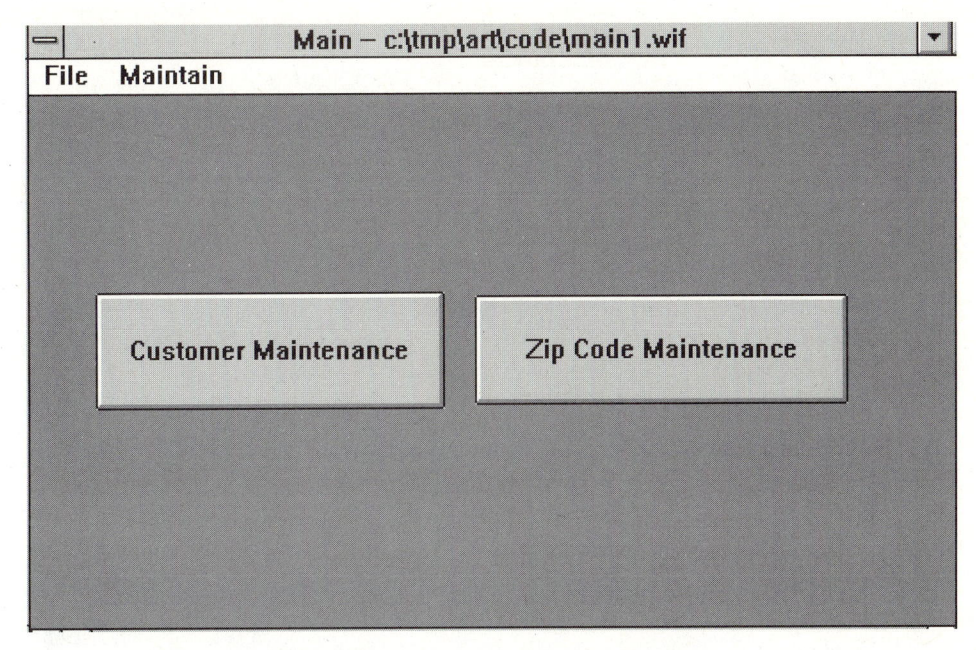

Chapter 7: Creating Application Windows with NewEra

Figure 7-17 - Main Customer Maintenance Window

Establishing Window References

Since the windows for the customer window and the zip code window can be opened from this menu window, the menu window must be able to reference the window objects. This is accomplished by including the header files for the two windows in the pre-header section of the main menu window as shown below.

```
include "custx.4gh"
include "zip2.4gh"
```

The pre-body code section of the menu window must also include statements that define object variables for these windows, as shown below.

```
GLOBAL VARIABLE MainWN MainWindow
global variable CustWN CustWindow
global variable ZipWN  ZipWindow
```

This creates variables for the main window (`MainWN`), the customer window (`CustWN`), and the zip code window (`ZipWN`). These variables are declared with global scope because the windows are referenced in other modules, notably the source code modules that were created with the window.

If developed as separate startup windows, the customer and zip code windows must now be modified to act as different window types. The properties section of the window should be changed to a window type other than `MainTop`. And the pre-header section of the windows should include a declaration for the external variable for the window object, as shown below.

```
external variable CustWN       CustWindow
external variable ZipWN        ZipWindow
global   variable CustListWN   CustListWindow
global   variable FindWN       FindWindow
global   variable CustListLoaded boolean = FALSE
```

This section of code creates external references for the customer window (`CustWN`) and the zip code window (`ZipWN`). These objects are created in the main menu module where the variables are declared as global variables. There are global variables declared for the searchable customer list window (`CustListWN`) and the find window (`FindWN`) which works in conjunction with the search window. These window object variables are declared global because the objects are created in this source code module, not in the main menu window module or some other module.

Opening, Hiding, and Closing the Windows

The `start` event handler of the main menu window is called when the window is opened (it is raised by the `open ixWindow` member function). It is used to create the window objects for the customer and zip code windows as shown below.

```
HANDLER MainWindow::MainWN_start() RETURNING VOID

let CustWN = new CustWindow()
let ZipWN  = new ZipWindow()

call ixSqlConnect::getImplicitConnection().connect("AR")

END HANDLER -- MainWindow::MainWN_start
```

This start event handler will create the window objects for the customer and zip code windows, and then create a connection to the accounts receivable database. The windows are not opened at this point; that will occur when either the user presses a button to execute the option, or the user executes a menu option to start the window. The code to open or show the window will be executed at that point, as shown below.

```
HANDLER ixButton::MainWN_Button145_activate()
    RETURNING VOID
```

Chapter 7: Creating Application Windows with NewEra

```
   if CustWN.getAvailability() = ixVisualObject::unopened or
      CustWN.getAvailability() = ixVisualObject::closed
   then
      call CustWN.open()
      call CustWN.show()
   end if

   END HANDLER -- ixButton::MainWN_Button145_activate

   HANDLER ixButton::MainWN_Button147_activate() RETURNING
   VOID

   if ZipWN.getAvailability() = ixVisualObject::unopened or
      ZipWN.getAvailability() = ixVisualObject::closed
   then
      call ZipWN.open()
      call ZipWN.show()
   end if

   END HANDLER -- ixButton::MainWN_Button147_activate
```

These button handlers test for the whether or not the window is unopened or closed. A call to the `getAvailabilty` member function returns the current state of the window.

The process of creating and opening a window after it's been closed can be tedious and expensive in terms of the memory allocation that must occur to re-create the window object. It is more efficient and requires less code to simply hide the window using the hide member function, and then show the window when the user has elected to use the window again. (One possible problem with this approach is that memory continues to be used by the *hidden* window. On a system with limited memory resources, the programmer may elect to close windows that are not in use in order to free more memory.)

In order to avoid having the window closed by the user, the programmer must avoid using the close member function for the window. But even if the programmer has avoided using this function call, the user still has the capability of closing the window using the GUI system menu. This can be prevented by writing a handler for the window `finish` event triggered by the system menu close. The code for such a handler is shown below.

```
   HANDLER CustWindow::CustWN_finish(byWhom smallint)
            RETURNING BOOLEAN
```

```
if byWhom = ixWindow::ClosedbySysMenu then
   call self.hide()
   return FALSE
else
   return TRUE
end if

END HANDLER -- CustWindow::CustWN_finish
```

Because of the generic window reference (`self.hide`), this code is identical to the code shown above for the finish handler for the customer list window. The code checks to determine that the window has in fact been closed by the system menu. This can be checked since a parameter indicating how the window has been closed is passed into the window.

If the window has been closed via the system menu, then the `byWhom` parameter is set to the value `ixWindow::ClosedbySysMenu`. In this case, the window `hide` function is called (we can use the `self` implicit formal argument since the `finish` handler is part of the window) and the handler returns FALSE indicating that the window should not be closed.

If the window has not been closed by the system menu, then the handler merely returns TRUE allowing the window to be closed.

Chapter 8
Developing Interacting Windows in NewEra

It is not uncommon for business applications to become very complex, largely due to the complexity of the underlying data relationships. Managing this complexity is made easier in a GUI environment with an object-oriented language because portions of the application can be broken into smaller, more manageable components. These components, as demonstrated in this chapter, are often windows which manage portions of the data. Interaction between these components in NewEra simply involves making calls to the member functions of the window objects for the various windows. These windows must continually interact and communicate.

This chapter demonstrates the use of multiple, connected NewEra windows. The example provided is a series of windows used to manage the accounting batches input into the accounts receivable database. There will ultimately be three windows displayed. Each window will interact with another window as the user manipulates their selected data set.

BATCH INPUT WINDOW

Data entry for the accounts receivable data is performed using batches. These batches represent an accounting control that groups a set of source documents together. Batch entry is used for both receivables entry for the entry of bills and associated line items, and payments entry for the recognition of a payment against a bill.

This example will demonstrate the creation of batch data entry for the batch table for the batch header, the bill table for the receivables header record, and the items table for the line items data entry. The application provides three windows to perform these operations.

The first window displayed is the *batch* window (see Figure 8-1). This window contains a set of radio buttons to select either data entry for a receivables batch or a payments batch. The selection of either button will change the title for the "Update" button so that it can be used to enter the receivables or payables batch requested by pressing the radio button.

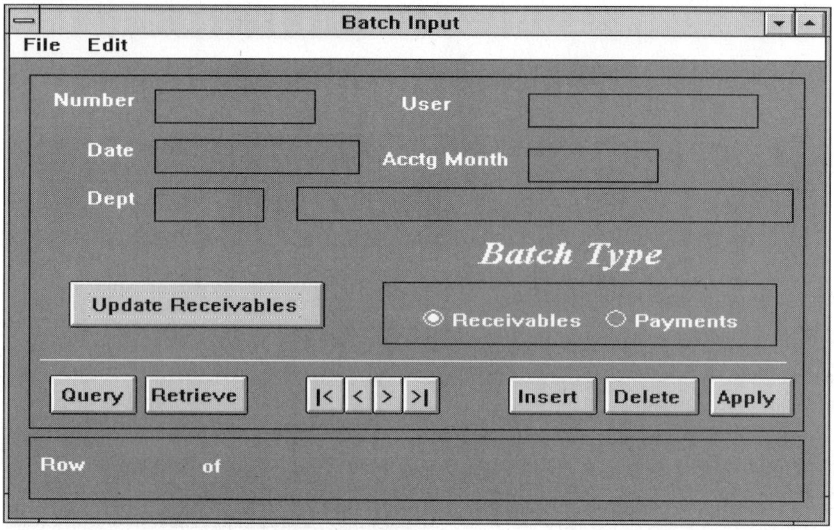

Figure 8-1 - Batch Entry Window

If the payables batch type is chosen using the radio buttons, "enter receivables" is displayed to the button in the middle, left portion of the screen. If this button is pressed by the user, then the receivables input window is displayed (see Figure 8-2). This window is a standard template window that allows record traversal just as the customer window does. But it is bound to the batch header window. If the user has queried or entered a batch number on the batch header window, this batch number is used to retrieve the related receivables entry for that batch.

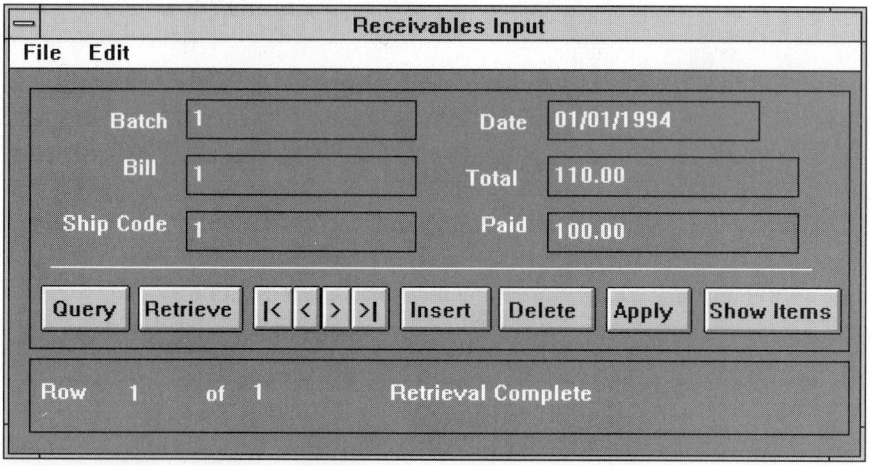

Figure 8-2 - Receivables Entry Window

Both windows can be used simultaneously (see Figure 8-3), and as the user traverses the batch header entries, the related receivables records for the current batch are displayed in the receivables window. The user is given the option to override this functionality and use query by example to query for a batch entry, or they can use the insert key to enter a new batch.

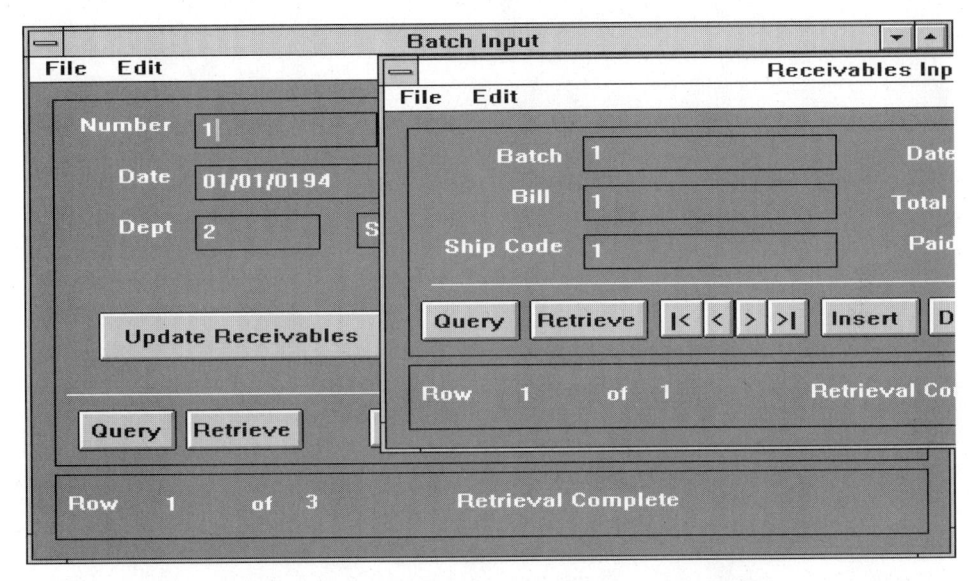

Figure 8-3 - Using Batch and Receivables Entry Windows

Once the user has selected a receivables batch, they can press the "enter items" button to enter the line items for the batch. The line items window will be displayed and will retrieve data based on the receivables number that is currently contained in the receivables window. As the user traverses the data set in the receivables window, the line items window will automatically retrieve and redisplay the data for the receivables header using the new receivables number.

The query-by-example buttons are not available on the line items window since this window requires that the data in it be related to the current data record in the receivables window.

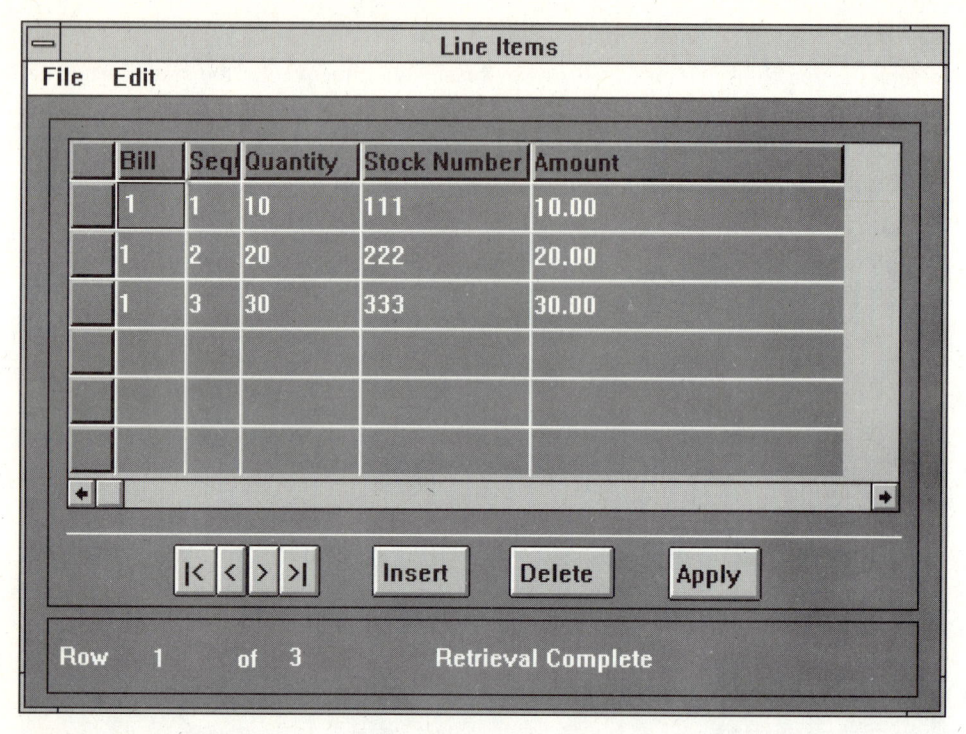

Figure 8-4 - Line Items Entry Window (Connected to Receivables Window)

With all three windows displayed, the user can traverse data in the batch window and trigger a retrieve operation in the receivables window which will in turn trigger a retrieve operation in the line items window (see Figure 8-5). This three-way update of windows is fairly simple to create using the extensive functionality of SuperTable member functions. Retrieval is achieved by calling the retrieve button for the related window. The code for these operations is discussed later in this chapter.

The "Batch Type" Radio Button

The batch header window displays the data to be stored in the batch table and starts the receivables window. Its interaction is only with the receivables window; it is through statements triggered in the receivables window that the line items window is displayed.

The batch type radio button is used to set the batch type. When this button is pressed, the following code is executed:

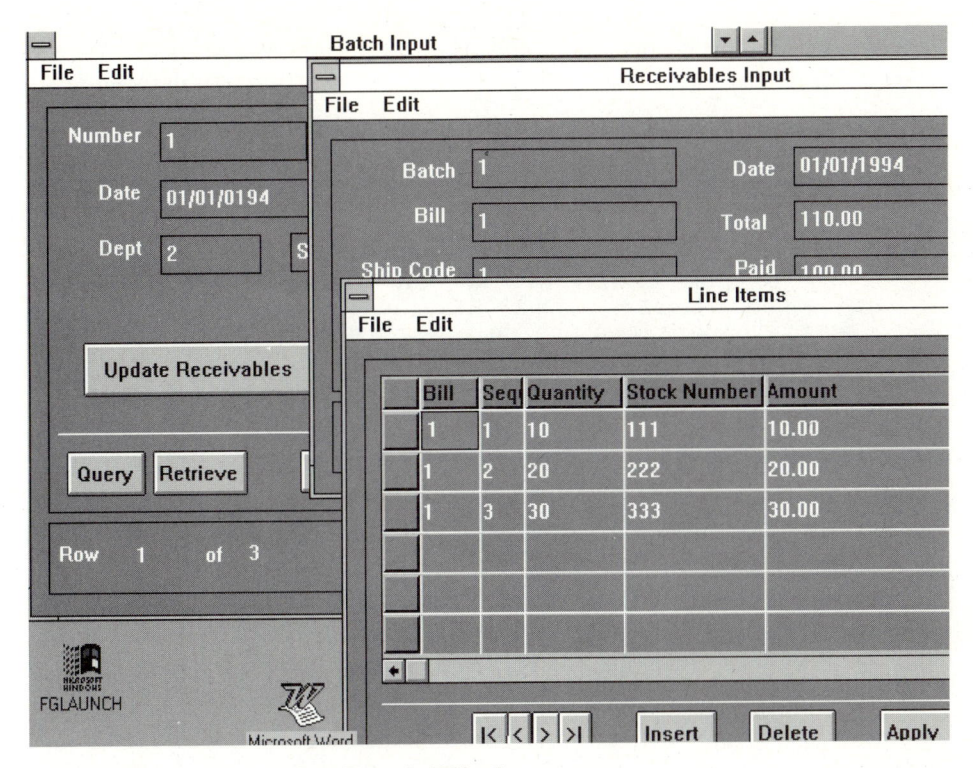

Chapter 8: Developing Interacting Windows in NewEra   157

Figure 8-5 - Interacting Batch Windows

```
HANDLER
ixRadioButton::batchWN_receivables_batchRB_focusIn()
        RETURNING VOID

if self.ispushed() then
   call batchWN.upd_docsBN.setTitle(
                  "Update Receivables" )
end if

END HANDLER

HANDLER ixRadioButton::batchWN_payments_batchRB_focusIn()
        RETURNING VOID

if self.ispushed() then
   call batchWN.upd_docsBN.setTitle( "Update Payments" )
end if

END HANDLER
```

This code sets the button label for the update documents (`upd_docsBN`) button to the correct label. It does this through the `setTitle Ixlabel` member function call.

The Retrieve Operation

The "retrieve" button will call the usual template code to retrieve the data set records and display messages to the window. It will then call the `retrRevPay` function to retrieve receivables records.

```
-- retrieve data for the receivables window
call retrRecvPay()
...
```

The code for the `retrRecvPay` function is shown below. This function is declared in a separate source code module, so it is necessary to include the various window header files before declaring references to the windows. This function will first declare external references for the various window objects it must reference.

The body of the function begins with the declaration of an `ixValue` object used to retrieve the batch number. If the receivables window has not been created for some reason, then the function will return since there is no window for retrieval of the batch information. If the receivables window exists but is unopened, the function will call the `ixWindow open` member function; otherwise the function will call the `ixWindow show` member function.

The function will then retrieve the batch number from the `batchST` SuperTable cell. If the batch number retrieved is non-null, the number is used to create the `selectFilterPart` for the `billST` SuperTable.

Once this step is complete, the `activate` handler for the "retrieve" button in the receivables window is called to retrieve the data. This allows us to take advantage of the additional functionality of the retrieve button that has been coded with the template window. But while doing this, we need to allow the button to be executed from the activate event in the receivables window. This requires that the QBE parameter to the retrieve SuperTable member function be set correctly.

If this parameter is set to TRUE, then the SuperTable will retrieve the query set (the query parameters entered by the user on the keyboard) and build the query string using those values. This behavior is desired if the user has pressed the query button and entered query criteria in the receivables window. In the function shown below, that is not the case. The user has not entered query criteria, instead the code in the function has entered the only query criteria to be used. Setting the QBE parameter to FALSE will cause the SuperTable to ignore the query set and build the query from the SQL string parts that it contains; one of these SQL strings, the `selectFilterPart`, has been set in this example.

Chapter 8: Developing Interacting Windows in NewEra

The QBE mode is set using a member variable for the receivables window. This value defaults to TRUE and is set to that value in the window `start` handler.

```
include "batch2.4gh"
include "recvbl2.4gh"
include "items2.4gh"

external variable itemsWN    itemsWindow
external variable recvblsWN  recvblsWindow
external variable batchWN    batchWindow
function retrRecvPay()
variable batchNumbIV ixValue

-- update and retrieve from the recvbls table,
-- if the recievables window is open
if recvblsWN IS NULL then
    return
end if

if recvblsWN.getAvailability() =
        ixVisualContainer::closed  or
    recvblsWN.getAvailability() =
        ixVisualContainer::unopened  then
        call recvblsWN.open()
else
        call recvblsWN.show()
end if

-- get the batch number from the batch window
let batchNumbIV = batchWN.batchST.getCellvalue(
                colnum:
batchWN.batch_numbSF.getColNum() )
if batchNumbIV IS NULL then
    return
end if

call recvblsWN.billST.selectFilterPart.setValuestr(
        " batch_numb = " ||
        batchNumbIV.getvaluestr() )

let recvblsWN.qbe_mode = FALSE

-- use the retrieve activate button to retrieve records
```

```
-- and display template messages
call recvblsWN.recvbl_retrBN.activate()

end function
```

The Pre-Body Code Section

In the pre-body code section, both the receivables window and the batch window objects are declared as global variables as shown below. The batch window is created in the main module for the window. The receivables window is created when the user presses the "retrieve receivables" button.

```
global variable batchWN batchWindow
global variable recvblsWN recvblsWindow
```

The Receivables Window

The receivables window displays and allows modification of receivables master table information. The records displayed in this window are related to the batch header record using the batch number. The retrieve operation for this window is described below.

The Receivables Window Retrieve Operation

As mentioned above, the retrieve operation uses the standard template code to perform the retrieve. A few changes are made to this code as shown below.

The receivables window must distinguish between programmatic execution of the "retrieve" button event handler by the batch window, or execution by the user pressing the "retrieve" button in the receivables window. This is accomplished by simply determining whether or not the "retrieve" button in the receivables window has received keyboard focus.

Before the retrieve button is pressed, it will receive keyboard focus. This is an indication that the retrieve operation has been started by a button press event from the receivables window and **not** by a call to the retrieve button activate event handler from the batch window. When this is the case, the QBE mode flag will be set to TRUE, which will prompt the SuperTable to retrieve the receivables window query set (as stored in the SuperTable) and use that information to build the query.

```
HANDLER ixButton::recvblsWN_recvbl_retrBN_focusIn()
        RETURNING VOID

let recvblsWN.qbe_mode = TRUE
```

Chapter 8: Developing Interacting Windows in NewEra

```
END HANDLER—ixButton::recvblsWN_recvbl_retrBN_focusIn
```

The retrieve button code will use the QBE flag when it calls the retrieve function as shown below.

```
LET ok = superTable.retrieve(
                QBE: recvblsWN.qbe_mode )
...
-- get the line items for this bill
call retrItems()
```

The retrieve button will also retrieve data for the line items window, if the window is opened. It performs this function with a call to the `retrItems` function as shown below.

This function declares an `ixValue` variable to retrieve the bill number from the receivable window. It then runs a series of tests to determine the state of the items window. Once the function is reasonably certain that the window is opened, it then retrieves the bill number from the receivables window. This bill number is then used to build the `selectFilterPart` of the query string for the items SuperTable table. The activate handler for the items window "retrieve" button operation is then called directly to retrieve the data. Since the user is not allowed to query on this screen, the code for the "retrieve" button activate event can set the QBE mode to FALSE as shown below.

```
-- query criteria is set elsewere !
LET ok = superTable.retrieve( QBE: FALSE )
   ....

function retrItems()
variable bill_numbIV ixValue
variable okval       Boolean

if itemsWN IS NULL then
    return
end if

if itemsWN.getAvailability() = ixVisualObject::closed or
   itemsWN.getAvailability() = ixVisualObject::unopened
                                                    then
     call itemsWN.open()
else
     call itemsWN.show()
end if
```

```
-- retrieve the line_items, if they exist
let bill_numbIV = recvblsWN.billST.getCellvalue(
    colnum: recvblsWN.bill_numbSF.getColNum())

call itemsWN.itemsST.selectFilterPart.setValuestr(
    " bill_numb = " || bill_numbIV.getvaluestr() )

-- activate this button
call itemsWN.items_rtrBN.activate()

end function
```

Calling the activate handler directly allows all of the handler code to be used. This is a convenient way to gain access to the functionality of that handler.

The Line Items Window

The line items window displays line items for the receivables or bill chosen in the receivables window. The retrieval of data in this window is controlled completely by the receivables window; query-by-example is not allowed; this is enforced by removing the standard SuperTable Query button. Once there is an active data set, the user can move through the data using standard grid-form SuperTable facilities.

The Retrieve Operation

The retrieval operation for the window is controlled by the receivables window. The receivables window will call the activate handler for the SuperTable retrieve button. In order to assure that the SuperTable uses the query criteria that has been inserted into the `SelectFilterPart` programmatically, the QBE mode is set to false in the "retrieve" button activate handler as shown above.

ADDING ADDITIONAL FUNCTIONALITY

This example has demonstrated a number of the more useful features available in GUI environments: interacting multiple windows and the use of radio buttons and grid-form SuperTables. But there are other issues to consider in the programming of data entry windows.

Using Transactions with SuperTables

In order to maintain the integrity of the database, transaction managment should be used. By default, the SuperTable class has no facilities for transaction logging. Most notably, it does not automatically commit transactions after completion of SQL operations.

Chapter 8: Developing Interacting Windows in NewEra 163

The NewEra Connectivity Class Library (CCL) operates with an implicit *begin work*; there is no explicit "begin work" operation; there is only a `commit work` statement. All activity in the logging database is performed within a transaction. What is needed, therefore, are commit work statements after SQL operations.

These `commit work` statements are not part of the SuperTable class as provided by Informix. But they could easily be added to a template or to an extended SuperTable class to be used with transactions. What must be considered, however, is the particular set of SQL operations to be grouped together in a transaction. In the example above, an insert into all three tables, the `batch`, `bill`, and `line_items` tables, should be grouped as a single transaction. The `commit work` should come after the completion of the `apply` SuperTable member function call that applies an insert into all three tables.

If there were no explicit CCL/Informix transaction call with an explicit "commit work" request in a NewEra application being used in a logging database, then all of the database actions of the SuperTable would be rolled back when the application terminates. Placement of the CCL/INFORMIX commit work statement is therefore crucial.

Example: Transaction Management in SuperTable Handlers

The following provides an example of handling a transaction within a SuperTable `SQLinsert` handler. This is one possible alternative to handling transactions with SuperTables.

In this example, the `SQLInsert` handler is overridden to manage transactions. This handler is passed an `ixRow` object which contains the row to insert into the database.

It calls the `doSQLInsert` member function to insert the data into the database. This function returns an integer variable indicating the status result of the insert operation. This variable is tested to determine whether or not the insert was successful. If the insert was successful, the status variable will be set to a value of `SQL_Success`. If this is the case, then the `transact` SuperTable member function is called for the implicit database connection as returned by the `getConnection ixSQLStmt` member function. The `transact` function is passed the value of `ixSQLConnect::SQL_Commit` and will commit the transaction to the database. If the status returned is some value other than `SQL_Success`, then the insert operation is rolled back.

```
HANDLER ixSuperTable::CustWN_custST_SQLInsert(
        theRow ixRow)
    RETURNING INTEGER

variable stat integer = doSQLInsert( theRow )
```

```
    if stat = ixSQLConnect::SQL_Success then
       call getConnection().transact(
                     ixSQLConnect::SQL_Commit )
    else
      call getConnection().transact(
                     ixSQLConnect::SQL_Rollback )
    end if

    return stat

    END HANDLER -- ixSuperTable::CustWN_custST_SQLInsert
```

Transactions with Multiple Rows

The approach shown above provides for the successful insert of a single row and commits each row after insert. But this approach does not provide for the successful insert of multiple rows. If multiple related rows were being inserted into a set of tables, then the commit should follow the call to the `ixSuperTable apply` SuperTable member function. Some logic would be needed to determine whether any of the related insert operations failed. If any one of the inserts failed, then the entire transaction would have to be rolled back.

When a number of rows are being applied, the apply function would be called (this is the member function called when the "Apply All" SuperTable button is pasted into the window). If it were desirable to treat the set of inserts as a set, then it would be best to manage the transaction after the `apply` call. This would be the case with a detail set of rows inserted into a grid-form SuperTable; rows which could represent the line items for a customer invoice. This transaction management could be accomplished by adding code to the `afterApply` SuperTable event handler as shown below.

Transaction Management in the `afterApply` Event

In this example, the transaction management is handled in the SuperTable `afterApply` event. In the event that the apply sequence has updated all rows to the database without error, this handler will commit the complete set of data.

In the event there has been an error during apply processing, the apply loop will cease processing and set the `errorStmt ixSQLstmt` object to the statement that caused the error. The `afterApply` handler will then be called and, after examining the `errorStmt`, will roll-back all the statements that have been executed. This handler appears in the line items grid-form SuperTable window where this roll-back logic is appropriate.

The `afterApply` handler will first examine the `errorStmt`. If this `ixSQLStmt` object is NULL, then there were no errors and the `ixSQLConnect` transact member function is called to commit the previously applied rows to the database. The handler will then return TRUE.

If the `errorStmt` is not null and the ODBC error code indicates there has been an error, the `transact` member function is called to rollback **all** rows that have been applied previously. The `getConnection ixSuperTable` member function is called to return a reference to the `ixSQLConnect` object for the SuperTable. This reference is used to call the transact function to roll back the rows previously updated to the database. The `afterApply` event handler will return FALSE under these conditions.

If the `errorStmt` object exists but does not indicate an SQL error has occurred, the transact `ixSQLConnect` member function will be called to commit all rows that have been previously applied.

```
HANDLER ixSuperTable::itemsWN_itemsST_afterApply()
        RETURNING BOOLEAN

if errorStmt IS NULL   then    -- there was no error
   call getConnection().transact(
               ixSQLConnect::SQL_Commit )
   return TRUE

end if

if errorStmt.getODBCErrorCode() != ixSQLStmt::SQL_Success
                                                      then
   call getConnection().transact(
           ixSQLConnect::SQL_Rollback )
   return FALSE
else
   call getConnection().transact(
                   ixSQLConnect::SQL_Commit )
   return TRUE
end if

END HANDLER -- ixSuperTable::itemsWN_itemsST_afterApply
```

Locking Issues

With NewEra *optimistic* locking, there is an assumption that there is little contention for the data. With optimistic locking, the rows are retrieved from the database without locks. When the rows are applied to the database, a lock is set before the update operation, the row is then updated, and the lock is released. This process is repeated on all of the rows in the data set.

With optimistic locking, there is significant potential for stale data, a situation where a user attempts to update a row that has already been updated by another user.

NewEra provides a stale data event, but it is up to the programmer to write an effective handler.

With *pessimistic* locking, rows are locked as soon as the user modifies the data. This locking will occur during the data set traversal operation. When the user modifies a row and then attempts to move to the next row, the `lockrow` SuperTable member function is called to lock the changed row in the database. This lock is then held until the changed data row is applied.

Pessimistic locking reduces the possibility that the row will be modified by another user while the user using the application modifies the data. Still, there is that possibility with pessimistic locking since there is a period of time where the user has retrieved the row and not yet modified the row. During this period of time another user could update the row in the database.

A solution that would eliminate the possibility of stale data would lock the row when the user displays the row to the window. The `beforeRow` handler could be used to lock the row. Once the user was finished with the row, the `afterRow` handler could be used to release the lock.

Programming Field Validations and Lookups

One of the strengths of Informix-4GL was the ability to control and handle screen input field traversal. That capability is still present in the NewEra language with several additional capabilities.

The following example demonstrates field validation and data retrieval and display with the NewEra language. This code is used in the batch input window in the `afterCell` event for the department code field. The user enters a department code. After the focus leaves the department code field, the field is validated. If the field is valid, then the department name is retrieved and displayed to the department name field.

An `ixValue` object is first declared to hold the department code retrieved from the department code field. An `ixSQLStmt` object is declared and instantiated using the implicit connection (the default for the `ixSQLStmt` constructor). An `ixRow` variable is declared to contain the department record and a Boolean variable is declared to hold the return value.

The department code is retrieved from the SuperTable cell containing the department code and stored in an `ixValue` data object. The department code value is then used to create an SQL statement to retrieve the department name from the database. Note that single quotes are placed around the department code. Because of the data type conversion capabilities of Informix-SQL, the department code will be converted correctly to the data type of the column of the left side of the `where` clause expression.

Once the SQL statement has been prepared and executed, the rows can then be fetched into the `ixRow` object declared earlier. Since we assert there should be only one row available in the department code table for the department code the user has entered,

Chapter 8: Developing Interacting Windows in NewEra 167

there is no need to create a loop to retrieve the data. A single `fetch ixSQLStmt` member function call is used to retrieve the data.

If no data have been found by the `fetch` call, then we can assume that the user has entered an invalid department code. The ODBC error code of the ixSQLStmt object is tested for this condition using the `getODBCErrorCode ixSQLStmt` member function call.

If an error has been found, then an error message is displayed using the `msgbox` function described in chapter 9. The current cell is set to the department code SuperTable cell using the `ixSuperTable setCurrentCell` member function. This will effectively force the user to enter a correct department code.

If a valid department code has been entered, the `setCellValue` SuperTable member function is called to insert the name of the department for the department code the user has entered. The value of the department name is retrieved from the `ixRow` object that holds the values retrieved from the database with the select statement. Note that the `ixRow getVal` member function returns an `ixValue` data type. The `getValueStr` member function call is then used to retrieve a character string pointer for the value stored in the `ixValue` object.

```
HANDLER ixSuperField::batchWN_deptCodeSF_afterCell(
          rowNum INTEGER)
       RETURNING VOID
variable deptCode ixValue
variable sqlStmt ixSqlStmt = new ixSqlStmt()
variable deptRec ixRow
variable ok Boolean

-- validate the dept code and get the description
let deptCode = batchWN.batchST.getCellValue(
          colnum: batchWN.deptCodeSF.getColNum() )

call sqlStmt.prepare(
  "select description from department where dept_code = "
   || "'"
   || deptCode.getValueStr()
   || "'" )

call sqlStmt.execute()
call sqlStmt.fetch() returning deptRec

if sqlStmt.getODBCErrorCode() =
                ixSqlStmt::SQL_No_Data_Found  then
```

```
          call msgBox( message: "Invalid Department Code" )
          call batchWN.batchST.setCurrentCell(
                  colnum: batchWN.deptCodeSF.getColNum() )
              returning ok
   else
       call batchWN.batchST.setCellValue(
              colnum: batchWN.deptNameSF.getColNum(),
              newstrval: deptRec.getVal(1).getValueStr() )
                returning ok
   end if

   END HANDLER -- ixSuperField::batchWN_deptCodeSF_afterCell
```

Using Help with NewEra

Providing application help is an important component of any application. Informix-NewEra provides application help in two flavors: Informix-4GL style help windows and Windows-style help. The following example demonstrates the use of Informix-4GL style help windows with NewEra, but the use of Windows style help would only involve changing the `helpStyle ixApp` member variable to `ixApp::systemHelp` and preparing the correct files with help text.

In the example below, the `start` event for the window is used to initialize the help. The `ixApp helpStyle` member variable is set to the `ixApp I4GLHelp` constant. The `ixApp helpFile` is set to an `ixString` object containing the name of the help file.

```
HANDLER CustWindow::CustWN_start() RETURNING VOID

-- initialize help
let ixApp::helpStyle = ixApp::I4GLHelp

-- use this line if Windows help is used
-- let ixApp::helpStyle = ixApp::systemHelp
let ixApp::helpFile = new ixString(
"c:\\tmp\\art\\code\\cust.iem" )
   ...
```

The application controls must then be assigned help numbers. These help numbers will be used to retrieve the help for the window controls. Virtually any object that can take focus can be assigned help. The general properties for an object are used to assign a help number (see Figure 8-6).

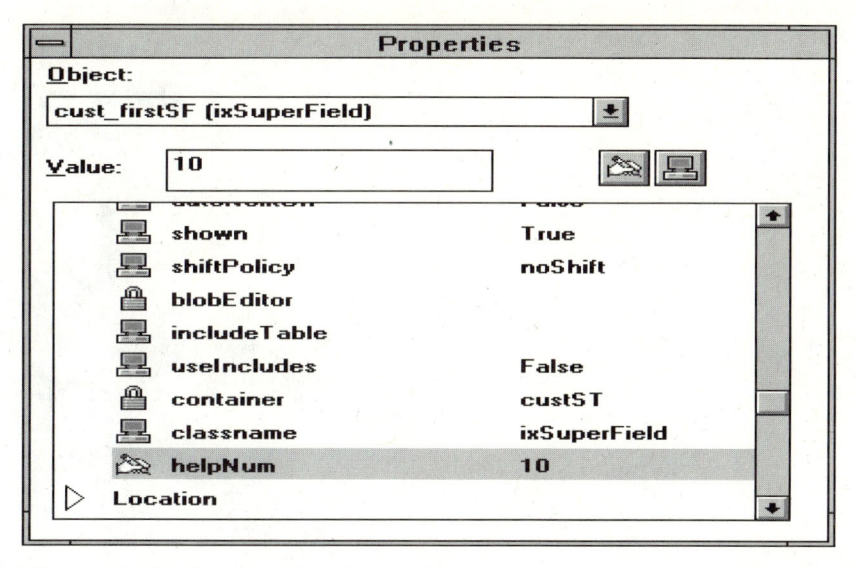

Chapter 8: Developing Interacting Windows in NewEra — 169

[Properties dialog showing Object: cust_firstSF (ixSuperField), Value: 10, with a list including shown=True, shiftPolicy=noShift, blobEditor, includeTable, useIncludes=False, container=custST, classname=ixSuperField, helpNum=10, Location]

Figure 8-6 - Setting the Help Number

The final step in adding help to a NewEra application is to insert the `displayHelp ixApp` member function call into the application. In this example, the `displayHelp` call is inserted into the menu. The menu handler then makes the call to get the current control focus. The `displayHelp` call is then made from that control. The `displayHelp` function will then determine the help number of the control with focus and display the help for that number (see Figure 8-7).

```
HANDLER ixMenu::CustWN_Menu120_activate() RETURNING VOID
call ixApp::getCtrlwithFocus().displayHelp()
END HANDLER -- ixMenu::CustWN_Menu120_activate
```

Using Error Logging with NewEra

The default error handling for NewEra does not log the errors to a file. Since users are notorious for removing and forgetting error messages, it is often useful to log errors to a file to be inspected at a later time. An example of such error logging is shown below.

```
Module name   : module1
Line number   : 0
Error number  : 0
Error           0 has occurred at 03:07:18
Module name   : module1
Line number   : 0
Error number  : 0
Error           0 has occurred at 03:07:22
```

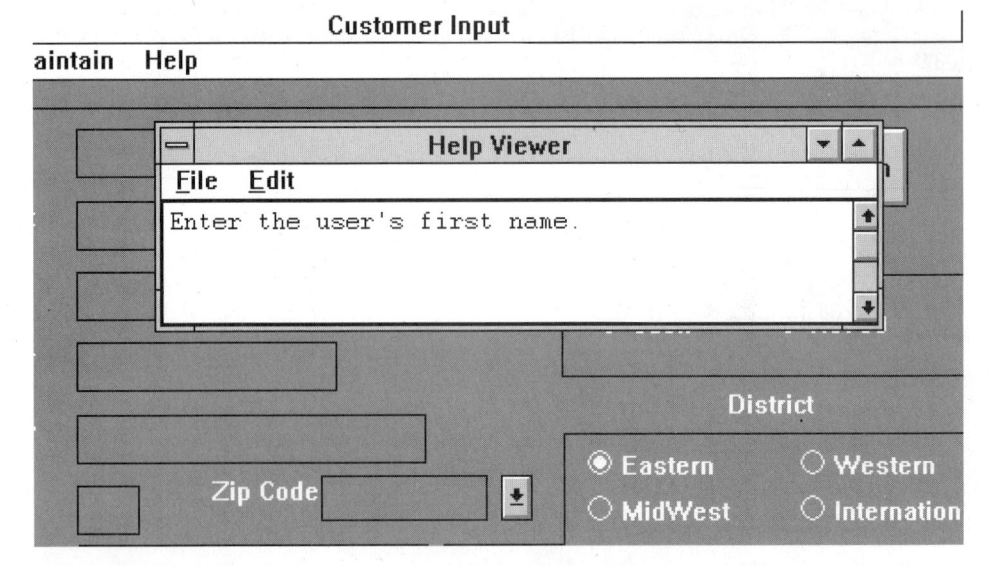

170   Informix-NewEra: A Guide for Application Developers

Figure 8-7 - NewEra Informix-4GL Style Help

The NewEra `rtError` event handler handles NewEra errors by default. This default handler calls the `showRtError` function to display the error number and message and then returns (see Figure 8-8). In this example, the default event handler is extended. Note that the `showRtError` function called by the default handler is still called in this solution to display the error message, but before the function is called, a log entry is made to an error log with the time, error number, and other information as shown above.

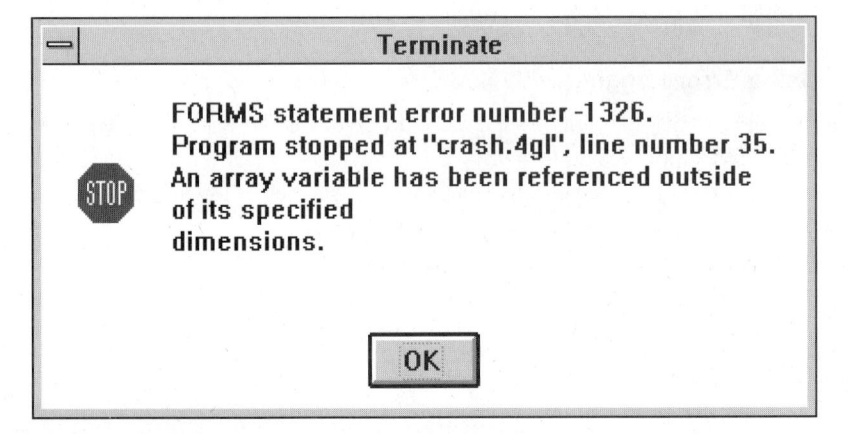

Figure 8-8 - Default NewEra Error Message

Chapter 8: Developing Interacting Windows in NewEra

The code below contains a fragment of the source code module for a NewEra window. An error log object is declared to be a class `ixErrorLog` and is instantiated with the name of the error log. An `ixApp` object is also declared to gain a reference to the current application.

The handler code appears next. The handler receives a number of parameters containing information about the error. A character string variable is declared to hold the string of error information. The `ixErrorLog logError` member function is then used to write the character string to the error log. The `showRtError` function is then called to display information on the error to the screen.

```
GLOBAL VARIABLE Window1 Window1
variable errlog ixErrorLog = new ixErrorLog(
                                 "crash.log" )
variable thisApp ixApp = ixApp::getApp()

handler ixApp::rtErrorLog( errnum integer,
                           severity smallint,
                           errData1 char(*),
                           errData2 char(*),
                           errData3 char(*) )

variable str char(*)

let str = "Error " || errnum
        || " has occurred at "
        || time

call errLog.logError( "module1", 0, errnum, str )

call showrtError( errnum,
                  severity,
                  errData1,
                  errData2,
                  errData3 )

end handler
```

The main module for the window creates the window object and opens the window. The handler for the crash demonstration button appears next in the source code. This handler will force an array bounds violation which will be trapped by the p-code runner. It does this by creating an array with a dimension of 10 and then attempting to reference element 100 of the array in a NewEra `let` statement. This will trigger the error handling event for the application.

```
MAIN

  LET Window1 = NEW Window1()
  CALL Window1.open()
  RETURN

END MAIN

HANDLER ixButton::Window1_CrashBN_activate()
          RETURNING VOID
variable x array[10] of char(1)
variable n smallint

let n = 100
let x[n] = "1"
END HANDLER -- ixButton::Window1_CrashBN_activate
```

The following code is the constructor for the error log demonstration window. This contains the standard NewEra window constructor code. The window instantiation parameters are passed to the constructor for `ixWindow` and a button is created to start the demonstration application. A `handle` statement is then used to attach the `rtError` event to the `rtErrorLog` event handler.

```
FUNCTION Window1::Window1(
   geometry ixGeometry,
   appearance ixAppearance,
   windowStyle SMALLINT,
   title CHAR(*),
   containingWindow ixWindow,
   enabled BOOLEAN,
   icon CHAR(*),
   shown BOOLEAN,
   helpFile CHAR(*),
   helpNum INTEGER,
   name CHAR(*)
)
  : ixWindow(
     containingWindow : containingWindow,
     name : name,
     enabled : enabled,
```

Chapter 8: Developing Interacting Windows in NewEra

```
      shown : shown,
      helpNum : helpNum,
      geometry : geometry,
      appearance : appearance,
      helpFile : helpFile,
      title : title,
      icon : icon,
      windowStyle : windowStyle
)

VARIABLE itemList ixVector
VARIABLE includeTable ixRow
VARIABLE result INTEGER

LET result = 0

LET CrashBN = NEW ixButton(
   geometry : NEW ixGeometry(
         top : 1095,
         left : 1230,
         height : 1140,
         width : 2910
   ),
   appearance : NEW ixAppearance(
         fontName : NULL,
         fontSize : NULL,
         fontBold : NULL,
         fontItalic : NULL,
         fontUnderline : NULL,
         foreColor : NULL,
         backColor : NULL
   ),
   title : "CrashIT",
   enabled : TRUE,
   tabIndex : NULL,
   tabEnabled : TRUE,
   shown : TRUE,
   helpNum : 0,
   theDefault : FALSE,
   name : "CrashBN",
   container : SELF
)
```

```
    HANDLE CrashBN.activate WITH
      ixButton::Window1_CrashBN_activate

    handle thisApp.rtError with ixApp::rtErrorLog

END FUNCTION -- Window1::Window1
```

Chapter 9
Creating Class Libraries

Much has been said about the power of object-oriented programming. Beyond the hype, object-oriented programming, in essence, is a convenient means of packaging code. It is a means of writing code that goes beyond structured programming and provides facilities that add safety and controls to the process of packaging code.

In structured programming with languages like Informix-4GL, function libraries could be created and distributed to programmers. These libraries could also contain global variables for use by the programmers. These libraries could contain internal functions and variables that were used by the library functions but were not designed for programmer use.

A weakness of the structured languages was that there was no facility for restricting programmers from functions and data shared among the library functions. A resourceful programmer could modify a global variable or could rewrite a shared function. Informix-4GL and most 3GL languages could not prevent programmers from making these changes.

But object-oriented languages have provided this functionality almost from their inception. Most of the object-oriented facilities and controls found in C++, one of the most robust and used object-oriented languages, have found their way into Informix-NewEra. The result is a language with the object-oriented power of C++ combined with the safety of COBOL or BASIC and the structured language facilities of C or ALGOL.

With Informix-NewEra, class functions and data can be declared to have *public*, *private*, or *shared* scope, thus providing programmers with a means of limiting user access to library components.

And much of the robustness lacking in Informix-4GL has been added to Informix-NewEra. Dynamic memory allocation and call-by-reference have been added through the object facilities. Constants are available, a Boolean data type has been added, external variable references are available, and files can be *included* in source code modules.

The language parser is also more robust and complete than its Informix-4GL counterpart. A very significant capability is the ability of the language to return an object reference from a function call. This is the core capability that allows a piece of generic code to access a component of that window using a call to `getWindow` to retrieve the object reference.

Using inheritance, a set of functions can be built upon the features of other functions. This can be done in a structured manner. Programmers familiar with the functions of a class low on the hierarchy can transfer the knowledge of those calls to the higher level functions. The functions contained in the `ixVisualObject` class are available throughout virtually all of the window facilities. A programmer familiar with many of these core functions knows that they can use these functions in the classes that have inherited from the `ixVisualObject` class. There is no need to learn a new set of functions since the core functionality has been *inherited* for the programmer.

These are not trivial features. The strength of a language begins to become an issue as the complexity of an application grows. As more and more complex logic must be coded into an application, the ability for a language to express complexity in an elegant manner becomes more of an issue. This is where simple tools without a language component begin to fail. This is where Informix-NewEra will shine.

BUILDING A CLASS LIBRARY

The process of building a class library involves only a few simple steps. This chapter will present the common example of deriving a class from an existing class. This is how the capabilities of a class library can be modified. The beauty of object-oriented programming is that it can be done in a manner that will allow the derived class to inherit all of the functionality of its parent class. And since it is possible for the designer of the class to limit the ability of the programmer to override and thus change the operation of specific class functions, an element of safety is added to the process.

The Database Aware List Box Class

The example below presents the process of creating a database aware list box shown in chapter 7; it allows a list box to be bound to a SuperTable cell and a database table or tables. The list box will load data from the database table or tables. When the user selects an item from the list, the SuperTable cell is automatically updated with their selection (see Figure 9-1).

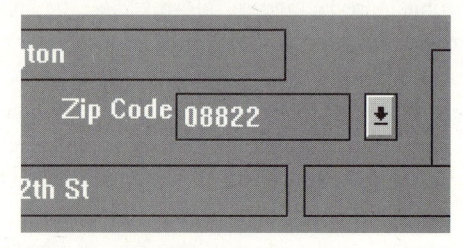

Figure 9-1 - The Zip Code List Box

The goal of creating this class was to allow a list box to be created to display a list of data from a table or tables in the database. When the user has chosen an item from this list, the item chosen will be placed in a predesignated SuperTable cell.

The object was to make using this list box as simple as possible. The list box should automatically handle the select event to place the data in the designated SuperTable cell. And starting the list box should be as simple as making a single function call.

To use the `dbelist` list box, the programmer must perform two steps. First, the programmer must paste the list box control over the SuperTable cell that will be supplied with data from the list box. The list box class property should be set to the `dbelist` class. The list box should be sized correctly to hide the SuperTable cell beneath the list box. And as with all other list boxes, the height of the list box should be adequate enough to display several rows of data.

The next and last step in using the list box is to insert an initialization function call into the `start` event handler or the window constructor for the window. This function call will take parameters for building the SQL statement to retrieve the data for the list box, and the SuperTable and SuperField reference for the SuperTable cell where the data will be inserted.

Programming a list box to perform this functionality from scratch would be difficult. Since several list box controls already exist, it would be best to use the code for one of these list boxes and customize the behavior to suit our needs.

In this example, we have chosen the `ixEditListBox` class to be the class from which to derive our list box. Our list box expands on this list box class by populating the list box with data and retrieving the selected item and inserting it into a SuperTable field. In order to load the list box, the list box class will have to be extended to include several functions for the retrieval of data from the database. This data can be inserted into the list box using existing `ixEditListBox` member functions.

In order to take the selected item and insert it into a SuperTable cell, a reference to the SuperTable cell would have to be retained by the class and the `select` event for the list box class would have to be bound to a customized handler. This custom handler would retrieve the selected item from the list box and insert it into the SuperTable cell. The following sections discuss a custom list box class that performs these functions.

The `dbelist` Class Header File

The header file for the database aware list box contains a set of include statements and the class definitions for the expanded list box class. The include statements retrieve definitions for the Informix-supplied edit list box class (`ixelstbx.4gh`). This is the class from which the `dbelist` class is being derived. The `general.4gh` file is included because it contains a variety of general use functions that are included in this file and are used by the database aware list box. The SuperField class is included because the `ixSuperField` data type must be recognized by the compiler.

```
include system "ix4gl.4gh"
include system "ixelstbx.4gh"
include system "ixSupFld.4gh"
include "general.4gh"
```

The class definition for `dbelist` follows. The class is derived from the `ixEditListBox` class and the class definition statement indicates this with the "derived from" clause.

Next, several variables are declared to contain values needed by the `dbelist` object in order to service the list box. A `query_string` variable will be used to hold the query string to be executed to retrieve the data for the list box. The `bind_SuperTable` is declared to be type `ixSuperTable` and `bind_SuperField` is declared to be of type `ixSuperField`. These variables will hold an object reference to the SuperTable and SuperField where the expanded list box class must insert the item the user selected.

```
class dbelist derived from ixEditListBox
-- store the data retrieval query
public variable query_string      ixString
public variable bind_SuperTable ixSuperTable
public variable bind_SuperField ixSuperField
```

The `init_list` function is called for the object to register the database aware list box. This function call makes the object aware of the table, columns, and optional filter criteria to be used to create the SQL statement to be used to load the list box. It is also passed the name of the SuperTable and SuperField to be used to store the selected list box item.

The assumption is that this function will be called before the user begins to manipulate the window with the list box. This would be done best within a window `start` event handler or as part of the code for the constructor extension, where the function would be called when the window is instantiated.

```
-- Call this from window start() event or constructor
   extension
-- Stores appropriate values into the public variables
public  function init_list( bind_SuperField ixSuperField,
            bind_SuperTable ixSuperTable,
            list_table      char(*),
            list_column     char(*),
            where_clause    char(*) : NULL )
```

Chapter 9: Creating Class Libraries

The constructor for the database aware list box is called when the list box is created. It is currently necessary for the constructor for the class being created to receive **all** of the parameters for the base class, the Informix supplied class the Window Painter has knowledge of. This is because the Window Painter will generate the constructor for the Informix class (in this case, the `ixEditListBox` class) in the Window Painter generated code. This constructor will include all of the parameters for the default class for the tool selected from the tool bar, the `ixEditListBox` class, but the code will be created to call the constructor for the new class, the `dbelist` class. The constructor for the `dbelist` class is shown below.

```
-- dbelist class constructor
function dbelist(container    ixVisualContainer,
           name        CHAR (* )       : NULL,
           enabled     BOOLEAN         : TRUE,
           shown       BOOLEAN         : TRUE,
           helpNum     INTEGER         : 0,
           geometry    ixGeometry      : NULL,
           appearance  ixAppearance    : NULL,
           tabIndex    SMALLINT        :
ixControl::defaultTabOrder,
           tabEnabled  BOOLEAN         : TRUE,
           style       SMALLINT        : singleSelect,
           sorted      BOOLEAN         : TRUE,
           itemList    ixVector        : NULL ,
           dropDown    smallint        : 0
   )
```

The next section of the header file contains the function signatures for the `dbelist` class member functions. Several of these functions will be used to service the handlers for the class. The `getSelection` member function will be used to handle the `select` event for the list box. And the `loadData` function will be used to load the data into the list box.

```
-- This will insert the selected value from the listbox
-- into the bind_to_field
public function getSelection( )

-- loads the data for the list box
public function loadData( )

end class
```

The `dbelist` Class Member Functions

A separate source code module is used for the `dbelist` class member functions. These functions can be entered in the include file with the class definition, but in the event the include file is included in more than one file in a set of source code modules being linked together, the link process will indicate that the functions have been multiply defined. For this reason, it is best to include the member functions in another source code module.

In the `dbelist.4gl` file is listed below, the handlers for the `dbelist` events are declared. These handlers do little more than call the member functions for the `dbelist` class. The self designation can be used since the handlers belong to the class and the `self` notation will resolve to the current object class. The `select` event for the handler will call the `getSelection` `dbelist` member function. And the `activate` event will call the `loadData` `dbelist` member function.

```
include "dbelist.4gh"

handler dbelist::dbelist_select()

    call self.getSelection()

end handler

handler dbelist::dbelist_activate()

    call self.loadData()

end handler
```

The `getSelection` Member Function

The code for the `getSelection` `debelist` member function is shown below. This function is called by the `select` event for the list box. The select event is inherited from the `ixList` box class.

The `getSelection` function must retrieve the data selected in the list box and insert that data into the bound SuperTable cell. It will then shift the focus to that cell. (It is this shift of focus that allows the insertion of data into that field to raise other events.)

A character string variable is declared to hold the string returned by the `getItembyNumber` call. The `getItembyNumber` `ixEditListBox` member function call is used to retrieve the character string of the selected item. Since the `getItembyNumber` call requires an integer to indicate the position of the selected item in the list, the `getSelectedItem` call is used to retrieve the item number of the selected item. The character string retrieved is then inserted into the bound SuperTable cell. The stored reference to the bound SuperTable (`bind_SuperTable`) is used to call the `ixSuperTable setCellValue` member function. The bound SuperField reference is used to get the column number of the bound SuperField to be used in the `setCellValue` function call.

Once the data item has been placed in the bound SuperTable cell, the focus is placed into the SuperField using the reference to the bound SuperField. An event handler written for the focus event on the SuperField could use this focus event to initiate some other action, such as a lookup or validation.

```
function dbelist::getSelection( )
variable str char(11)
variable retval smallint

-- get the string value of the selection
let str = self.getItembyNumber( itemnum:
self.getSelectedItem() )

-- insert this into the bound SuperTable cell
call self.bind_SuperTable.setCellValue( colnum:
self.bind_SuperField.getColnum(),
                    newStrVal: str )
        returning retval

-- shift the focus to the superfield
call self.bind_SuperField.focus()

end function
```

The `init_list` Member Function

The `init_list` member function is used to set the parameters for the list box and build the `select` statement that will retrieve the data. It will first assign the parameters passed into the function to the object's member variables used to store the parameters. The `bind_SuperTable` and `bind_SuperField` will be used to store these parameters. The `getSelection` function uses these parameters to insert the user's list box selection into the SuperTable cell.

Next, the query string is built by creating a new `ixString` object with the concatenated values of `list_table` and `list_column`. Note that the SQL clause keywords "select" and "from" are automatically inserted into the query string to make it a syntactically correct SQL query statement.

If the `where` clause parameter has been passed to the function, then the value of this parameter will be non-null, the default assigned in the function signature in the class definition. If the `where_clause` parameter has a value, it is inserted onto the end of the string using the `ixString` insert member function. The `getLength ixString` member function is used to set the insert position for the `where` clause to start at the end of the string. The `loadData` function is also called at this point to load the list box with data.

```
function dbelist::init_list(
            bind_SuperField  ixSuperField,
            bind_supertable  ixSuperTable,
            list_table       char(*),
            list_column      char(*),
            where_clause     char(*) )

-- store the bound Superfield
let self.bind_SuperField = bind_SuperField
let self.bind_SuperTable = bind_SuperTable

-- store the data retrieval query
let self.query_string = new ixString(
            " select " ||
            list_column clipped ||
            " from " || list_table )

if where_clause IS NOT NULL then

    call self.query_string.insert(
            string: new ixstring( " where " ||
                where_clause ),
            pos: self.query_string.getlength() )

end if

-- load the data
-- would prefer to put this elsewhere
call self.loadData()

end function
```

The Class Constructor

The constructor function for `dbelist` class is virtually identical to the constructor for the `ixEditList` class from which this class is derived. Since this class is derived

Chapter 9: Creating Class Libraries

from the `ixEditList` class, the actual constructor for the `ixEditList` class must be included in the constructor.

The only other code in the constructor is the handler statement for the `activate` and `select` events. These statements attach dbelist class handlers for these list box events.

```
-- constructor function
function dbelist::dbelist( container  ixVisualContainer ,
                          name        CHAR ( * )     ,
                          enabled     BOOLEAN        ,
                          shown       BOOLEAN        ,
                          helpNum     INTEGER        ,
                          geometry    ixGeometry     ,
                          appearance  ixAppearance   ,
                          tabIndex    SMALLINT       ,
                          tabEnabled  BOOLEAN        ,
                          style       SMALLINT       ,
                          sorted      BOOLEAN        ,
                          itemList    ixVector       ,
                          dropDown    smallint

                        ) : ixEditListbox( container: container,
                          dropdown: TRUE,
                          geometry: geometry,
                          appearance: appearance,
                          tabIndex: tabindex,
                          tabEnabled: tabenabled,
                          sorted: sorted,
                          shown: shown
                        )

handle self.activate with dbelist::dbelist_activate
handle self.select   with dbelist::dbelist_select

end function
```

The `loadData` Member Function

The `loadData` member function is used to load the list box using a select statement generated from the parameters passed in to the `dbelist` object in the `init_list` member function.

The function first declares variables to hold the query string and a position parameter to store the position within the list box. An `ixVector` variable is also declared to store the values for the list box.

The `getNumItemsixListBox` member function is called first to determine whether or not the list box has been loaded with values. If it has, then `getNumItems` will return a value greater than zero and the `loadData` function will return. This prevents the list box from being unnecessarily loaded should the `loadData` function be called more than once while the application is being run.

Next, the value of the query string is retrieved from the `dbelist` `query_string` class member variable and stored in a character string pointer as required by the NewEra SQL statements. This is necessary since embedded SQL statements in NewEra will not accept an `ixString` object variable as a host variable.

A cursor is then prepared and declared for the query string and then a NewEra `foreach` loop is started for the cursor. The `foreach` statement will retrieve the values in a character string variable. The value in the character string variable is then converted into an `ixString` object and inserted into the `ixVector` object using the `ixVector` `insert` member function. This function returns the position of the inserted item which is ignored.

When the `foreach` loop has completed, the `ixVector` object contains all of the items for the list box. The `ixVector` object is then inserted into the list box using the `ixListBox` `insertList` member function. At this point, the list box has been loaded and is ready to be displayed.

```
function dbelist::loadData( )
-- retrieve the data and load the list, if it has not
been done yet
variable str char(*),
         qstr char(500),
         pos integer,
         ret smallint,
         iv  ixVector = new ixVector()

-- check to see whether or not the list box has data
-- If the list already has data, quietly return
if self.getNumItems() > 0 then
   return
end if

let str = self.query_string.getValueStr()

prepare _dbes1 from str
declare _dbec1 cursor for _dbes1
```

```
   foreach _dbec1 into  str

      call iv.insert( new ixString( str ) )
             returning pos

   end foreach

   -- insert the list into the list box
   call self.insertList( iv ) returning pos

   end function
```

THE GENERAL USE LIBRARY FUNCTIONS

The general use library contains several functions used throughout the examples in this text. Many of these are effectively *wrapper* functions for the NewEra library functions. They perform the same function as the NewEra library functions, but they require fewer parameters to be passed into the function and, when a return value is not needed, they do not return a value.

In this text, these functions are not grouped together into a class library. A better implementation would be to group these functions, and any constants or variables that may be added, into a class library. This approach would allow the consumers of these functions to use them with all of the benefits of object-oriented programming.

The General Functions Header File

The header file for the general use functions provides a good overview of the usage of these functions. The first function in the file is the `msgbox` function. This function is designed to provide a simple mechanism for displaying a pop-up message box to the screen. It can be called with a single parameter, the message to be displayed, and does not require a return parameter.

The `msgbox` function takes a parameter for the title as a character string pointer; it defaults to a title of "Message" (see Figure 9-2). The required parameter of message is a character string message. By using character string pointers as parameters, the size of the input string is not restricted. Had a fixed length character string been used, the parameter would have been clipped at the defined length of the character string parameter.

Figure 9-2 - The msgbox Call

The `alert_message` function is used to display a message box to the screen that indicates an alert condition to the user (Figure 9-3). It takes a single parameter for the message and does not return a value.

Figure 9-3 - The `alert_msg` Call

The `warn_message` function is similar to the `alert_message` function. It displays a message box with a title of "Warning". It takes a single parameter for the message and does not return a value.

The `message` function displays a message to the text label in a given window. There are two required parameters: a character string message parameter and a window reference parameter. It does not return a value.

The `browse_status` function displays current row and total row information for the current SuperTable data traversal. This function is designed to be used with the template windows shown in chapter 6. It takes three parameters: a row number, a total rows parameter, and an `ixWindow` reference.

The `setMessageFont` function sets the font for the message line in a given window. It takes four parameters; three of the parameters have defaults: a Boolean parameter for italic which defaults to FALSE, a Boolean parameter for underline which defaults to FALSE, and a Boolean parameter for bold font which defaults to font. An ixWindow parameter is supplied to provide a reference to the window where the message text label exists. The function does not return a parameter.

Chapter 9: Creating Class Libraries

The `setVObjFont` is identical to the `setMessageFont` function with the exception that the ixWindow parameter is replaced by an `ixVisualObject` parameter. The function does not return a parameter.

```
external function msgbox( title char(*) : "Message", message char(*) )
returning void
external function alert_message( message char(*) ) returning void
external function warn_messsage( message char(*) ) returning void
external function message( message char(*), window ixWindow )
    returning void
external function browse_status( row smallint,
                 totalrows smallint, window ixWindow )
    returning void

external function setMessageFont( font_italic    boolean : FALSE,
                                  font_underline boolean : FALSE,
                                  font_bold      boolean : FALSE,
                                  window ixWindow )
        returning void

external function setVObjFont( font_italic    boolean : FALSE,
                               font_underline boolean : FALSE,
                               font_bold      boolean : FALSE,
                               VisObj ixVisualObject )
        returning void
```

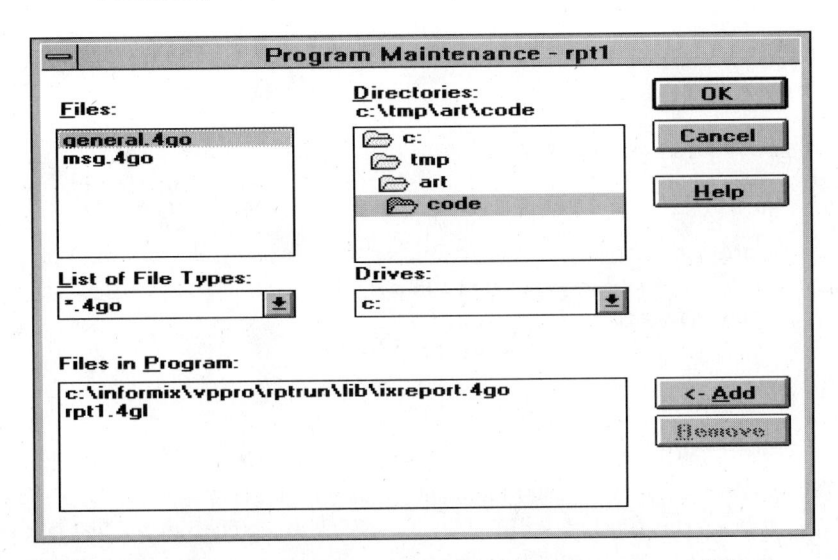

Figure 9-4 - Application Builder Program Maintenance Window

The General Function Source Code Module

The source code module for the general functions is compiled to object code and then is linked to other applications at runtime. It would be added to the Program Maintenance window in the Application Builder (see Figure 9-4).

The msgBox Function

The msgBox function displays a message box to the screen. This function acts as a wrapper function to the slightly more complex messageBox function. The function accepts two parameters: the title parameter and the message parameter. If no title parameter is passed into the function, the title "Message" will be used. The message parameter is required. The function simply calls the messageBox function using the default button style and then returns. The return value of the messageBox function is ignored.

```
include system "ixviscon.4gh"
include system "ixlabel.4gh"
include system "ixwindow.4gh"
include system "ixvisobj.4gh"
include system "ix4gl.4gh"
include "general.4gh"

function msgbox( title char(*) : NULL , message char(*) )
variable ret smallint
variable title_str ixString

if title IS NULL then
   let title_str = new ixString( "Message" )
else
   let title_str = new ixString( title )
end if

   call messagebox( Message: new ixString( message ),
                    Title: title_str )
      returning ret

end function
```

The message Function

The message function is used in conjunction with the window templates shown in chapters 6 and 7. This function will display a message to a predesignated text box in the

Chapter 9: Creating Class Libraries

window reference passed into the function. This emulates the functionality of the Informix-4GL `message` statement.

The function takes two parameters: a character pointer message parameter and an `ixWindow` object reference parameter. The window reference parameter is used to search for a reference to a visual object named "messageLbl" in the window. (The window reference is used to allow the `getWindow ixWindow` member function to be used to pass the a generic reference into the function.)

The `getContainedObjbyName` member function is first used to retrieve the reference to the message text label. If the reference to the text label is NULL, then the window reference passed does not have the message label. The current version of this function displays an error message in a message window if there is no message text label available. This function could easily be rewritten to quietly fail and return in this case.

If the message label does exist, then the `setText` function is used to set the text label in the function to the message character string passed into the function.

```
function message( message char(*),
            window ixWindow ) returning void
variable msglbl ixLabel

let msglbl = window.getContainedObjbyName(
            "messageLbl" ) cast ixLabel
if msglbl IS NOT NULL then
   call msglbl.setText( message )
else
   call msgbox( message: "NULL message label" )
end if
end function
```

The browse_status Function

The `browse_status` function is used in conjunction with the template windows shown in chapter 6. It displays information on current row and total number of rows in the browse data set.

This function takes parameters for the current row, the total number of rows and a window reference. The `getContainedObjbyName` function is used to retrieve references to text labels with the name "rowNumLbl" and "TotalRowsLbl." The return value is cast as an `ixLabel` object reference. The text label references are then tested to determine if they are NULL or not. If the `rowNumLbl` or the `TotalRowsLbl` is NULL, indicating that the label reference was not found, an error message window is displayed indicating the label does not exist. If the label references are NOT NULL, then the appropriate values are output to the label.

```
function browse_status( row smallint, totalrows smallint,
window ixWindow )

variable rowLbl, totLbl ixLabel

let rowLbl = window.getContainedObjbyName(
             "rowNumLbl" ) cast ixLabel
let totLbl = window.getContainedObjbyName(
             "totalRowsLbl" ) cast ixLabel

if rowLbl IS NOT NULL then
   call rowLbl.setText( row )
else
   call msgbox( message: "NULL rowLbl" )
end if

if totLbl IS NOT NULL then
   call totLbl.setText( totalrows )
else
   call msgbox( message: "NULL rowLbl" )
end if

end function
```

The `alert_message` and `warn_message` Functions

The `alert_message` and `warn_message` functions provide a simple access to the `messageBox` function. They take a single parameter, a character string message. With the `alert_message` function, the message box title is "Alert," the message string is the character string message parameter passed into the function, and the icon style is the exclaim icon. The `warn_message` function performs the same function but displays a title of "Warning."

```
function alert_message( message char(*) )
variable retval smallint

call messagebox( title: new ixString( "Alert" ),
                 message: new ixString( message ),
                 iconstyle: ixExclaimicon )
   returning retval

end function

function warn_message( message char(*) )
```

Chapter 9: Creating Class Libraries

```
variable retval smallint

call messagebox( title: new ixString( "Warning" ),
                 message: new ixString( message ),
                 iconstyle: ixExclaimicon )

    returning retval

end function
```

The setMessageFont and setVObjFont Function

The `setMessageFont` and the `setVObjFont` functions allow the font characteristics of visual objects to be changed at runtime. They supply a simpler access than the Informix supplied functions used to perform these functions. This functionality can be used to draw attention to a message in the current window as is done in the browse window templates shown in this text.

The `setMessageFont` function is used to set the font properties for the message text label. It takes three Boolean parameters for various font characteristics. These parameters match the parameters of the `setFont` function used to set the font characteristics of an `ixVisualObject`. The font name and font size are retrieved using the `getFontName` and `getFontSize` functions. If the message label does not exist (a NULL reference), then an error message is displayed in a message box.

The `setVObjFont` function performs the same function as the `setMessageFont` functions, with the exception that the parameter passed into the function is an `ixVisualObject` reference. This provides a more generic access to the capability to change font appearance at runtime, requiring only a visual object reference instead of a window reference.

```
function setMessageFont( font_italic    boolean,
                         font_underline boolean,
                         font_bold      boolean,
                         window ixWindow )
variable msglbl ixLabel

let msglbl = window.getContainedObjbyName( "messageLbl" )
cast ixLabel

if msglbl IS NOT NULL then

    call msglbl.setFont( fontname: msglbl.getFontName(),
                         fontsize: msglbl.getFontSize(),
                         bold:     font_bold,
```

```
                          italic:    font_italic,
                          underline: font_underline )
else

   call msgbox( message: "NULL message label" )

end if


end function
-------------------------------------------------

function setVObjFont( font_italic     boolean,
                      font_underline  boolean,
                      font_bold       boolean,
                      VisObj ixVisualObject )

if VisObj IS NOT NULL then

   call VisObj.setFont( fontname: VisObj.getFontName(),
                        fontsize: VisObj.getFontSize(),
                        bold:      font_bold,
                        italic:    font_italic,
                        underline: font_underline )
else

   call msgbox( message: "NULL Visual Object" )

end if

end function
```

Chapter 10
NewEra Reports

The NewEra language has retained all of the powerful report generation statements of the Informix-4GL language. Informix-4GL reports can be migrated to NewEra virtually intact. The only additional consideration in moving reports to NewEra would be the impact of running complex reports in client-server mode. The performance impact of moving large amounts of data over a network could significantly impact report performance. Future additions to the NewEra language should reduce this performance impact by adding features such as *application partitioning*.

Application partitioning allows portions of an application to run in a location other than the client. In a client-server environment, portions of an application that required large amounts of data retrieval could be run on the server, thus reducing the impact of the network.

Fixed and Proportionally Spaced Fonts on Reports

Character-based reports have generally been created using fixed fonts (as opposed to proportional fonts). When using the NewEra report writing statements to create a columnar report, data is aligned on a column position. If a proportional font is used, the data will not align on columns and the report may appear as shown below.

```
======================================================
Date: 03/07/1995                         Page: 1
          Accounts Receivable Aging Report
======================================================


          Under 30  Over 30   Over 60  Over 120
  1   01/01/1994              110.00
  2   02/01/1994              110.00
  3   03/01/1994              110.00
  4   03/01/1995  100.10
  5   02/01/1995           1000.00
======================================================
Total       100.10   1000.00     330.00
```

If a fixed font is used, each character will use the exact same amount of space and the report columns will align correctly. The same report is shown below using a fixed courier font to create the report output.

```
============================================================
Date: 03/07/1995                                    Page: 1
            Accounts Receivable Aging Report
============================================================


                          Under 30   Over 30   Over 60   Over 120
     1      01/01/1994                                   110.00
     2      02/01/1994                                   110.00
     3      03/01/1994                                   110.00
     4      03/01/1995   100.10
     5      02/01/1995             1000.00
============================================================
     Total                100.10   1000.00              330.00
```

FUNCTIONALITY OF A/R AGING REPORT

The Accounts Receivable Aging Report produces a listing of accounts receivable bills that are currently unpaid. The bills are categorized as being under 30 days old, over 30 days (and under 60 days), over 60 days (and under 120 days), and over 120 days old. A total is printed under each category. This report allows accounting staff to determine how well the business entity is collecting money owed.

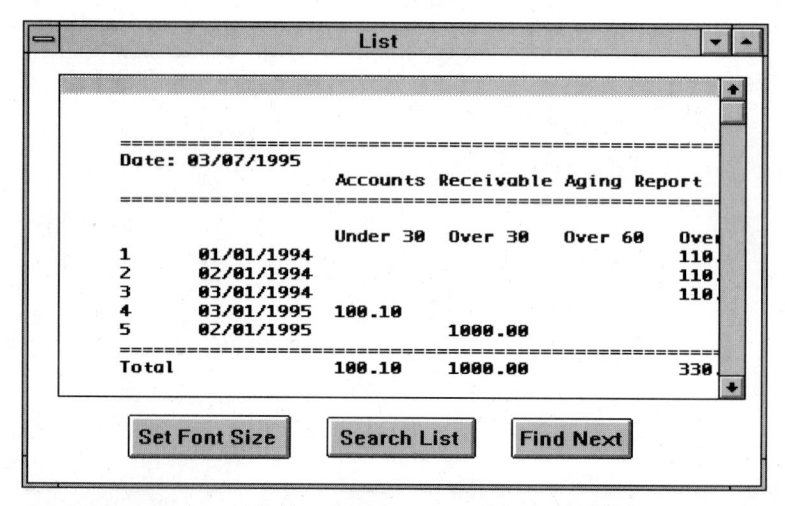

Figure 10-1 - Accounts Receivable Aging Report

Chapter 10: NewEra Reports

This report will first be run as a simple report output to an ASCII file. This file will then be read and inserted into a list box (see Figure 10-1). The user can then scroll through the list box and optionally adjust the display font size.

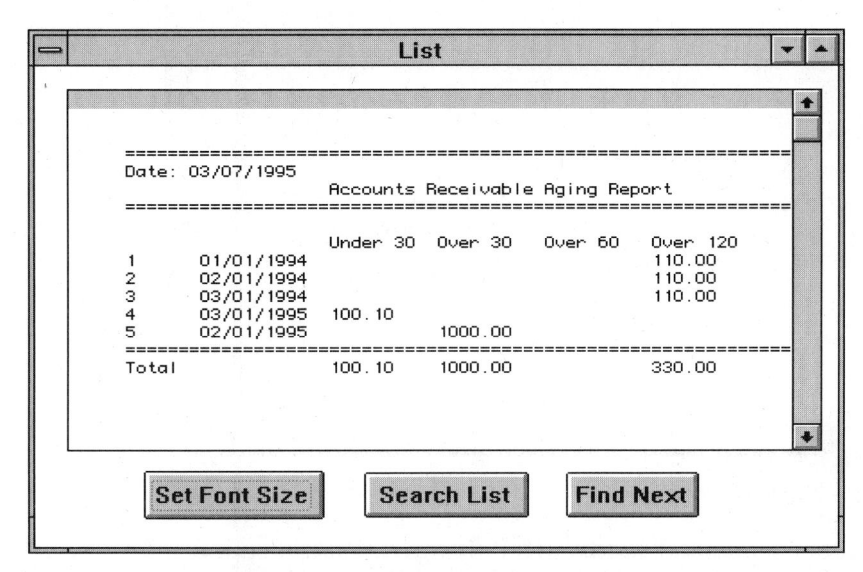

Figure 10-2 - Accounts Receivable Aging Report after Font Size Change

To adjust the font size, a prompt box will be displayed to prompt the user for the point size. If the font being displayed is a scalable font and can be scaled to the point size entered, the point size will be changed and the contents of the window redisplayed (see Figure 10-2). This will allow wide reports to be displayed in the list window.

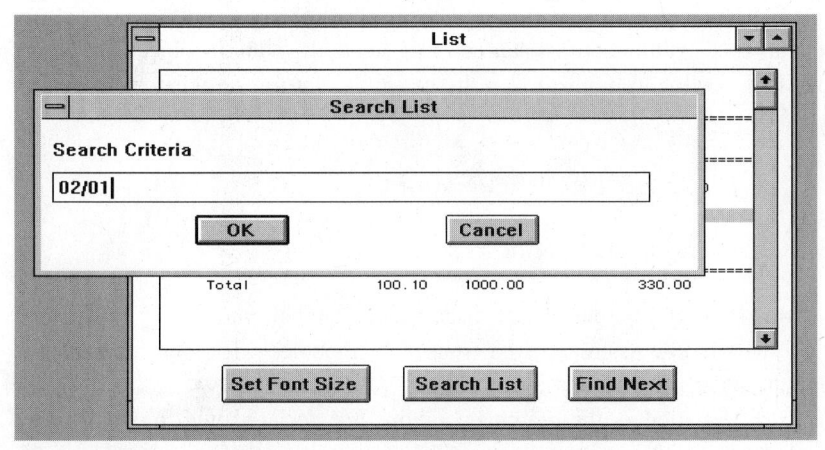

Figure 10-3 - Row Search Criteria Prompt Box

A search option is also available to allow the user to search through the report for a pattern (see Figure 10-3). A find next button allows the user to find the next occurrence of a pattern in the document.

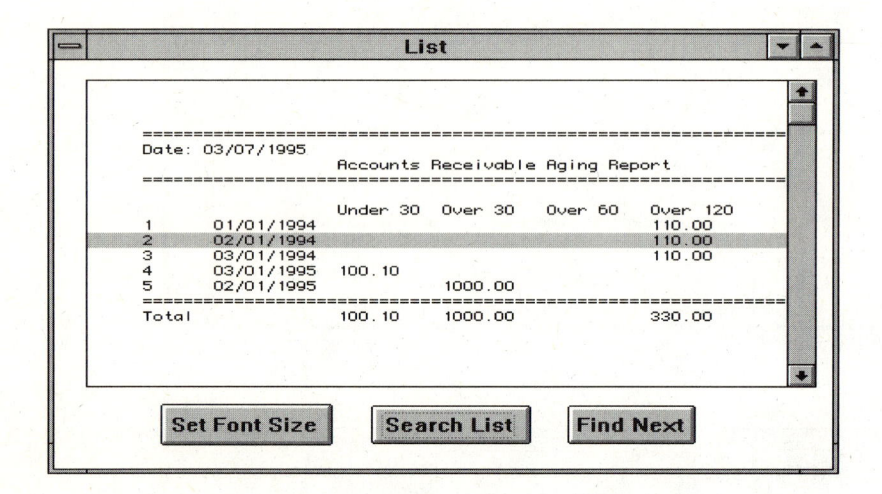

Figure 10-4 - Report Window after Row Search/ Selection

The Accounts Receivable Aging Report

The Accounts Receivable Aging Report is executed using several functions. One function is used to run the A/R aging report and another is used to display a file to a list box. This allows a generic function to be created to take the contents of a file and display them to a scrollable list box.

In order for the list window to be used to display the report, the window from which the accounts receivable report is started must create the window object for the list window. This is generally accomplished in the `start` event for the window, as shown below.

```
global variable ListWN listWindow
...
let   ListWN = new listWindow()
```

The `listWN` object variable is first declared as a global variable. It is declared global to allow the window to be accessed from other modules. The object variable is then created in the `start` event for the window.

Several variables used in the search operations are declared with module scope. This will allow these variables to retain their value during successive calls to the search handlers. The current position in the list (`CurrListPos`) and the find start position (`FindStartPos`) are declared with module scope. A find next flag (`FindNext`) is used to indicate the mode for the search list. A variable is also created to hold the search string (`SearchStr`). The `listwnd.4gh` include file is needed to allow the list window object to be created in this module.

```
include "listwnd.4gh"

external variable listWN listWindow
variable CurrListPos smallint = 1,
FindStartPos smallint = 1,
FindNext boolean = FALSE
variable SearchStr ixString
```

The Set Font Size Button Activate Handler

The "set font" button is used to allow the user to change the font size of the list window. The activate handler for this button is shown below.

This handler declares an `ixString` object as the return value from the `promptBox` function. The `promptBox` function is called to request a font size from the user. If the user presses the escape key in the `promptBox` window, the `promptBox` function will return a NULL. The return value of the `promptBox` function is therefore tested for a NULL value. If the user has entered a non-NULL value, then the `setFont` member function is called for the `ListBox` control. If the value of the `fontSize` variable is an invalid font size, the `setFont` function will quietly fail; no error message will be displayed.

Other than the test for a NULL object, there are no edit checks performed on the `fontSize` variable returned from the `promptBox` function. Since the `setFont` function where this is used as a parameter is fairly tolerant of invalid values, this is not a problem. (An attractive alternative to using the `promptBox` function to input font size would be a list box that displays only valid values for font size.)

The call to `setFont` retrieves the current font of the list box control with a call to the `getFontName` member function. This function will return the font name of the list box font as a character string. The `fontSize` parameter is passed as a character string returned by the call to `getValueStr` for the `fontSize` variable. The other `setFont` parameters, used to set font attributes, are set to FALSE to create a normal font.

```
HANDLER ixButton::ListWN_setFontBN_activate() RETURNING
VOID
variable fontSize ixString
```

```
call promptbox(
        title: new ixString( "Report Font Size" ),
        prompt: new ixString( "Font Size" ) )
             returning fontSize

if fontSize IS NULL then
   return
end if

call
   listWN.reportList.setfont( fontname:
                     listWN.reportList.getFontname(),
                     fontsize: fontSize.getValueStr(),
                     bold:      FALSE,
                     italic:    FALSE,
                     underline: FALSE )

END HANDLER—ixButton::ListWN_setFontBN_activate
```

The Search Button Activate Handler

The search button activate handler contains the code that actually conducts the search. This search routine operates in a manner similar to that of the list box search shown in chapter 8.

Variables are declared to store various return values and a Boolean variable is used to indicate whether or not a value was found during the search.

An `ixString` object is first created for the storage of the return from the `ixListBox` member function `getItembyNumber` call. This string is created at this point to avoid the overhead of instantiating the `ixString` object on each loop iteration. The `ixString` object is used to store the returned line from the list box object. This allows the `ixString` `find` member function to be used to search the list box string.

If the `findNext` flag is set, then the user has chosen to continue searching for the search string in the list. If this is the case, then the user does not need to be prompted for a search string. If the `findNext` flag is not set, then the user is prompted for a search string.

If the search string returned from the `promptBox` function is NULL, then the handler will return. If the `promptBox` function returns a valid non-NULL object, then the search loop begins.

```
HANDLER ixButton::ListWN_searchBN_activate()
        RETURNING VOID
variable pos smallint
variable ListStr    ixString
```

Chapter 10: NewEra Reports

```
variable retval, itemnum, n smallint
variable found Boolean

let ListStr = new ixString( " " )

-- get the search criteria
if NOT FindNext then
   call promptBox(
            title: new ixString( "Search List"),
            prompt: new ixString ("Search Criteria ") )
         returning SearchStr
end if

if SearchStr IS NULL then
    return
end if
```

Before the loop starts, the found flag is set to FALSE. A variable (FindStartPos) is used to store the search starting position in the list. If this value is 0, it will be set to 1.

A for loop is then started to conduct the search. The loop will be executed from the stored starting position (FindStartPos) to the number of stored items in the list (getNum Items). For each iteration of the loop, the value of the list is retrieved with a call to the getItembyNumber call. The getItembyNumber call is passed an integer parameter indicating the current list number to retrieve. This integer parameter is the counter variable from the for loop. The character string value returned by getItembyNumber is passed to the setValueStr function for the ixString data type. (The setValueStr function is used instead of instantiating a new ixString on each pass to avoid the overhead of object creation.)

The ixString find member function is passed the search string returned by the promptBox function. If the find function returns TRUE, then the found flag is set to TRUE and the for loop is exited. If the find function returns FALSE, then the for loop continues executing.

```
let found = FALSE
if  FindStartPos = 0   then
    let FindStartPos = 1
end if

for n = FindStartPos  to listWN.ReportList.getNumItems()

    call ListStr.setValueStr(
```

```
                    ListWN.ReportList.getItembyNumber( n ) )

      if ListStr.find( searchStr )   then
         let found = TRUE
         exit for
      end if

   end for
```

If the search string value has been found, then execution will continue after the end of the `for` loop. At this point, the current list position (`CurrListPos`) is set to the index value for the `for` loop, thus storing the position of the found item. This index value is also used to select this list box item as the current list box item. This is accomplished using the `selectItem ixListBox` member function.

If the search string was not found, then the `for` loop will exit without the `found` flag being set to TRUE. In this case, the `messageBox` function will be called to display a message to the user indicating that the search string was "Not Found" and the current list position (`CurrListPos`) will be set to 1. (The current list position is used with the "Find Next" button to set the find list start position (`FindStartPos`) to the current list position plus one.) Before the handler returns, the `findNext` flag is reset allowing a regular search to be conducted the next time the handler is executed.

```
if   found   then
     let CurrListPos = n
     call ListWN.ReportList.selectitem( n )
else
     call messagebox(
                title: new ixstring( "Message"),
                message:  new ixstring( "Not Found" ) )
          returning retval
     let CurrListPos = 1

end if

let FindNext = FALSE
END HANDLER       -- ixButton::ListWN_searchBN_activate
```

If the "find next" button has been set previously, then the `FindStartPos` variable would be set to the value set during the previous search, an incorrect value for the "find" search being conducted. The "find" value search should start at the first position. Therefor this code will set the `FindStartPos` value to one. And since the "find next" search sets the `FindNext` flag to TRUE to indicate that a "find next" search

Chapter 10: NewEra Reports

is being conducted, this code will set that variable value to FALSE thus indicating that a "find next" search is **not** being conducted.

The `findNext` Button Activate Handler

The `findNext` button activate handler allows the user to continue searching the list at the current list position using the previously entered search string. This search is accomplished by assigning the current position in the list (`CurrListPos`) as the search start position (`FindStartPos`).

The handler will set the start position for the search to be the current list position plus one. This sets the search position to one item past the current list position.

The search start position is then tested to determine whether or not the start position has been incremented beyond the end of the list. If the starting position has gone beyond this limit, the list search is set to the first item in the list. This is accomplished by setting the search start position to the value of one.

Next, the `findNext` flag is set to TRUE. This will have the search button handler code skip the step of prompting the user for a search string.

To initiate the search, the "search" button activate handler is called synchronously. This will execute the search button handler and thus trigger the list search operation.

```
HANDLER ixButton::ListWN_FindNextBN_activate()
    RETURNING VOID

let FindStartPos = CurrListPos + 1

if FindStartPos > ListWN.ReportList.getNumItems()   then
    let FindStartPos = 1
end if

let FindNext = TRUE
call ListWN.SearchBN.activate()

END HANDLER—ixButton::ListWN_FindNextBN_activate
```

The Search Button `focusIn` Handler

Since the handler for the search button is called synchronously by the "Find Next" button, it is necessary to set the flags for the search operation correctly if the button is pressed from the keyboard. If this were not done, then when the user pressed the search button after having previously pressed the "Find Next" button, the search start position (`FindStartPos`) would be set incorrectly. When the user presses the search button using the mouse, the `focusIn` event for the button will be executed as the cursor moves over the button. By executing the following code in the `focusIn` handler, the search start position can be set correctly.

```
HANDLER ixButton::ListWN_searchBN_focusIn()
    RETURNING VOID

let FindStartPos = 1
let FindNext = FALSE

END HANDLER-ixButton::ListWN_searchBN_focusIn
```

The `runARAge` Function

The Accounts Receivable Aging Report is generated using two functions: a report *driver* function that retrieves the data for the report, and a NewEra *report*, essentially a special case of a NewEra function. The `runARAge` function is the report driver and takes a character string file name as a parameter as shown below.

```
call runARage( fileName: "arage.out" )
```

Note that since the report driver will use the NewEra `like` clause in the variable declaration statement, the NewEra `database` statement is needed at the start of the report source code module as shown below.

```
database ar
```

This will indicate to the NewEra source code compiler that the current database is the `ar` database and will allow variable declarations such as the one shown below to be used in the source code module.

```
variable bill_rec record like bill.*
```

The `runARAge` function is shown below. The single file name parameter defaults to NULL if not passed into the function. A record is declared to have the structure of the `bill` table in the `ar` database.

An `ixSQLStmt` object is declared. This will be used to manage the database access required by the report. An `ixRow` object is declared to receive the rows for the report. But since the NewEra report writer cannot use the `ixRow` data type, the ixRow object must be converted to a NewEra record (the `bill_Rec` variable) before being output to the `ARAge` report. This conversion is accomplished using the `unpackrow` function as shown below.

Chapter 10: NewEra Reports

The `sqlstatmt` object is instantiated on the same line as the ixSQLconnect object creation. Once this statement object has been created, the SQL statement for the report is prepared. The prepared statement is then executed to begin retrieving rows and the report is started to the file name parameter passed into the function. Each row retrieved is unpacked and then output to the Accounts Receivable Aging Report.

At the end of the `while` loop, the report is complete and can be finished via the NewEra `finish report` statement. This will close the report output file. At this point, the completed report is contained in the output file produced by the NewEra report *function*. This file will be opened and viewed using the `listFile` function shown below.

```
function runARAge( fileName char(*) : NULL )
variable sqlstmt ixSQLStmt
variable bill_rec record like bill.*
variable ar_row ixRow
variable rptFile ixFile

-- assert we have an implicit connection to ar database
let sqlstmt = new ixSQLStmt( new ixSQLConnect() )

call sqlstmt.prepare( " select * from bill " )
call sqlstmt.execute()

start report arAgeReport to fileName

while ( 1 )
     call sqlstmt.fetch() returning ar_row
     if ( getImplicitConnnection().getODBCErrorCode() !=
          ixSQLStmt::SQL_Success )  then
             exit while
     end if

     call unpackrow( ar_row ) returning bill_rec.*
output to report arAgeReport( bill_rec.* )

end while

finish report arAgeReport
end function
```

The `listFile` Function

The `listFile` function is used to read a file that currently exists on disk and display the file in a NewEra list box control. It is passed the name of the file to read and the reference to a list box object.

In the code shown below, an `ixFile` object is declared to read the file, a character string pointer is declared to read the lines of the file, and an `ixVector` object is declared to hold the lines of the file. The `ixVector` object will then be passed to the list box function for display.

An attempt is first made to open the report file. This is accomplished by instantiating a new `ixFile` object. In this example, the file is opened in `readOnly` mode. If the `ixFile` status after this operation indicates that this operation did not succeed, then the function will quietly return.

If the file open was successful (indicated by a `getStatus` return value of zero), then the function makes sure the list window is currently displayed. A reference to the list window is obtained through the `getVisualContainer ixVisualContainer` member function. If the window is not opened, it is *opened*; otherwise it is *shown*.

Next, a `while` loop is started to read the file and insert each line into an `ixVector` object. Each line of the file is read with a `readLine ixFile` member function call. The status of the `readLine` operation is checked after each call. If successful, this function returns a character string.

The character string returned by `readLine` is converted into an `ixString` object and inserted into an `ixVector` object. The `while` loop will continue until a non-zero status is returned by the `ixFile getStatus` member function call. When this occurs, the `while` loop will be exited and the `ixVector` object will be inserted into the list box using the `insertList ixListBox` member function call.

```
function listFile( fileName char(*), listBox ixListBox )
variable rptFile ixFile
variable rptLine char(*), pos smallint
variable iv ixVector = new ixVector()
variable LstWindow ixWindow

let rptFile = new ixFile( fileName, ixFile::readOnly )
if rptFile.getStatus() != 0 then    -- not successful open
   return
end if

let LstWindow = listBox.getVisualContainer() cast
ixWindow

-- open the window if necessary
```

```
if LstWindow.getAvailability() != ixWindow::opened then
   call LstWindow.open()
else
   call LstWindow.show()
end if

while ( 1 )
    call rptFile.readLine() returning rptLine, pos
    if rptFile.getStatus() = 0  then
       call iv.insert( new ixString( rptLine ) )
           returning pos
     else
       exit while -- at EOF or error
     end if
end while

call listBox.insertList( iv ) returning pos

end function
```

The `arAgeReport` Report

The `arAgeReport` NewEra `report` block generates the report that is displayed to the list box window. This report applies some formatting and uses NewEra report aggregates to produce the Accounts Receivable Aging Report.

The `report` code shown below contains several variable declarations. An `ixString` variable is declared as a general purpose string. This will be used to provide formatting for the report header. And an array of decimals is declared; this will be used to hold report summary totals.

As with Informix-4GL, the `first page header` section is available to initialize the static local variables available in the report section of the language. In this example, the `concatRep ixString` member function is used to create a string of equal signs which will appear in the report as a double underline. This will be used on the top and bottom of the report header. This string is printed using the `getValueStr ixString` member function.

The remainder of the report `first page header` section is used to print the portions of the page header. The date and the page number (`pageno`) are printed, as well as the report title. The column titles are then printed at specific column positions. These columns represent the different accounts receivable aging categories. The page header of the report is then printed using much of the same code used in the `first page header` section.

```
report arAgeReport( bill_rec )
variable bill_rec record like bill.*
variable istr ixString = new ixString( "" )
variable total_amt array[4] of decimal(13,2)

format
first page header
    call istr.concatRep( new ixString( "=" ), 80 )
    call istr.clip()
    print istr.getValueStr()
    print "Date: ", today,
          column 75, pageno using "Page: <<<<"
    print column 20, "Accounts Receivable Aging Report "
    print istr.getValueStr()
    skip 1 line

    print column 20, "Under 30", column 30, "Over 30",
          column 40, "Over 60", column 50, "Over 120"

page header
    print istr.getValueStr()
    print "Date: ", today,
          column 75, pageno using "Page: <<<<"
    print column 20, "Accounts Receivable Aging Report "
    print istr.getValueStr()
    skip 1 line
    print column 20, "Under 30", column 30, "Over 30",
          column 40, "Over 60", column 50, "Over 120"
```

A case statement is used in the `on every row` section of the report. The case statement is used to segregate the data coming into the report. Since the aging is based on the age of the bill, the age of the bill can be calculated as shown below.

```
( today - bill_rec.bill_date )
```

The `today` variable used in the equation above is a NewEra keyword that resolves to the current date. The value of the current date is subtracted from bill date to get the number of days the bill has gone unpaid, the *age* of the bill. The `case` statement below is

Chapter 10: NewEra Reports

used to segregate the `bill_rec` rows into 4 categories based on the *age* of the bill. The age category of the bill will determine the column where the bill total will be printed.

```
on every row
case
    when (today - bill_rec.bill_date) < 30
         print column 1, bill_rec.bill_numb using "<<<",
               column 8, bill_rec.bill_date,
               column 20, bill_rec.bill_total
                     using "<<<<.##"
    when (today - bill_rec.bill_date) > 30   and
         (today - bill_rec.bill_date) < 60
         print column 1, bill_rec.bill_numb using "<<<",
               column 8, bill_rec.bill_date,
               column 30, bill_rec.bill_total
                     using "<<<<<.##"
    when (today - bill_rec.bill_date) > 60   and
         (today - bill_rec.bill_date) < 120
         print column 1, bill_rec.bill_numb using "<<<",
               column 8, bill_rec.bill_date,
               column 40,bill_rec.bill_total
                     using "<<<<.##"
    when (today - bill_rec.bill_date) > 120
         print column 1, bill_rec.bill_numb using "<<<",
               column 8, bill_rec.bill_date,
               column 50, bill_rec.bill_total
                     using "<<<<.##"
end case
```

The `on last row` section of the report is used to print the grand totals for the columns listed on the report. A double underline is first printed to separate the totals from the regular data.

The totals are then stored in an array of decimals. The totals make use of the report language where clause that can be attached to built-in aggregate functions such as the sum function used in the code below. The criteria used to create the totals are identical to the criteria to segregate report information in the "`on every row`" section of the report shown above. The totals are segregated based on the *age* of the bill and are then printed to the output file using the NewEra `print` statement.

```
on last row
    print the grand totals
    print istr.getValueStr()
```

```
    let total_amt[1] = sum( bill_rec.bill_total )
            where ( today - bill_rec.bill_date )  < 30
    let total_amt[2] = sum( bill_rec.bill_total )
        where ( today - bill_rec.bill_date ) > 30 and
              ( today - bill_rec.bill_date ) < 60
    let total_amt[3] = sum( bill_rec.bill_total )
        where ( today - bill_rec.bill_date ) > 60 and
              ( today - bill_rec.bill_date ) < 120
    let total_amt[4] = sum( bill_Rec.bill_total )
        where ( today - bill_rec.bill_date ) > 120

print column 1, "Total",
      column 20, total_amt[1] using "<<<<<.##",
      column 30, total_amt[2] using "<<<<<.##",
      column 40, total_amt[3] using "<<<<<.##",
      column 50, total_amt[4] using "<<<<<.##"

end report
```

RUNNING VIEWPOINT PRO REPORTS FROM NEWERA APPLICATIONS

NewEra Viewpoint Pro is a graphical development tool that provides the capability to quickly create data entry forms, perform database maintenance, and create graphical reports (see Figure 10-5). This product is bundled with NewEra and through the ixReport class library, ViewPoint Pro reports can be run from NewEra applications. Parameters can be supplied to the report, a query can be supplied or a default query can be used, and the user can be prompted for report parameters. The following example demonstrates the ViewPoint Pro report running capability.

To run ViewPoint Pro reports from NewEra requires the ixReport.4gh file to be included with the application and the ixReport object file to be linked with the application at compile time. This file contains the function signatures for the NewEra report running class library member functions. Note that this file is **not** contained in the same include file directory with other NewEra include files. The include statement for the ixReport.4gh file must used the full pathname for the include file as shown below.

```
INCLUDE SYSTEM "ixrow.4gh"

INCLUDE SYSTEM "ixwindow.4gh"
INCLUDE SYSTEM "ixbutton.4gh"

include
"c:\\informix\\vppro\\rptrun\\incl\\ixreport.4gh"
```

Chapter 10: NewEra Reports   209

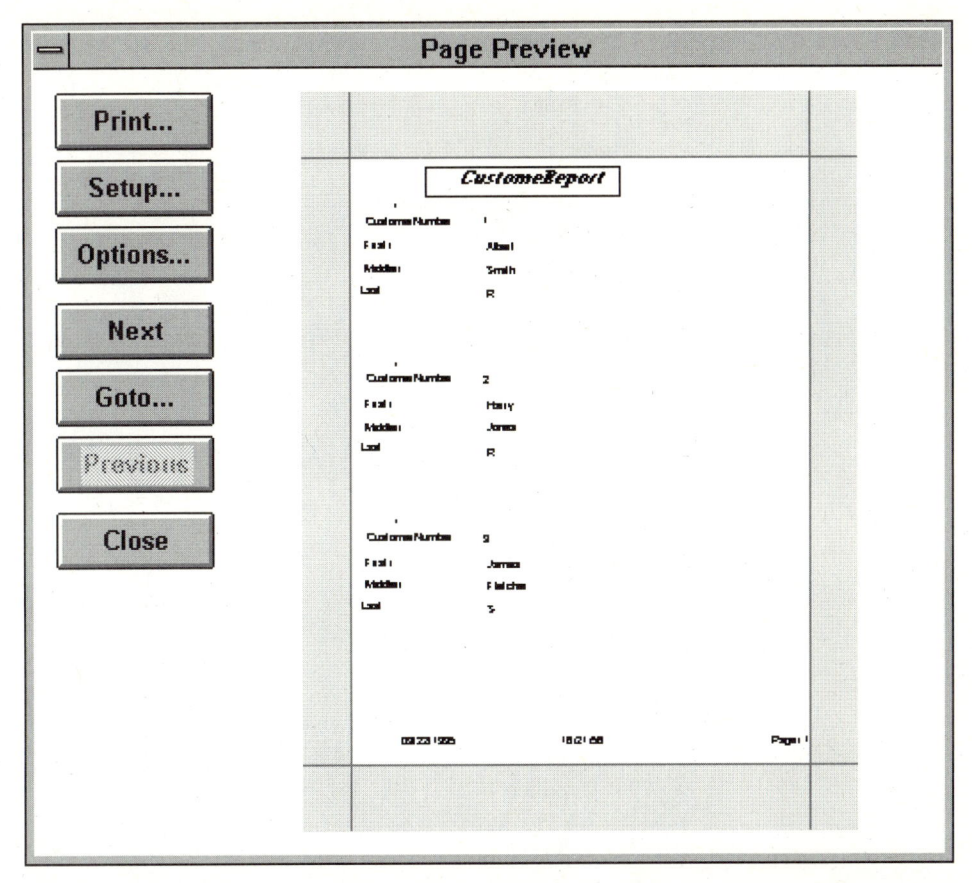

Figure 10-5 - ViewPoint-Pro Accounts Receivable Customer Report

Because the `ixReport.4gh` file is not in the NewEra default include directory, the `include system` NewEra statement cannot be used to include the file and the full pathname for the file must be supplied. Since the backslash character is interpreted as an escape character denoting that the next character is to be interpreted literally by NewEra, a double backslash is used in the pathname to indicate that this is a directory character for the DOS environment.

For this example, a button was used to start the report. The handler for the report button is shown below. An `ixReport` object is first declared and created. The `setPrinter` member function is then called to set the printer.

The report file is then set to the `custrpt.vpr` file, a customer report created with Viewpoint-Pro. The `ixReport print` member function is then called to print the report. At this point, the Viewpoint Pro reporting environment is started and the report is run in the background. The NewEra application can continue to run and process user input while the report is being run.

```
HANDLER ixButton::custRptWN_custRptBN_activate()
RETURNING VOID
variable rpt ixReport = new ixReport(),
         stat boolean

call rpt.setPrinter( )
call rpt.setReportFile( "custrpt.vpr" )

call rpt.print() returning stat
```

Chapter 11
Extending NewEra Classes

The template examples shown in chapters 6 and 7 demonstrated the benefits of using a template approach when developing NewEra applications (see Figure 11-1). By creating window templates, NewEra standard functionality can be extended and a common set of applications can be developed with the same *look and feel*.

Programmers can simply retrieve a template wif, select the SuperTable frame, paste fields into the frame and then save the template wif with a new name. The code generated by the wif can then be used to develop an application.

All of the template functionality described in chapters 6 and 7 is packaged in the template. The steps of pasting controls and menu items and setting menu properties for each window can be greatly reduced.

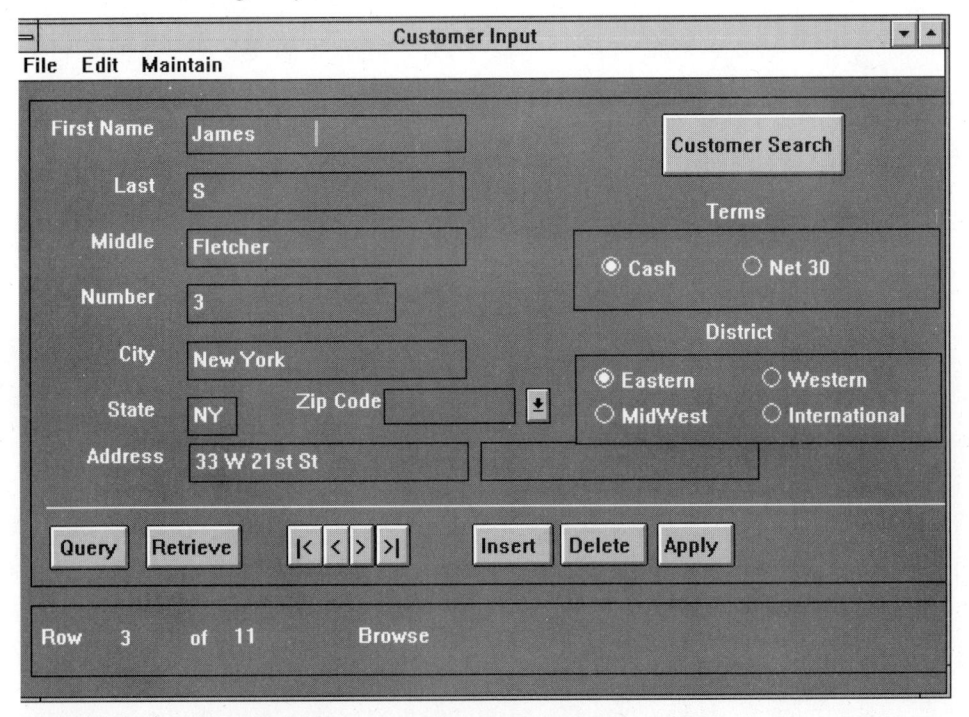

Figure 11-1 - Customized Browse Template

But there are limitations to the template approach shown in chapter 6. The window templates are essentially *wif* files that contain information about the controls and objects in the NewEra window. These definitions are optionally converted into NewEra code by the window painter when the window file is saved. A large part of this code is event handler code for the controls that were customized in the template window file.

Once the code is generated, there is no way to change the operation of the button handlers. Much of the customized functionality shown in chapter 6 is contained in the event handler. This code is duplicated for each window created. If the programmer wanted to alter the operation of the windows, they would have to recreate the windows using the Window Painter and then save and recompile the code.

It would be more desirable to allow the customized behavior of the template windows to be modified and then have the changes be recognized by all template-based applications. One solution would be to create library functions to perform the operation of each of the button handlers in the template window. But this could be a tedious process and would still not allow this extended functionality to be used in non-template windows should that be desired.

An improved approach to defining common behavior for the button handlers would be to make the button handlers part of a class. This would have the effect of encapsulating the template behavior in a class library. Then, when the application is compiled, the class name could be substituted in the Window Painter for the class of the object. The object would then inherit all of the capabilities of the extended class.

Should a developer want to modify the behavior of some aspect of the template, the class library could be modified. A recompile of all template applications would then recognize the change since all template applications make use of the same classes.

PACKAGING THE SUPERTABLE BUTTONS: EXTENDING THE ixFrame CLASS

The SuperTable buttons pasted by the SuperTable editor are **not** part of the SuperTable class. These buttons contain the NewEra code to perform the SuperTable function associated with the button. They do call some methods of the same class.

A convenient way to package the capability of the SuperTable buttons would be to place the buttons together in a class. The `ixFrame` class is a package for a visual object that can be used to group controls. By painting the buttons into a frame within the Window Painter, the buttons can be grouped together.

But the SuperTable buttons must be able to access a reference to the SuperTable object that they control. When pasted into the window using the SuperTable editor, this SuperTable reference is automatically set by making the container for the buttons the SuperTable that has been painted into the window. This allows the SuperTable reference to be obtained with a call to the `getVisualContainer` function within the button handler as shown below.

```
-- SuperTable button handler
variable supertable ixSuperTable

let supertable = getVisualContainer() cast ixSuperTable
....
```

The `getVisualContainer` function is a member function of the `ixVisualContainer` class. It returns an `ixVisualContainer` reference that is cast within the button handler as an `ixSuperTable` object reference. The `getVisualContainer` function returns a visual container reference that was in place at *construction* time. If the control has been painted into the visual container by the Window Painter, then the container parameter for the object is set by the Window Painter to the visual container where the control is painted.

This means that the `ixFrame` used to group the SuperTable buttons must be painted into the SuperTable that the buttons will control. This is necessary to achieve a correct reference for the `getVisualContainer` call in the SuperTable button handlers.

The `browseFrame` Class Definition

The class definition for the `browseFrame` class is shown below. This class is based on the `ixFrame` class. This custom frame class will be used to group the customized SuperTable buttons for the browse template.

The class definition indicates that the class is derived from the `ixFrame` class. The constructor for this class must therefore contain a call to the constructor for the base class. Since the call to instantiate an object of this class will be initiated by the Window Painter which will assume the object is an `ixFrame` class, all of the parameters accepted by the `ixFrame` class constructor are used in the `browseFrame` class constructor. The function prototype for the class constructor is required in the class definition and is shown below.

Following the function prototype for the class constructor are the variable declarations for the SuperTable buttons. These button objects will be instantiated in the constructor for the `browseFrame` class. A variable is also declared to hold a reference for the containing SuperTable for the frame.

```
CLASS browseFrame DERIVED FROM ixFrame

  function browseFrame (
    geometry ixGeometry: NULL,
    appearance ixAppearance: NULL,
    enabled boolean: TRUE,
    borderWidth  integer: 20,
    shown boolean: TRUE,
    helpFile char(*): NULL,
    helpNum integer: 0,
    name char(*): NULL,
    container ixVisualContainer : NULL
  )

  public variable
          QueryBN    ixButton,
          RetrieveBN ixButton,
          FirstRowBN ixButton,
          PreviousRowBN ixButton,
          NextRowBN ixButton,
          LastRowBN ixButton,
          InsertBN ixButton,
          DeleteBN ixButton,
          ApplyBN ixButton

  public variable supertable ixSuperTable

  END CLASS -- BrowseFrame
```

The `browseFrame` Constructor Function

The constructor function for the `browseFrame` class is shown below. This class receives parameters that are identical to the parameters passed into the `ixFrame` constructor. Since the `browseFrame` class is *derived from* the `ixFrame` class, the constructor for the `ixFrame` class is called in this constructor. All of the parameters received by the `browseFrame` class are passed to the `ixFrame` class constructor.

The constructor then contains entries to instantiate or create the objects for the buttons. The code shown below creates the SuperTable query button. Since the query button object is a member variable of the `browseFrame` class, there is no need to precede the object reference with a class reference (`browseFrame::queryBN`). The container parameter for the button is set to `self`, an object reference that resolves to the `browseFrame` object being created.

Chapter 11: Extending NewEra Classes

The geometry reference for the button contains a `top` and `left` parameter. The values for these parameters are relative to the container in which the button is placed. Since the container reference for the button is the `browseFrame` object being instantiated, these buttons will be placed relative to the left-hand corner of that visual object.

Following the creation of the query button is a `handle` statement that references the handler for the query button activate event. The handler referenced appeared in the source file before the handle statement (and the `browseFrame` constructor). The code for the button handler is shown below. Other identical button handle statements exist in the code but have not been shown here for brevity.

The final statement that appears in the constructor is a statement that stores the container reference passed into the `browseFrame` constructor. This reference will be used to obtain a reference to the containing SuperTable as needed by the button handlers.

```
-- constructor function
function browseFrame::browseFrame (
    geometry ixGeometry,
    appearance ixAppearance,
    enabled boolean,
    borderWidth integer,
    shown boolean,
    helpFile char(*),
    helpNum integer,
    name char(*),
    container ixVisualContainer
) :
ixFrame (
   geometry: geometry,
   appearance : appearance,
   enabled : enabled,
   borderWidth : borderWidth,
   shown : shown,
   helpFile : helpFile,
   helpNum : helpNum,
   name : name,
   container : container
              )
```

```
        LET QueryBN = NEW ixButton(
          geometry : NEW ixGeometry(
                top : 160,
                left : 180,
                height : 450,
                width : 830
          ),
          appearance : NEW ixAppearance(
                fontName : NULL,
                fontSize : NULL,
                fontBold : NULL,
                fontItalic : NULL,
                fontUnderline : NULL,
                foreColor : NULL,
                backColor : NULL
          ),
          title : "Query",
          enabled : TRUE,
          tabIndex : NULL,
          tabEnabled : TRUE,
          shown : TRUE,
          helpNum : 0,
          theDefault : FALSE,
          name : "QueryBN",
          container : self
        )
        HANDLE QueryBN.activate WITH
          ixButton::wind1_QueryBN_activate

...

-- store the supertable reference
let self.supertable = container cast ixSuperTable

end function
```

Query Button Activate Event Handler

The button handler for the SuperTable query button first obtains a reference to the SuperTable which it will manipulate. It does this by first obtaining a reference to the `browseFrame` container and then examining the SuperTable `browseFrame` public member variable contained within the `browseFrame` class. As shown above, the SuperTable variable has been assigned the value of the container for the `browseFrame`. Since the `browseFrame` has been placed into the SuperTable using the Window

Painter, the `browseFrame` container will be the SuperTable which the buttons will control.

Once the SuperTable reference has been obtained, the remainder of the button handler is identical to the button handler shown in chapter 7 for the template application. (The call to the `message` function uses a frame that is also derived from the `ixFrame` class; the class definition for that is shown below.) A button handler would be declared for each of the SuperTable template buttons shown in chapter 7.

```
HANDLER ixButton::wind1_QueryBN_activate() RETURNING VOID
VARIABLE superTable ixSuperTable

    LET superTable =
    (getVisualContainer() cast browseFrame).SuperTable

    CALL
superTable.setDisplayMode(ixSuperTable::displayQuery)

    CALL message( message: "Query", window: getWindow() )

END HANDLER -- ixButton::wind1_QueryBN_activate
```

DISPLAYING BROWSE INFORMATION: THE STATUS FRAME

The bottom portion of the browse window contains a section that displays information on the state of the browse process (see Figure 11-2). This frame and the references to the labels within the frame should also be encapsulated in a class as shown below.

| Row 1 of 8 | Retrieval Complete |

Figure 11-2 - The Browse Status Frame

The `statusFrame` class will be used to group the text labels used to display browse information. The `statusFrame` class is derived from the `ixFrame` class. The class definition contains a constructor function for the class that mirrors the constructor for the `ixFrame` class. As with the `browseFrame` class, the Window Painter will generate a call to the constructor for this class using the parameters associated with the `ixFrame` class.

Public variables are declared to hold references for the labels in the window. text label objects are declared for the current row number (`rowNumLbl`), the total number of rows (`totalRowsLbl`), and the message label (`messageLbl`). Other label objects are also declared and will be used to hold fixed text for the window.

```
class statusFrame derived from ixFrame

  function statusFrame (
    geometry ixGeometry: NULL,
    appearance ixAppearance: NULL,
    enabled boolean: TRUE,
    borderWidth  integer: 20,
    shown boolean: TRUE,
    helpFile char(*): NULL,
    helpNum integer: 0,
    name char(*): NULL,
    container ixVisualContainer : NULL
  )

public variable
  rowNumLbl ixLabel,
  totalRowsLbl ixLabel,
  messageLbl ixLabel,
    Label48 ixLabel,
    Label50 ixLabel

end class
```

The `statusFrame` Constructor Function

The `statusFrame` constructor function receives parameters identified in the constructor function signature shown above. These parameters are then passed to the constructor for the `ixFrame` class from which the `statusFrame` class is derived.

The constructor contains a series of statements that instantiate the `ixLabel` objects contained in the status frame. The container for the object is declared to be `self` which resolves to the `statusFrame` object being created. The geometry for the labels is then relative to the geometry (or location) of the `statusFrame` object being created. An object is created for each of the labels contained within the frame (only the first label object instantiation is shown below).

Chapter 11: Extending NewEra Classes

```
function statusFrame::statusFrame(
  geometry ixGeometry,
    appearance ixAppearance,
    enabled boolean,
    borderWidth integer,
    shown boolean,
    helpFile char(*),
    helpNum integer,
    name char(*),
    container ixVisualContainer
  ) :
  ixFrame (
    geometry: geometry,
    appearance : appearance,
    enabled : enabled,
    borderWidth : borderWidth,
    shown : shown,
    helpFile : helpFile,
    helpNum : helpNum,
    name : name,
    container : container
            )

  LET rowNumLbl = NEW ixLabel(
    geometry : NEW ixGeometry(
         top : 200,
         left : 900,
         height : 360,
         width : 630
    ),
    appearance : NEW ixAppearance(
         fontName : NULL,
         fontSize : NULL,
         fontBold : NULL,
         fontItalic : NULL,
         fontUnderline : NULL,
         foreColor : NULL,
         backColor : NULL
    ),
```

```
        shown : TRUE,
        name : "rowNumLbl",
        labelJustify : ixLabel::leftJustify,
        text : NULL,
        container : self
    )

    ...
    end function
```

EXTENDING THE SUPERTABLE CLASS: THE browseSuperTable CLASS

The template application shown in chapters 6 and 7 contained an extension of the SuperTable class. This extension allowed the user to reach the maxRows number of rows and then optionally continue retrieving another set of rows. Rather than package this functionality in the template *wif*, it would be better to extend the SuperTable class to contain this added functionality. The SuperTable class shown below provides this added capability.

The class definition for the `browseSuperTable` class indicates that it is derived from the `ixSuperTable` class. The constructor function prototype for the `ixSuperTable` class must therefore contain parameters identical to those of the `ixSuperTable` class.

```
    class browseSuperTable derived from ixSuperTable

        function browseSuperTable (
            geometry      ixGeometry,
            appearance    ixAppearance,
            updateTable char(*),
            enabled              boolean,
            selectUnique         boolean,
            numDisplayedCols     integer,
            selectFromPart       char(*),
            selectJoinPart       char(*),
            selectOrderbyPart char(*),
            borderWidth          integer,
            shown                boolean,
            helpNum              integer,
            name                 char(*),
            lockMode    integer,
            layout      integer,
            numDisplayedRows integer,
```

Chapter 11: Extending NewEra Classes

```
        dbConnection ixSQLConnect,
        selectFilterPart char(*),
        displayMode integer,
        maxRows     integer,
        container ixVisualContainer
    )
end class
```

The `browseSuperTable` Constructor

The `browseSuperTable` constructor receives the parameters identified in the constructor function prototype shown above. These parameters are merely passed to the constructor for the `ixSupertable` class contained in the `browseSuperTable` class constructor.

The constructor contains a `handle` statement for the `rowRetrieved` `browseSuperTable` event (an event inherited from the `ixSuperTable` class). This statement attaches the `rowRetrieved` event to the `browseRowRetrieved` handler for the `browseSuperTable` class.

```
function  browseSuperTable::browseSuperTable(
    geometry      ixGeometry,
    appearance    ixAppearance,
    updateTable char(*),
    enabled           boolean,
    selectUnique      boolean,
    numDisplayedCols  integer,
    selectFromPart    char(*),
    selectJoinPart    char(*),
    selectOrderbyPart char(*),
    borderWidth       integer,
    shown             boolean,
    helpNum           integer,
    name              char(*),
    lockMode   integer,
    layout     integer,
    numDisplayedRows integer,
    dbConnection ixSQLConnect,
    selectFilterPart char(*),
    displayMode integer,
    maxRows     integer,
    container ixVisualContainer
    ) :
```

```
        ixSuperTable(
geometry              : geometry,
appearance            : appearance,
updateTable           : updateTable,
enabled               : enabled,
selectUnique          : selectUnique,
numDisplayedCols      : numDisplayedCols,
selectFromPart        : selectFromPart,
selectJoinPart        : selectJoinPart,
selectOrderbyPart     : selectOrderbyPart,
borderWidth           : borderWidth,
shown                 : shown,
helpNum               : helpNum,
name                  : name,
lockMode              : lockMode,
layout                : layout,
numDisplayedRows      : numDisplayedRows,
dbConnection          : dbConnection,
selectFilterPart      : selectFilterPart,
displayMode           : displayMode,
maxRows               : maxRows,
container             : container )

handle rowRetrieved with
browseSuperTable::browseRowRetrieved

end function
```

The `browseSuperTable rowRetrieved` Handler

The `browseSuperTable` handler appears in the source code module before the constructor for the browseSuperTable constructor and thus before the `handle` statement for the `rowRetrieved` event. The NewEra compiler must know the signature for the handler before the `handle` statement that binds an event to that handler.

As shown in chapter 7, this handler will be called for each row retrieved from the database. As each row is received, the total number of rows currently stored in the SuperTable (as returned by the `getNumStoredRows` member function) is evaluated against the `ixSuperTable::maxRows` value. If the `maxRows` value is about to be reached, the user is prompted to retrieve more rows or to stop retrieving rows. If the user requests more rows be retrieved, the maxRows parameter is incremented by 25 rows, thus allowing another 25 rows to be retrieved.

This handler sets an upper limit (set to 100 in this example) on the number of rows retrieved. If this upper limit is reached, an error message is displayed and the handler

Chapter 11: Extending NewEra Classes

returns. The `maxRows` parameter is set equal to 100 and the handler returns. The `maxRows` parameter setting at that point will stop the retrieval of records by the SuperTable.

```
handler browseSuperTable::BrowseRowRetrieved(
         theRow ixRow )
                returning boolean
variable retval smallint
variable str char(10)

-- set upper limit for rows retrieved
if self.getNumStoredRows() = 100 then

   call messagebox( title: new ixString( "Message" ),
                 message: new ixString(
     self.getNumStoredRows() ||
   "Rows Retrieved. No more rows allowed." )
                                      )
           returning retval

end if

if self.getnumstoredrows() = (self.maxrows - 1 ) then

   call messagebox( title: new ixString( "Alert" ),
                 message: new ixString(
           "Maxrows reached. Retrieve 25 More Rows ?" ),
                 iconstyle: ixQueryicon,
                 buttonstyle: ixYesNo )
                         returning retval

   if retval = ixYesButton then
      let self.maxrows = self.maxrows + 25
   end if

end if

return TRUE

END HANDLER -- ixSuperTable::CustWN_custST_rowRetrieved
```

EXTENDING THE WINDOW CLASS

By creating a custom window class, certain window properties and functionality can be made consistent throughout the application. This example demonstrates such a class.

This example of a custom window class demonstrates the setting of certain window properties, the creation of a menu, and the inclusion of a *splash* window (see Figure 11-3). The splash window displays some information about the application and remains on the screen for a number of seconds before being closed.

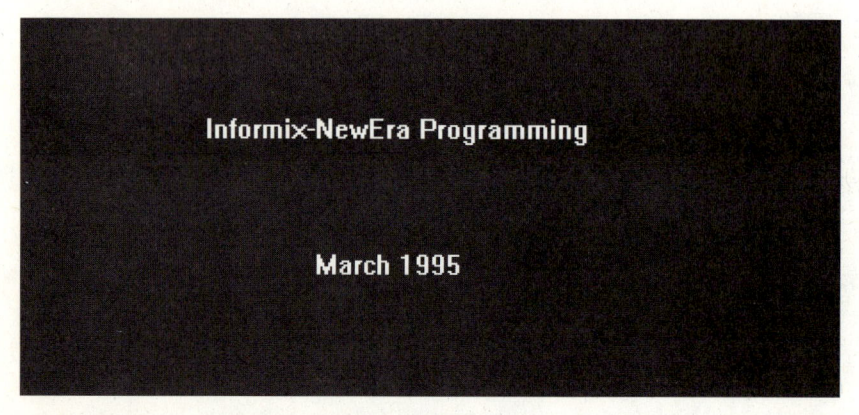

Figure 11-3 - NewEra Splash Window

The window class definition defines the `browseWindow` class derived from the `ixWindow` class. The constructor function for the `browseWindow` class receives parameters identical to those received by the `ixWindow` class.

Variables are declared for the standard menu items used in the template window. These menu items will be created in the constructor for the `browseWindow` shown below.

```
class browseWindow derived from ixWindow

function BrowseWindow(
   geometry ixGeometry,
   appearance ixAppearance,
   windowStyle SMALLINT,
   title CHAR(*),
   containingWindow ixWindow,
   enabled BOOLEAN,
   icon CHAR(*),
   shown BOOLEAN,
   helpFile CHAR(*),
```

```
    helpNum INTEGER,
    name CHAR(*) )

public variable
   Menu38 ixMenu,
   Menu39 ixMenu,
   Menu40 ixMenu,
   Menu41 ixMenu,
   Menu42 ixMenu,
   Menu43 ixMenu

end class
```

The `browseWindow` Constructor

The constructor for the `browseWindow` receives the parameters identified in the constructor definition shown above. These parameters are then passed to the constructor for the `ixWindow` class from which the `browseWindow` was derived.

A variable is then declared for the splash window to be of class `splashWindow`. This will be used to create the visual object for the splash window to be created and the window to be displayed.

The menu objects are then created for the various menu items. An `ixMenu` object is created for each of the menu items (they are not all shown here). Menu items that have actions associated with them are assigned handlers. Menu items with no actions (menu titles) are not assigned handlers.

```
FUNCTION BrowseWindow::BrowseWindow(
   geometry ixGeometry,
   appearance ixAppearance,
   windowStyle SMALLINT,
   title CHAR(*),
   containingWindow ixWindow,
   enabled BOOLEAN,
   icon CHAR(*),
   shown BOOLEAN,
   helpFile CHAR(*),
   helpNum INTEGER,
   name CHAR(*)
)
      : ixWindow(
        containingWindow : containingWindow,
        name : name,
        enabled : enabled,
```

```
      shown : shown,
      helpNum : helpNum,
      geometry : geometry,
      appearance: appearance,
      helpFile : helpFile,
      title : title,
      icon : icon,
      windowStyle : windowStyle
   )

variable splash splashWindow,
         retval smallint

   LET Menu38 = NEW ixMenu(
      appearance : NEW ixAppearance(
            fontName : NULL,
            fontSize : NULL,
            fontBold : NULL,
            fontItalic : NULL,
            fontUnderline : NULL,
            foreColor : NULL,
            backColor : NULL
      ),
      title : "File",
      enabled : TRUE,
      checkState : ixMenu::notACheck,
      accelerator : NULL,
      helpNum : 0,
      name : "Menu38",
      parentMenu : SELF.getMenuBar()
   )
   LET Menu39 = NEW ixMenu(
      appearance : NEW ixAppearance(
            fontName : NULL,
            fontSize : NULL,
            fontBold : NULL,
            fontItalic : NULL,
            fontUnderline : NULL,
            foreColor : NULL,
            backColor : NULL
      ),
      title : "Exit",
      enabled : TRUE,
```

Chapter 11: Extending NewEra Classes

```
            checkState : ixMenu::notACheck,
            accelerator : NULL,
            helpNum : 0,
            name : "Menu39",
            parentMenu : Menu38
         )
         HANDLE Menu39.activate WITH
            ixMenu::wind1_Menu39_activate
...
```

After the menu items have been created, the `setColor` function is used to set the color for the window. In this example, the foreground and background color are assigned specific color numbers that were determined from the creation of the template window.

Next, the splash window is created using specific geometry to place the window in the center of the screen. (Since the window has no containing window, the geometry will be relative to the left corner of the screen.) The splash window is opened and the `splashWindInit` function is called to set the text labels in the window. The window is displayed for five seconds using the NewEra sleep statement to pause for 5 seconds, after which the splash window is closed.

```
      call self.setColor( foreColor: 16777215,
                 backColor : 8421504 )

      let splash = new splashWindow( geometry : NEW ixGeometry(
            top :     570,
            left :    1140,
            height :  2865,
            width :   6375) )

      call splash.open()
      call splash.splashWindInit( )
      sleep 5
      call splash.close() returning retval

      end function
```

USING THE EXTENDED NEWERA CLASSES

Accessing the functionality of the extended classes discussed here in NewEra applications involves very few steps. First, the *class* property for the visual object must be assigned to the class name identified above. To have a SuperTable to use the extended SuperTable `rowRetrieved` handler, the SuperTable frame would be selected, the SuperTable properties window would be accessed and the class name propery for the SuperTable would be set to `browseSupertable` (see Figure 11-4).

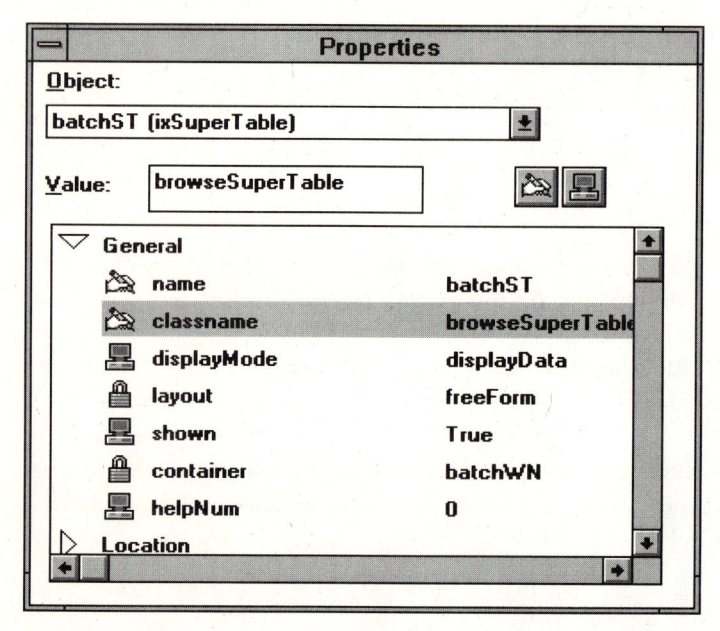

```
┌─────────────────── Properties ───────────────────┐
 Object:
 ┌──────────────────────────────────────┬──┐
 │ batchST (ixSuperTable)               │▼ │
 └──────────────────────────────────────┴──┘
 Value:   ┌──────────────────────┐
          │ browseSuperTable     │
          └──────────────────────┘

   ▽ General
      🖉  name                   batchST
      🖉  classname              browseSuperTable
      🔒  displayMode            displayData
      🔒  layout                 freeForm
      🔒  shown                  True
      🔒  container              batchWN
      🔒  helpNum                0
   ▷ Location
```

Figure 11-4 - Setting SuperTable Class Property

Next, the `browse.4gh` file must be included in the pre-header code section for the window. This will include the class definition for the extended SuperTable, `browseSuperTable` (see Figure 11-5).

```
┌─────────────────────── Code ───────────────────────┐
        Object:  ┌─────────────────────────┬──┐
                 │ CustWN (ixWindow)       │▼ │
                 └─────────────────────────┴──┘
         Event:  ┌─────────────────────────┬──┐
                 │ pre_header              │▼ │
                 └─────────────────────────┴──┘
   Handler For:  pre_header()

 ┌────────────────────────────────────────────────┐
 │ include system "ix4gl.4gh"                     │
 │ include system "ixapp.4gh"                     │
 │ include "dbelist.4gh"                          │
 │ include "custlst1.4gh"                         │
 │ include "custlst2.4gh"                         │
 │ include "browse.4gh"                           │
 │ include "general.4gh"                          │
 │ include "zip2.4gh"                             │
 │                                                │
 └────────────────────────────────────────────────┘
```

Figure 11-5 - Pre-header Section

Chapter 11: Extending NewEra Classes 229

And finally, the `browse.4gl` object file (`browse.4go` or `browse.obj`) and the `general.4gl` object file must be included in the link step for the application. This can be added in the application builder using the program manager (see Figure 11-6).

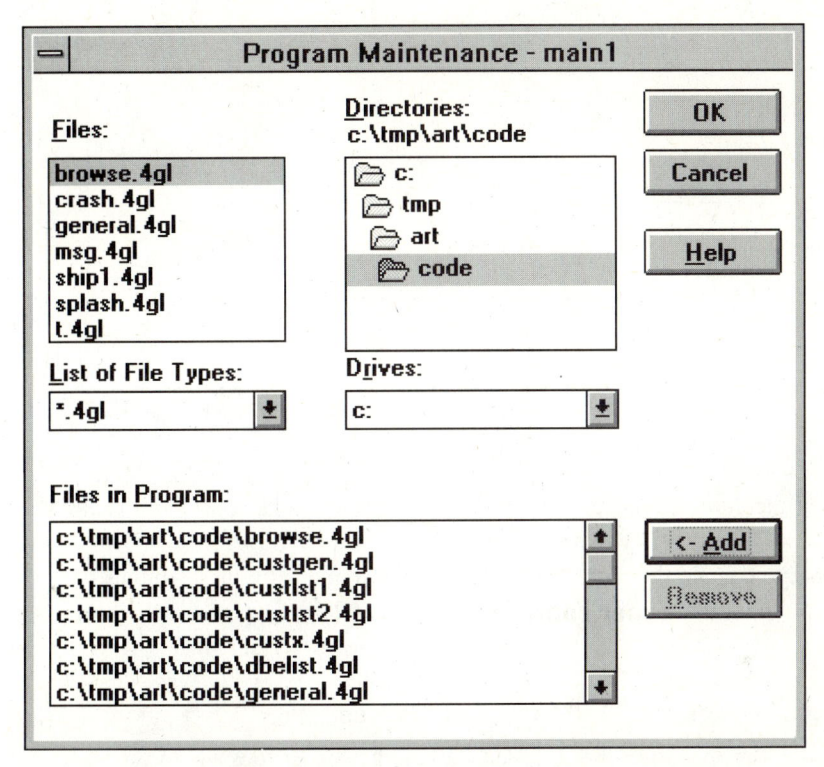

Figure 11-6 - Adding Modules to the Application Builder

As a result of these few steps the application can begin using the extended functionality outlined above. If changes are made to the customized classes, the applications using the classes would only have to be recompiled to recognize the changes.

Combining the Extended Classes into the Template Application

A template can be created using the extended classes shown in this chapter. A new window could be created with an empty SuperTable. The window and the SuperTable could be assigned properties for the classname of the extended classes.

Two frames should then be pasted into the window: a frame for the browse buttons which should be pasted **into** the SuperTable frame, and a frame for the status labels which should be pasted onto the bottom of the screen. The resulting screen would resemble the wif shown in Figure 11-7.

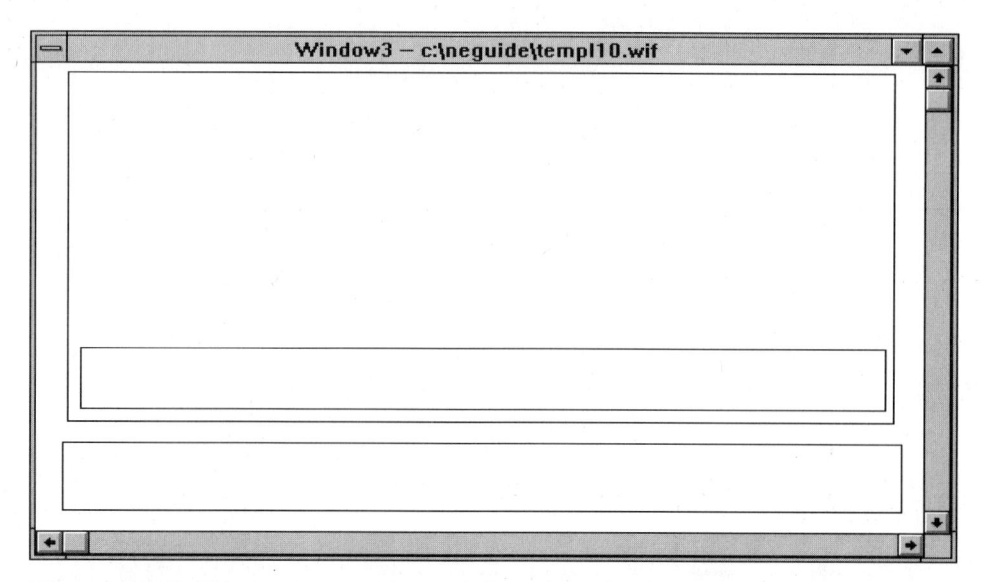

Figure 11-7 - Template Using Customized Classes

Note that the current implementation of the Window Painter does not display the controls within a frame class. The button frame pasted into the SuperTable shown above does not appear to contain the buttons that exist in that frame. But these buttons will be displayed at runtime and the full functionality discussed in chapter 6 and 7 will be available.

Changing Functionality of Extended Classes

To change the behavior of the extended classes, the header files and the appropriate source code file must be changed. The applications that contain the extended classes must then be recompiled. If they have been compiled using the Application Builder, then dependency lists will detect the changes and recompile and relink the applications that use the altered header files.

Chapter 12
Migrating Informix-4GL Applications to NewEra

The Informix-NewEra language was built on the foundation of the Informix-4GL language. The majority of the Informix-4GL language statements have found their way into the NewEra language, with the important exception of the Informix-4GL screen interaction statements. This means that the migration of legacy Informix-4GL applications to NewEra requires a rewrite of the screen interaction code.

While on the surface this may appear to be a serious impediment, the character-based interface and the GUI-based interface are significantly different. The logic which drives a character-based data entry application is very different from the logic which drives a GUI application. Exploiting the power of the GUI environment ultimately requires portions of the character-based application to be rewritten.

In a character-based screen, the programmer can assert that data entry will proceed serially through the screen fields. In a GUI environment, the programmer can no longer make assumptions about the serial flow of screen field input. In a GUI environment, users have the ability to move easily to different parts of the application, a difficult task to manage with character-based environments.

CONVERTING INFORMIX-4GL APPLICATIONS

The conversion of character-based Informix-4GL applications to a GUI-based Informix-NewEra primarily involves the conversion of the screen interaction statements of Informix-4GL. There is no straightforward correspondence of Informix-4GL screen statements to NewEra screen interaction functions. In fact, the process of retrieving data from the screen and inserting the data into the database changes dramatically in Informix-NewEra. Informix-NewEra combines the retrieval of data from the screen and the database update process together into the SuperTable class library.

CHARACTER-BASED VERSUS GUI SCREEN DEVELOPMENT

A character-based data entry application usually centered around one or more data entry screens. Screen *controls* were primarily menus and function keys. Other GUI-type controls were sometimes emulated with mixed success. Users would initiate actions in the program using the limited controls. The code driving the application would then be executed in a generally serial fashion.

The process of programming a GUI application involves the creation of one or more *windows*. Within these windows are GUI controls and screen objects. The GUI window is *event-driven*: The user controls the flow of the program by triggering *events* associated with the controls in the data entry window or windows. These events are queued. The window manager "event loop" removes events from the queue and dispatches them as needed. Program execution proceeds from event handler to event handler. Within each event handler, program execution proceeds in a generally serial fashion.

INFORMIX-4GL *EVENTS*

Several Informix-4GL language statements do have event-driven clauses. The Informix-4GL `input` statement will create a loop that scans for user input. If the user enters a character string, this is interpreted as input for the current field. If the user enters a control character, the control character could trigger an *event*. If the control character were a carriage return, the `after field/before field` *events* would be triggered. (If auto-next were in effect, then filling the field to its defined length would trigger these events.) If the user pressed a function key or control key, a specific code block associated with the control key could be triggered by the *event*.

These Informix-4GL events can be easily mapped into Informix-NewEra events. The `before field/after field` logic can be moved into `beforeCell/afterCell` SuperField event handlers in Informix-NewEra. The control key logic could be moved to the menu or to button *activate* event handlers.

This process of mapping could be made easier if the Informix-4GL program logic is concise and modular, and the *event* triggered code is in the form of a function call. But if that is not the case, a cut-and-paste operation using an editor that recognizes the Windows clipboard can be used to make the process of code conversion easier.

THE STRUCTURE OF INFORMIX-4GL APPLICATIONS

Informix-4GL is a structured programming language. If programs are structured, then they are composed of small and specific functions. Source code modules are composed of logically grouped sets of these functions.

Informix-4GL provided a rich set of structured screen interaction statements. These statements allowed a number of screen *events* (`before field/after field/ on key`) to be programmed within these structured statements. While large blocks of code could be entered in these *event* blocks, modular function calls were preferred as shown below.

```
after field cust_code
    if  NOT valid_cust_code( cust_rec.cust_code )  then
        error "Invalid Customer Code"
        next field cust_code
    end if
```

Informix-4GL Reports

The Informix-4GL report language has been retained in the Informix-NewEra language. Informix-4GL reports can be migrated directly from Informix-4GL to Informix-NewEra.

If an Informix-4GL report is a columnar report, then it was developed with the assumption that each character position is the same length. In a GUI environment, this is not always the case. If a *proportional* font is being used, the space taken by a character differs depending on the character being displayed. This is not true with *fixed* size fonts in a GUI environment. With fixed size fonts, each character uses the same amount of space.

If an Informix-4GL columnar report is to be displayed in a GUI window, then it will be necessary for the window to use a fixed size font. A fixed size font is usually the default for NewEra applications.

CONVERSION OF INFORMIX-4GL LEGACY APPLICATIONS

Though the Informix-4GL screen interaction statements do not appear in the NewEra language explicitly, there are a few NewEra window interaction facilities that can be used to emulate Informix-4GL screen input/output statements. These facilities are listed in the table below.

Informix-4GL Screen Interaction Statements and NewEra Equivalents

Informix-4GL Statement/Event	NewEra Equivalent
before field/after field	beforeCell/afterCell SuperField event
before row/after row	beforeRow/afterRow SuperTable event
on key	<menu handler> (associate menu handler with control key)
fgl_lastkey	cellKeyPress SuperField member function
display <character string>	display statement
message	setText ixLabel or ixTextBox member function
display <character string > at row, col	<none>

Informix-4GL Statement/Event	NewEra Equivalent
message	setText ixLabel or ixTextBox member function
menu	<menu handler>
<none>	beforeDataChanged/AfterDataChanged

Though these NewEra statements do not provide a simple, direct conversion into Informix-NewEra, they can help in the conversion process. They are explained in more detail in the section below.

Language Conversion

The process of converting Informix-4GL legacy applications to the NewEra language primarily involves re-engineering the screen interaction. This is accomplished by isolating and making this portion of the application more modular. The following section suggests a strategy for migrating Informix-4GL applications to NewEra (see Figure 12-1).

- ✓ Isolate Screen I/O Modules
- ✓ Isolate before field/after field Logic
- ✓ Convert Specific Statements
- ✓ Convert Menu Blocks

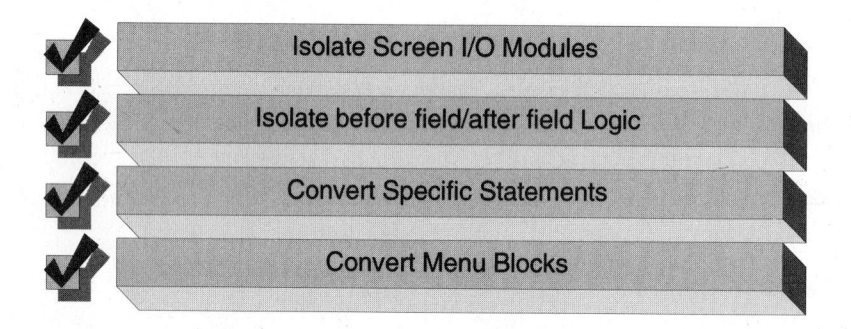

Figure 12-1 - Steps in Informix-4GL to NewEra Conversion

Isolate Screen I/O Modules

The screen interaction portion of an Informix-4GL application should be separate from the rest of the application code. The functions which drive the screen should reside in a separate source code module.

Informix-4GL did not require this logical division of screen interaction code. With few exceptions, screen interaction statements could be coded anywhere in the application. Preferably, Informix-4GL screen code should be located in a separate module or modules.

The occasional Informix-4GL `message` or `error` statement does not need to be placed in a separate module. (These statements can be mapped to function calls to display modal dialogue boxes.) But the statements that interact with screen forms such as the `input/input array, construct,` and `display/display array` statements should be grouped in separate modules. This will help expedite the process of converting these statements.

Isolate `Before Field`/`After Field` Logic

Any code blocks that can be mapped into NewEra screen oriented event logic should be isolated. This logic could be isolated by moving large portions of the code to functions. Small portions of code, Informix-4GL *event* blocks that are only two or three lines, could be left intact and moved to NewEra using a cut-and-paste operation.

Isolating the event-driven code into functions makes the process of moving the code to NewEra fairly simple. The related NewEra event can be identified, the code window for the event can be opened, and the function call inserted. The Informix-4GL screen interaction module containing the isolated functions can then be linked together with the NewEra application to produce the runnable NewEra application.

Code can be isolated by taking the block of code between the Informix-4GL `input` statement clause and the start of the next `input` statement clause and placing this code into a function. The example below demonstrates this process.

```
before field cust_code

    select  code_descr
    into    pcode_descr
    from    cust_codes
    where   cust_code = cust_rec.cust_code

    display pcode_descr to code_descr
```

To isolate this code it would be placed in a function that could be easily called from a SuperField handler. The following code demonstrates this process.

```
function dispCustCodeDescr( custCode char(*) )
variable pcode_descr like cust_codes.descr

  -- retrieve the code
    select  code_descr
    into    pcode_descr
    from    cust_codes
    where   cust_code = custCode
```

```
-- display the value
call window1custST.setCellValue(
        newStrVal: pcode_descr,
        colnum: window1.codeDescrSF.getColnum() )

end function
```

This function takes a single parameter, a character string pointer of the value of the customer code. An embedded SQL statement is then executed to retrieve the customer code description from the database. The next line of code displays this description to the SuperTable cell for the customer code description using the `setCellValue` `ixSuperTable` member function call.

This code will be placed in a module to be linked with the application. The call to the function will be inserted into the `afterCell` handler for the customer code SuperField as shown below.

```
variable custCodeIV ixValue

custCodeIV = window1.getCellValue(
            colnum: window1.custCodeSF.getColNum() )

call dispCodeDescr( custCodeIV.getValueStr() )
```

An `ixValue` variable is declared to hold the return value of the `getCellValue` call. The `getValueStr` `ixValue` member function call is used to retrieve a character string value of the customer code which is then passed to the `dispCodeDescr` function to display the customer code description.

Converting Informix-4GL on key Statements

Informix-4GL provided the ability to trap the action of a user pressing a specific control key. These were the `on key` input statement clauses. Informix-NewEra does not provide an equivalent to the Informix-4GL `on key` statement, but it does provide accelerator keys for menu items that will trap function key execution.

To trap a function key press in NewEra involves creating a menu for the data entry window and providing menu options for what were previously control key options. These menu options can then be assigned control key or function key accelerators that are identical to the control keys used in the Informix-4GL application. The code within the `on key` clause can be moved to the menu item handler with a cut-and-paste operation, or by isolating the code and creating a function as shown previously.

Providing menu items for what were formerly control keys has the added advantage of making the functionality visible to the user as a pull-down menu option. This will represent an improvement over the character-based application where function keys were not always labeled due to lack of screen space.

Another alternative to converting function keys is to move the function key operation to a button handler. By creating a button for the function key operation, the user is more likely to be aware of the operation. The code in the `on key` block for the function key can simply be moved to the button *activate* event handler.

Converting Informix-4GL `message`, `error` and `display` Statements

Some screen output statements may lie outside of the regular screen interaction modules. These statements may be interspersed at random throughout the Informix-4GL code. They are the occasional `message` statements that are used to provide information to the user wherever such information may need to be conveyed. The `display` statement is often substituted for the `message` statement for intermittent screen output, and the `error` statement can appear with SQL statements to trap errors wherever they may occur in the code. Converting these statements is discussed in more detail below.

The `message` and `display` Statements

There is no single NewEra statement or function that is equivalent to the Informix-4GL `message` or `display` statement. But the NewEra language does provide for the dynamic display of character strings to specific locations in the window.

Unlike character-based screens, the GUI window is not a consistent size. With character screens, the programmer can generally expect the screen to be at least 24 rows by 80 character columns. Given this size, the programmer can safely address various points on the screen using a row and a column coordinate. The Informix-4GL display statement exploits this capability using a very simple syntax as follows:

```
display "this string" at 10, 20
```

This statement will display the character string "this string" at row 10, column 20. The NewEra language does not provide a statement or function to explicitly perform this same function. In a GUI environment, it is not always safe to assume that a specific "row, column" set of coordinates can be accessed. Given the varying size of GUI windows, it would be better to output character strings to a location that is known to be on the window.

This can be accomplished using the `setText` function. In NewEra, a text box or label can be pasted into the window. This text box or label can then accept output using the `setText` function. Assuming that an `ixLabel` object named `MessageLbl` has been painted into the window, the `setText` function can be used as follows:

```
call window1.MessageLbl.setText( "this is a message" )
```

This will display the text "this is a message" to the message label. This will perform the same function as using the `display at` statement would in Informix-4GL: A character string is output at a specific location on the screen. This was the technique used to display the browse status output presented in chapters 6 and 7.

The Informix-4GL `display` statement without an 'at' clause displays a text string at the current cursor location. This statement is supported in NewEra with slightly different functionality. The `display` statement in NewEra will open a new window and display the character string on the current line (see Figure 12-2). After displaying the character string, the cursor will move to the next line and display the next character string on that line. This has the effect of scrolling the rows upward. When the number of rows exceeds what can be displayed on a single line, a scroll bar will appear on the side of the window. A File and Edit menu appears on the top line of the window. These menu options allow the user to exit or close the display window, and to select and cut some or all of the contents to the GUI clipboard.

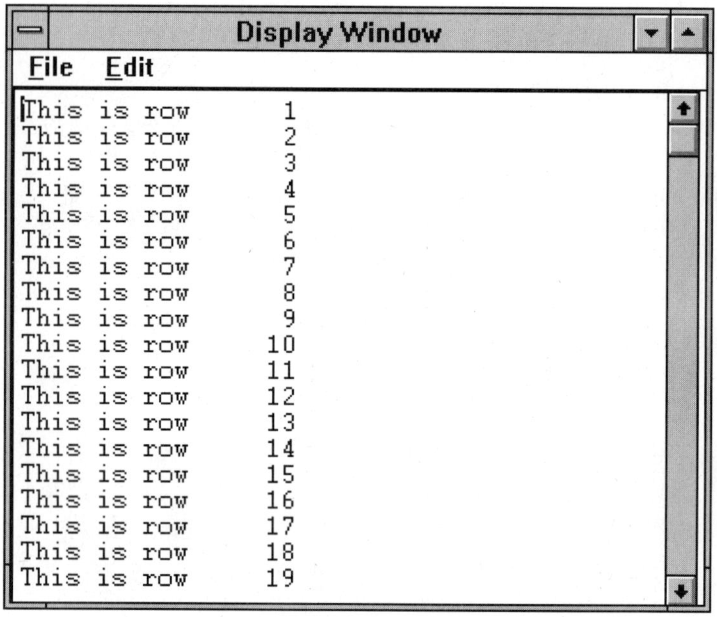

```
┌─────────────────────────────────────────────┐
│              Display Window              ▼▲ │
│ File  Edit                                  │
│ This is row    1                          ↑ │
│ This is row    2                            │
│ This is row    3                            │
│ This is row    4                            │
│ This is row    5                            │
│ This is row    6                            │
│ This is row    7                            │
│ This is row    8                            │
│ This is row    9                            │
│ This is row   10                            │
│ This is row   11                            │
│ This is row   12                            │
│ This is row   13                            │
│ This is row   14                            │
│ This is row   15                            │
│ This is row   16                            │
│ This is row   17                            │
│ This is row   18                            │
│ This is row   19                          ↓ │
└─────────────────────────────────────────────┘
```

Figure 12-2 - Output of the NewEra `display` Statement

Converting Informix-4GL `display` Statements

If an Informix-4GL `display` statement does **not** contain a row and column set of coordinates, then it can most likely be converted intact. The difference in functionality will probably represent an improvement in usability for the application.

Chapter 12: Migrating Informix-4GL Applications to NewEra

If an Informix-4GL `display` statement contains row and column coordinates, then a text box or text label will need to be painted into the window and a `setText` function call used to output the character string to the window.

If an Informix-4GL `display` statement outputs data to a screen form `formonly` field, then a text field or label has to be created and the `setText` function used to output text.

If the `display` statement outputs to a screen form field that was bound to a database table field and a SuperTable is being used to bind to the database table field, then the SuperTable `setCellValue` function is used to output data to this field.

Note that the SuperTable functionality eliminates the need for a number of the currently used Informix-4GL `display` statements. For instance, there is no need to execute a `construct` statement, build a query string, retrieve data from the database, and then display data to the screen form fields using a `display` statement. These functions can be handled by as few as two SuperTable member functions which can be pasted into the window with the SuperTable `query` button.

Converting Informix-4GL Menu Blocks

Informix-4GL menus are composed of a `menu` statement with blocks of code with `command` blocks. These command blocks contain code that is executed when the user chooses the corresponding menu option.

Informix-4GL menus can relate directly to NewEra menus. Instead of command blocks, the NewEra menus use menu event handlers. The code that previously resided in the menu command blocks will be placed in the appropriate menu handler.

Conversion of Informix-4GL code involves creating a similar NewEra menu using the NewEra menu editor. The code in the Informix-4GL menu command blocks is then cut and inserted into the menu handler code window for the corresponding menu handlers.

Another alternative for the conversion of Informix-4GL menus is to convert some of the menu options to other NewEra controls. Menu options that are used to simply set internal program parameters and flags could be converted to radio buttons or check boxes. And some menu options could be converted to text buttons and picture buttons, providing a clearer presentation of application options than could be accomplished with the character-based Informix-4GL.

Converting the Screen Forms and Browse Functionality

Informix-NewEra screen forms can be read by the NewEra Window Painter. Large portions of the form will convert to an Informix-NewEra data entry window.

The Informix-4GL data browse screen is a common approach to moving through a data set. Fortunately, this functionality is easily provided with the standard SuperTable buttons. Two possible approaches to conversion are outlined below.

Converting with the Standard SuperTable Functionality

A viable approach to converting existing Informix-4GL forms is to convert the Informix-4GL screen form with the Window Painter. Once the form is converted, the SuperTable editor can be selected and the SuperTable browse buttons (the query, retrieve, next row, and previous row, buttons) can be inserted into the window. This can provide a data entry window with a similar appearance to its Informix-4GL counterpart complete with the browse capability.

Converting with the Extended Classes

To convert an Informix-4GL screen form utilizing the extended classes shown in chapter 11 would involve several simple steps. First the ".frm" file is opened with the Window Painter and converted into a NewEra *wif* file.

Next, the SuperTable frame is selected and the SuperTable class changed to the `browseSuperTable` class discussed in chapter 11.

The frame for the SuperTable browse buttons should be pasted into the window. This frame should be pasted **into** the SuperTable frame since the SuperTable frame must be the container for the button frame. It should be sized so that the width is the full length of the SuperTable frame, and the height is about 1 inch. The class for the frame should then be changed to `browseFrame`.

The frame for the status window should be painted below the SuperTable frame. This frame need not be in the SuperTable frame. The class name property for the frame should be `statusFrame`. The status frame should be about the same size as the Browseframe to hold the SuperTable buttons detailed above.

The pre-header section of the window should then be set to include the `browse.4gh` and `general.4gh` NewEra header files.

The Application Builder or Makefile should include both the `browse.4gl` and `general.4gl` object files, in addition to any other object files or libraries that may be needed.

Index

—A—

A/R Aging Report, 194
accounts receivable aging, 43
Accounts Receivable Data Flow, 44
Accounts Receivable Module, 43
activate event
    list box, 76
adding graphics, 72
Adding Informational Messages, 115
after field statements, 232
afterApply event, 66
afterCell event, 166
afterRetrieve event, 66, 82
afterRow event, 66
afterRowApplied event, 66
Aging Report, 52
Aging Report Window, 52
alert_message, 186
alert_message function, 190
alignment buttons, 128
Application Builder, 33
Apply Button Activate Handler Code, 119
apply member SuperTable member function, 119
applyRowSql SuperTable member function, 121
arAgeReport Report, 205
Asynchronous Handler Calls, 11

—B—

Batch Entry Window, 154
batch header window, 51
Batch Input Window, 153
batch table, 55
Batch Type Radio Button, 156
batch windows
    Retrieve Operation, 162
before field statements, 232

beforeApply event, 66
beforeRetrieve event, 66
beforeRevert event, 66
beforeRowLocked event, 66
bill table, 57
browse_status function, 119, 186, 189
browseFrame Class Definition, 213
browseFrame Constructor Function, 214
browseSuperTable
    rowretrieved event handler, 222
browseSuperTable Class, 220
browseSuperTable Constructor, 221
browseWindow Constructor, 225
Building a Class Library, 176
Button Control, 71
Button Events, 71
button state, 72

—C—

Call By Reference, 8
CCL, 12
Check Box, 74
Check Box Events, 74
class, 3
    derived, 178
Class Definition, 9
class libraries, 11
class library, 3
class_extension, 29
class_extension Code Block, 29
click event, 70
clipboard, 109
color parameters, 24
commit work
    placement in SuperTable events, 163
Connectivity Class Library, 12
Constants, 6
constructor
    dbelist box class, 179

constructor_extension, 29
constructor_extension Code Block, 30
containers, 61
control table, 59
controls
   alignment, 128
Converting Informix-4GL, 231
   Converting the Screen Forms, 239
   display statements, 238
   menu blocks, 239
   message, error and display statements, 237
   on key statements, 236
copySelectedText
   ixApp member function, 109
Creating a NewEra Application
   steps, 34, 101
Creating NewEra Windows
   steps, 103
credit terms, 44
Custom Data Types, 8
customer codes table, 56
Customer data entry window
   expanded, 131
Customer Entry Window, 48
Customer List, 50
customer table, 55
cutSelectedText
   ixApp member function, 109

—D—

database aware, 25
Database Aware List Box Class, 176
database design
   accounts receivable module, 53
Database Properties, 147
database-aware list box, 123, 128
dataRowCheck event, 66
dbelist Box
   getSelection Member Function, 180
   registering, 129
dbelist box class
   constructor, 179
   getSelection member function, 179
dbelist class

bind_SuperField parameter, 129
bind_SuperTable parameter, 129
constructor, 182
database-aware edit list box, 128
header file, 177
init_list Member Function, 181
list_column parameter, 129
list_table parameter, 129
loadData Member Function, 183
member functions, 180
dbelist list box, 177
Default event handlers, 27
Delete Button Activate Handler
   Code, 120
disable event, 63
displayHelp event, 63
displayHelp ixApp member function, 169
districts table, 56
drop-down
   list box, 75
Dynamic Memory Allocation, 8

—E—

edit-list box
   database aware list box, 128
Embedded SQL, 13
enable event, 63
encapsulation, 2
   benefits, 3
end main statement, 85
errorStmt object, 165
event, 9
Event Code Window, 19
Event Handlers, 27, 88
event queue, 9
Extended NewEra Classes
   using, 227
   using in template applications, 229
Extending the ixFrame Class, 212
Extending the SuperTable Class
   browseSuperTable Class, 220
External Variables, 6

Index

—F—

Field Labels, 38
Field Name Properties, 146
Field Validations, 166
find member function
    ixString, 140
findNext Button Activate Handler, 201
finish Event, 144
fixed
    list box, 75
focus Event, 129
focusIn event, 201
formatting
    controls, 128
    text, 126
    window, 126
Frames, 128
    events, 69
    frameFocusIn event, 69
    frameFocusOut event, 69
Function parameters, 7
Function Prototypes, 6
functionality of the windows, 103

—G—

geometry parameter, 94
getAllSelecteditems
    list box member function, 78
getAnchor event, 63
getAvailabilty event, 63
getAvailabilty member function
    ixVisualObject, 151
getBackColor event, 63
getCellValue, 40
getCellValue function, 130
getCurrRowNum, 41
getFont event, 63
getFontName event, 64
getFontSize event, 64
getForeColor event, 64
getHeight event, 64
getItembyNumber
    ixListBox function, 180
    list box member function, 76
    member function, 199
getItembyNumber member function
    ixListBox, 142
getLeft event, 64
getNumItems
    ixListBox member function, 184
getNumStoredRows, 113
getSelectedItem
    list box member function, 76
getSelectedItem member function
    ixListBox, 142
getSelection
    list box member function, 76
getSelection Member Function, 180
getSize event, 64
getSubstring member function
    ixListBox, 142
getTop event, 64
getValueStr member function, 167
getVisualContainer, 89
    ixVisualContainer member function, 213
    member function, 118
getVisualContainer event, 64
getWidth event, 64
getWindow event, 64
Grid-form SuperTable, 67
    adjusting column widths, 147
GUI window, 15

—H—

handle statement, 11
Handler, 10
header file
    example, 177
helpStyle ixApp member variable, 168
Hidden SuperTable, 131
hide, 64
hide member function
    ixVisualContainer, 139

—I—

implicit *begin work*, 163
include Statement, 6
Informix-4GL, 5

converting legacy applications to NewEra, 234
screen interaction statements, 233
Informix-4GL Applications
structure, 232
Informix-4GL Reports, 233
Inheritance, 3, 9, 176
Insert Button, 91
Insert Button Activate Handler Code, 121
Interacting Windows, 148
isEnabled event, 64
isFontBold, 64
isFontItalic event, 64
isFontUnderline event, 64
isolating Informix-4GL statements, 235
isShown event, 64
ixApp helpFile, 168
ixAppearance object, 94
ixButton, 71
ixErrorLog class, 171
ixErrorLog logError member function, 171
ixFrame, 69
ixframe class
extending, 212
ixLabel, 70
ixLabel Constructor, 97
ixListBox, 75
getItembyNumber member function, 180, 199
ixPictureButton, 72
ixRadiobutton, 73
ixReport class, 209
ixReport.4gh, 208
ixRow, 13
ixRowArray, 13
ixRowArray class, 78
ixSQLConnect, 87
ixSQLConnect::SQL_Commit member constant, 163
transact member function, 163
ixString
find member function, 140
ixSuperTable, 65
ixTextBox, 69
ixvector object, 76

example, 184
ixVisualObject, 62
member functions, 63
ixVisualObject class, 85
ixWindow class, 85

—J—

journal entries table, 58

—K—

keyboard focus, 160
keyPress event, 69, 70

—L—

Label Control, 70
legacy Informix-4GL, 17
Line Items Entry Window, 156
line items table, 57
Line Items Window, 162
List Box, 75
dbelist box class, 177
events, 76
loading with data, 137
searchable, 137
searching for a value, 139
select event, 142
listFile Function, 204
LoadCustList function, 138
Locking Issues, 165
afterRow handler, 166
beforeRow handler, 166
transaction management, 46
locking mode, 82
lockMode Property, 81
Lookups, 166

—M—

Main Menu Window
example, 148
main program block, 85
Master-Detail Relationships, 39
master-detail window, 16

maxRows Property, 82
maxRowsExceeded event, 66
Menu Editor, 31
message function, 119, 188
messageBox, 113
messages, 2
msgbox function, 185, 188
multi-select
    list box, 75
Multi-Select List Box, 77

—N—

NewEra Code Blocks, 28
NewEra Error Logging, 169
NewEra Help, 168
NewEra Language Improvements, 5
NewEra program structure, 85
NewEra Screens
    Steps in development, 104
NewEra window
    object, 30
NewEra Window Hierarchy, 30
NewEra windows
    connected, 153
Next and Previous Buttons Activate
        Handler Code, 118
Next Button, 90
nolocking, 81

—O—

object reference, 61
object-oriented facilities, 8
Object-oriented Languages, 1
Objects, 2
optimistic, 47
optimistic locking, 82, 165
override, 4

—P—

pasteText
    ixApp member function, 109
pessimistic, 47
pessimistic locking, 81, 166
Picture Button, 72

events, 72
Polymorphism, 4
pre_body, 29
pre_body Code Block, 29
pre_header, 29
pre_header Code Block, 29
Pre-Body Code Section, 160
Pre-Header Section, 86
preheader Section, 143
Previous Button, 89
Primary Key Property, 126
primaryKey Property, 79
private variables, 9
program *by difference*, 4
projects, 33
protected variables, 9
public variables, 9

—Q—

Query Button Activate Handler Code, 115
Query Button Code, 88
queryRowCheck event, 67

—R—

Radio Button, 73
    events, 73
    handler example, 134
Radio Buttons
    binding to SuperTable cells, 134
    drawbacks, 134
Receivables Entry Window, 154
receivables header window, 51
Receivables Window, 160
report
    a/r aging report, 194
reports
    fixed fonts, 193
    font spacing, impact, 193
resizing columns
    grid-form SuperTable, 147
retrieve, 89
    SuperTable member function, 12, 89
retrieve button
    activate handler, 158

Retrieve Button Activate Handler
    Code, 116
retrieve member function
    QBE parameter, 158
retrItems function, 161
retrRevPay function, 158
rowRetrieved event, 67
    handler, 82
rtError event handler, 170
runARAge Function, 202

—S—

Scope
    class members, 9
Search Button
    activate handler, 198
    focusIn handler, 201
Search Function
    searchable list box, 140
Searchable List Box
    Find Next Button Handler, 144
searching
    list box, 139
security codes table, 58
security table, 58
select event
    list box, 76
    radio button, 73
selectFilterPart, 161
selectfromPart, 83
selectJoinPart, 83
selectUnique, 83
self keyword, 180
Set Font Size Button
    activate handler, 197
setAnchor event, 64
setCellValue member function, 181
setCellValue SuperTable member
        function, 167
setColor event, 64
setCurrentCell
    SuperTable
        member function, 89
    SuperTable member function, 82
setCurrentCell SuperTable member
    function, 118

setDisplayMode
    SuperTable member function, 88
setFont event, 65
setFont function, 197
setMessageFont function, 117, 186, 191
setSize event, 65
Setting Entry Properties, 26
Setting Format Properties, 24
Setting Location Properties, 23
setVObjFont function, 187, 191
ship codes table, 57
show event, 65
Shown Property, 133
showRtError member function, 171
single-select, 75
    list box, 75
splash window
    example, 224
SQLDelete event, 67
SQLFetch event, 67
SQLFreeSelect event, 67
SQLInsert event, 67
SQLInsert handler, 163
SQLPrepSelect event, 67
SQLUpdate event, 67
stale data, 47
staleData event, 67, 82
start event handler
    window, 150
Status Frame, 217
statusFrame
    class, 217
    constructor function, 218
stock items table, 58
stock table, 59
structured programming, 5, 15
SuperField, 12
    constructor, 95
    control, 78
    events, 19
    focus event, 181
    setting primary key property, 105
SuperFields
    bind to SuperTable, 95
SuperTable, 12, 25, 65
    buttons, 38
    constructor, 93

Index

control, 80
customizing functionality, 110
doSQLInsert member function, 163
editor, 37
events, 12, 66
frame, 37
free-form, 65
getNumStoredRows member function, 113
hidden in window, 131
maxrows parameter, 110, 112
maxRowsExceeded event, 111
query mode, 88
row retrieval modifications, 110
rowRetrieved event, 108, 111
SelectFilterPart, 158
transactions, 162
window, 37
SuperTable Fields
   pasting, 124
SuperTable reference, 62
Superviews, 39
Synchronous Handler Calls, 11

—T—

Template
   window menu options, 109
template applications
   using extended applications, 229
template window, 104
   create messages, 107
   creating, 104
   design and create, 107
   grid-form Template Window, 145
   limitations of approach, 212
   prompt for retrieval of additional rows, 107
   set color and font of window, 107
   standard menu options, 107
   status information, 107
   using custom classes, 212
   VCR type traversal buttons, 107
Template Windows
   creating simple windows, 123
   free-form and grid-form SuperTable Templates, 122

using, 121
terms table, 56
Text Box Control, 69
Text Box Events, 70
Transaction Management, 82
   rollback, 165
Transaction Management in SuperTable Handlers
   example, 163
transactions
   location of commit, 164
   SuperTables, 162
   transaction management in the afterApply event, 164
   with multiple rows, 164

—U—

updateTable property, 80
Using SuperViews, 39

—V—

valueChanged event, 70
Variable Initialization, 6
VCL, 11
ViewPoint Pro Reports, 208
ViewPoint-Pro, 39
Visual Class Library, 11
visual frame
   grouping visual objects, 69
Visual Frame Object, 69
Visual objects, 15

—W—

warn_message function, 186, 190
wif, 17, 39
window
   constructor, 92
   containership, 30
   formatting, 126
   header file, 98
   object, 85
   objects, 15
   objects and controls, 61
   start event, 196

start event handler, 150
　　　startup property, 104
　　　type property, 104
Window Class
　　　extending, 224
window manager event loop, 85
Window Painter, 15, 17
　　　code window, 28
　　　defining attributes, 20
　　　editing facilities, 28
　　　properties, 104
　　　Setting General Properties, 20
　　　setting properties, 20
Window Painter generated code, 85
Window Properties, 124

window references
　　　establishing, 149
Window Template, 49
windows
　　　closing, 150
　　　hiding, 150
　　　opening, 150
　　　three-way update, 156
wrapper functions, 185

—Z—

zip code table, 59

LICENSE AGREEMENT AND LIMITED WARRANTY

READ THE FOLLOWING TERMS AND CONDITIONS CAREFULLY BEFORE OPENING THIS DISK PACKAGE. THIS LEGAL DOCUMENT IS AN AGREEMENT BETWEEN YOU AND PRENTICE-HALL, INC. (THE "COMPANY"). BY OPENING THIS SEALED DISK PACKAGE, YOU ARE AGREEING TO BE BOUND BY THESE TERMS AND CONDITIONS. IF YOU DO NOT AGREE WITH THESE TERMS AND CONDITIONS, DO NOT OPEN THE DISK PACKAGE. PROMPTLY RETURN THE UNOPENED DISK PACKAGE AND ALL ACCOMPANYING ITEMS TO THE PLACE YOU OBTAINED THEM FOR A FULL REFUND OF ANY SUMS YOU HAVE PAID.

1. **GRANT OF LICENSE:** In consideration of your payment of the license fee, which is part of the price you paid for this product, and your agreement to abide by the terms and conditions of this Agreement, the Company grants to you a nonexclusive right to use and display the copy of the enclosed software program (hereinafter the "SOFTWARE") on a single computer (i.e., with a single CPU) at a single location so long as you comply with the terms of this Agreement. The Company reserves all rights not expressly granted to you under this Agreement.

2. **OWNERSHIP OF SOFTWARE:** You own only the magnetic or physical media (the enclosed disks) on which the SOFTWARE is recorded or fixed, but the Company retains all the rights, title, and ownership to the SOFTWARE recorded on the original disk copy(ies) and all subsequent copies of the SOFTWARE, regardless of the form or media on which the original or other copies may exist. This license is not a sale of the original SOFTWARE or any copy to you.

3. **COPY RESTRICTIONS:** This SOFTWARE and the accompanying printed materials and user manual (the "Documentation") are the subject of copyright. You may not copy the Documentation or the SOFTWARE, except that you may make a single copy of the SOFTWARE for backup or archival purposes only. You may be held legally responsible for any copying or copyright infringement which is caused or encouraged by your failure to abide by the terms of this restriction.

4. **USE RESTRICTIONS:** You may not network the SOFTWARE or otherwise use it on more than one computer or computer terminal at the same time. You may physically transfer the SOFTWARE from one computer to another provided that the SOFTWARE is used on only one computer at a time. You may not distribute copies of the SOFTWARE or Documentation to others. You may not reverse engineer, disassemble, decompile, modify, adapt, translate, or create derivative works based on the SOFTWARE or the Documentation without the prior written consent of the Company.

5. **TRANSFER RESTRICTIONS:** The enclosed SOFTWARE is licensed only to you and may not be transferred to any one else without the prior written consent of the Company. Any unauthorized transfer of the SOFTWARE shall result in the immediate termination of this Agreement.

6. **TERMINATION:** This license is effective until terminated. This license will terminate automatically without notice from the Company and become null and void if you fail to comply with any provisions or limitations of this license. Upon termination, you shall destroy the Documentation and all copies of the SOFTWARE. All provisions of this Agreement as to warranties, limitation of liability, remedies or damages, and our ownership rights shall survive termination.

7. **MISCELLANEOUS:** This Agreement shall be construed in accordance with the laws of the United States of America and the State of New York and shall benefit the Company, its affiliates, and assignees.

8. **LIMITED WARRANTY AND DISCLAIMER OF WARRANTY:** The Company warrants that the SOFTWARE, when properly used in accordance with the Documentation, will operate in substantial conformity with the description of the SOFTWARE set forth in the Documentation. The Company does not warrant that the SOFTWARE will meet your requirements or that the operation of the SOFTWARE will be uninterrupted or error-free. The Company warrants that the

media on which the SOFTWARE is delivered shall be free from defects in materials and workmanship under normal use for a period of thirty (30) days from the date of your purchase. Your only remedy and the Company's only obligation under these limited warranties is, at the Company's option, return of the warranted item for a refund of any amounts paid by you or replacement of the item. Any replacement of SOFTWARE or media under the warranties shall not extend the original warranty period. The limited warranty set forth above shall not apply to any SOFTWARE which the Company determines in good faith has been subject to misuse, neglect, improper installation, repair, alteration, or damage by you. EXCEPT FOR THE EXPRESSED WARRANTIES SET FORTH ABOVE, THE COMPANY DISCLAIMS ALL WARRANTIES, EXPRESS OR IMPLIED, INCLUDING WITHOUT LIMITATION, THE IMPLIED WARRANTIES OF MERCHANTABILITY AND FITNESS FOR A PARTICULAR PURPOSE. EXCEPT FOR THE EXPRESS WARRANTY SET FORTH ABOVE, THE COMPANY DOES NOT WARRANT, GUARANTEE, OR MAKE ANY REPRESENTATION REGARDING THE USE OR THE RESULTS OF THE USE OF THE SOFTWARE IN TERMS OF ITS CORRECTNESS, ACCURACY, RELIABILITY, CURRENTNESS, OR OTHERWISE.

IN NO EVENT, SHALL THE COMPANY OR ITS EMPLOYEES, AGENTS, SUPPLIERS, OR CONTRACTORS BE LIABLE FOR ANY INCIDENTAL, INDIRECT, SPECIAL, OR CONSEQUENTIAL DAMAGES ARISING OUT OF OR IN CONNECTION WITH THE LICENSE GRANTED UNDER THIS AGREEMENT, OR FOR LOSS OF USE, LOSS OF DATA, LOSS OF INCOME OR PROFIT, OR OTHER LOSSES, SUSTAINED AS A RESULT OF INJURY TO ANY PERSON, OR LOSS OF OR DAMAGE TO PROPERTY, OR CLAIMS OF THIRD PARTIES, EVEN IF THE COMPANY OR AN AUTHORIZED REPRESENTATIVE OF THE COMPANY HAS BEEN ADVISED OF THE POSSIBILITY OF SUCH DAMAGES. IN NO EVENT SHALL LIABILITY OF THE COMPANY FOR DAMAGES WITH RESPECT TO THE SOFTWARE EXCEED THE AMOUNTS ACTUALLY PAID BY YOU, IF ANY, FOR THE SOFTWARE.

SOME JURISDICTIONS DO NOT ALLOW THE LIMITATION OF IMPLIED WARRANTIES OR LIABILITY FOR INCIDENTAL, INDIRECT, SPECIAL, OR CONSEQUENTIAL DAMAGES, SO THE ABOVE LIMITATIONS MAY NOT ALWAYS APPLY. THE WARRANTIES IN THIS AGREEMENT GIVE YOU SPECIFIC LEGAL RIGHTS AND YOU MAY ALSO HAVE OTHER RIGHTS WHICH VARY IN ACCORDANCE WITH LOCAL LAW.

ACKNOWLEDGMENT

YOU ACKNOWLEDGE THAT YOU HAVE READ THIS AGREEMENT, UNDERSTAND IT, AND AGREE TO BE BOUND BY ITS TERMS AND CONDITIONS. YOU ALSO AGREE THAT THIS AGREEMENT IS THE COMPLETE AND EXCLUSIVE STATEMENT OF THE AGREEMENT BETWEEN YOU AND THE COMPANY AND SUPERSEDES ALL PROPOSALS OR PRIOR AGREEMENTS, ORAL, OR WRITTEN, AND ANY OTHER COMMUNICATIONS BETWEEN YOU AND THE COMPANY OR ANY REPRESENTATIVE OF THE COMPANY RELATING TO THE SUBJECT MATTER OF THIS AGREEMENT.

Should you have any questions concerning this Agreement or if you wish to contact the Company for any reason, please contact in writing at the address below.

Robin Short
Prentice Hall PTR
One Lake Street
Upper Saddle River, New Jersey 07458